GOD SENT REVIVAL

Asahel Nettleton D.D.
A copy of the official Nettleton portrait which hung for many years in the halls
of Hartford Theological Seminary.   It now gathers dust in an attic.

John F. Thornbury

GOD SENT REVIVAL

THE STORY OF ASAHEL NETTLETON
AND THE SECOND GREAT AWAKENING

EVANGELICAL PRESS

P.O. Box 5, Welwyn, Herts., AL6 9NU England
P.O. Box 2453, Grand Rapids, Mich. 49501, USA

© Evangelical Press

First published July 1977

ISBN Paperback 0 85234 099 0
ISBN Hardback 0 85234 100 8

Cover design by PETER WAGSTAFF Designs

Printed by Stanley L. Hunt (Printers) Ltd.,
Rushden, Northamptonshire, England

To my dear wife, Reta,
who gave me her valuable advice and
encouragement in the writing of this
book.

This favoured servant of Christ came, with no trumpet sounded before him, in the meekness of his master, and the Lord was with him in very deed.

Jonathan Lee.

CONTENTS

ILLUSTRATIONS

ABOUT THE AUTHOR

John Thornbury descended from a line of Baptist ministers beginning with his great grandfather, L. A. Thornbury, who preached in Elliott County, Kentucky and served as an officer in the Union Army. He was educated in the public schools of Ashland, Kentucky, graduated with a B.A. degree from the Lexington, Kentucky, Baptist College, and did further studies at the University of Kentucky. He was ordained to the ministry by the Ashland Avenue Baptist Church of Lexington, Kentucky while pastoring in Pulaski County, Kentucky.

He is the author of The Doctrine of the Church, a Baptist View, *and* David Brainerd, *a prize-winning biography included in* Five Pioneer Missionaries *published by Banner of Truth Trust. In addition to numerous articles for magazines and theological journals, he supplied the entries on David Brainerd and Andrew Fuller for* The Encyclopedia of Christianity.

He has served as pastor of independent, Southern Baptist, and American Baptist Churches in Kentucky and Pennsylvania, including the present pastorate at the Winfield Baptist Church, Winfield, Pennsylvania. Since 1967 he has been an instructor in the Central Pennsylvania Christian Training Institute. Other positions have included president of the Union County Sabbath School Association, vice moderator of the Northumberland Baptist Association, Pennsylvania, and vice president of the North Central Baptist Ministers' Fellowship. He is married and has two children.

FOREWORD

Asahel Nettleton is a name that is well known to students of American Church History and revivalism, but he is relatively unknown to most modern Christians. This book has been written because of the author's conviction that the quality of Nettleton's ministry was such that the story of his life is one that needs to be retold. He was an evangelist who was specially anointed by the Holy Spirit, and wherever he went town after town was visited with the power of God and transformations took place which seem today almost incredible. Decades after his labours in a community, living monuments to the genuineness of these revivals could still be found, and witness after witness declared that the vast majority of those who professed faith under Nettleton's evangelism were still serving the Lord. Spurious converts were the exception rather than the rule.

The record of this amazing ministry raises such questions as, what kind of a man was this who was so greatly used of God? What was his message? What methods did he use in winning men to Christ? These are some of the questions this book will seek to answer.

One who does research into the background of Nettleton's life and times soon discovers that the available data is more than adequate for a fairly thorough portrait of him. Although he wrote no books, which from a historian's standpoint is unfortunate, he left behind a considerable amount of correspondence and a volume of his sermons was published. His diligent and dedicated biographer, Bennet Tyler, a close personal friend, collected and published much valuable information about him.

My research into Nettleton's life and ministry has taken me across New York, Massachusetts, Connecticut, and Virginia where I have met many interesting people who have, almost without exception, cooperated to the fullest with this biographical project. Valuable books have been loaned for a considerable period of time and college libraries have willingly been made available to me. Custodians of

church records have shared their knowledge and citizens of
the town where he spent the last years of his life have taken
keen interest in this book and given me necessary assistance.
I have had the strong feeling, as I searched for details of
Nettleton's career and studied the movement of which he
was a part, that I was digging in a gold mine which needed
only to have its treasure brought to the surface for all to see
its great value.

I would especially like to thank Mr Nafi Donat, who is the
librarian at the Hartford Seminary Foundation and cus-
todian of the priceless Nettleton Collection which is housed
there. Mr Donat has personally organised all the Nettleton
letters and filed them in such a way as to make them acces-
sible to visitors to the Foundation. He also takes care of
Nettleton's personal effects which are still extant, and
willingly makes them available for others to see.

The primary sources for this biography are the original
works about Nettleton: Tyler's *Memoir* of his life, his *Remains*,
a volume of the sermons and sayings of Nettleton, collected
and published by Tyler, the British edition of his life edited
by A. A. Bonar, who reorganised somewhat Tyler's *Memoir*
and added occasional comments, and the *Letters on the New
Measures*, by Nettleton and one of his earliest coadjutors,
Lyman Beecher. Last but not least, the unpublished doctoral
thesis of George Hugh Birney, *The Life and Letters of Asahel
Nettleton*, has been relied upon to fill many of the gaps.
Students of Nettleton have been spared a vast amount of
time and research by Birney's thorough investigations into
his family origins, the developments at the historic New
Lebanon Conference, and the background of *Village Hymns*,
a collection which was the only literary effort of the evangelist.

Copyrighted material from the following works has been
used with the permission of the publishers. *The Social Ideas
of the Northern Evangelists*, by Charles C. Cole, Jr., Columbia
University Press; *Unvanquished Puritan*, by Stuart Henry,
William B. Eerdmans Publishing Co. (a biography of
Lyman Beecher); *Modern Revivalism, Charles Grandison Finney
to Billy Graham*, by William G. McLoughlin, Jr., Ronald
Press; *Life History of the United States*, Time-Life Books; and
The Oxford History of the American People, by Samuel Eliot
Morison, Oxford University Press.

PART I

ROOTS OF AN
EVANGELIST

(1783-1812)

He who has engraven Zion on the palms of his hands – who never wants means to fulfil his promises – has sent his heavenly influence to rouse the Christian world. He beheld the desolations of Zion and has come to rebuild her ruined walls. He heard the groans of his people as with harps on the willows they were weeping "by the rivers of Babylon", and has come to bring them again "to Zion with songs and everlasting joy upon their heads". Eternal thanks to God for what our eyes have seen and our ears have heard for the last four and thirty years.

Edward Griffin (1826)

CHAPTER I

AN EVANGELIST IS BORN

On 13th October, 1812, Captain John E. Wool led a small detachment of American soldiers across the Niagara river and attacked the British army of General Isaac Brock which was stationed at Queenston Heights, Canada. This ill-fated assault was the first autumn engagement of American land troops in the "War of 1812" which had been declared by Congress on 18th June.

About the same time a different type of offensive was taking place in the small Connecticut town of South Britain. Here the career of a young minister was being launched, which can safely be labelled an assault on the kingdom of Satan. At the time he was a most unlikely candidate for fame. His rural family origins, his less than brilliant college career, and his plain appearance made him seem to be just an ordinary man in every way. But his humble beginnings tended to obscure the fact that God, in him, was raising up one of the most formidable antagonists to sin and error that ever graced the American pulpit.

This young man, Asahel Nettleton, had stopped at South Britain on the way to his ultimate destination, South Salem, New York, where he was going to fulfil an appointment to preach. But he had been invited to pause, en route, to assist the pastor of the Congregational Church of South Britain which was in the midst of a common phenomenon in those days, a revival. A revival then meant not just a series of special meetings, but a genuine spiritual upheaval in which the interests of Christians were raised to great heights and large numbers of sinners were converted.

When the pastor of the church, Bennet Tyler, greeted his guest, it was the beginning of a close personal friendship.

17

Although they were the same age, twenty-nine, and had attended the same college, Yale, located at New Haven, they had not met because Tyler had graduated the year before Nettleton entered. But he knew of Nettleton's love for the truth and, having heard of his preaching abilities, he felt that he could safely entrust his pulpit to him.

Asahel arrived at a time when special meetings were being held in the local school building. The school house, or "academy" as it was sometimes called, was probably more commodious than the church building. It was also a neutral place where anyone, regardless of his spiritual inclinations, could come, without being identified necessarily as a religious person.

When the Sabbath for the "out of town" preacher arrived, the school building was packed to the walls. This reflected not only the excitement which the revival had generated in the community, but also the curiosity of the people to size up the new preacher. Scarcely anyone was much concerned about the "war talk" currently floating about (after all, as New Englanders, they were opposed to the war anyway), but were intent on coming to church and hearing their regular Sunday sermon.

Probably neither Tyler nor the townsfolk were particularly impressed with Asahel Nettleton when he took his stand behind the pulpit for the first time. He certainly was no elegant gentleman. His suit was neat but well worn, giving the appearance of a person not particularly endowed with material prosperity. His stocky frame and ruddy complexion suggested a man who had been accustomed to physical labour and outdoor life – probably that of a farmer.[1] Yet he, like the pastor, was a Yale graduate, so he must have had the intellectual and academic equipment for a preacher.

There was something arresting, almost unsettling about the countenance of the youthful preacher. In the first place he seemed awfully serious. Did he have some grave and terrible message to deliver? He obviously considered preaching a weighty responsibility.

And then those eyes of his! As they moved back and forth across the congregation they fixed now upon this person, then upon another, in each case locking their eyes in near hypnotic attention. Many sitting near the front may have wished they had taken a seat further back, as if to hide from this piercing glare.

The congregation sat in breathless silence as he began to speak. No graveyard could have been more quiet.

"What is that murmur I hear?" began the preacher.[2]

Not a lip had moved for several minutes; to what "murmur" could he be referring?

"I wish I had a new heart – what shall I do?" he continued.

His voice, though moderate in volume and low in pitch, reverberated through the building.

Obviously his probing question was addressed to the inner thoughts of some of the awakened sinners in the audience. Many were conscious that they had often asked, at least to themselves, "What must I do to be saved?" Did this mysterious stranger have some supernatural access to their hearts?

"They tell me to repent; I can't repent. I wish they could give me some other direction."

A profound curiosity now settled upon the congregation. Some probably gasped in astonishment. This somewhat dramatic style of preaching was something they had never heard before. Furthermore the words of the preacher revealed their thoughts as accurately as the mirrors in their parlours had imaged their physical appearance as they dressed to come to church. After all, weren't the unconverted dead in trespasses and sins, weren't they so chained by their pride and love of sin that they *would not*, and thus *could not* repent? Hadn't some even been heard to say that they wished salvation could be obtained on easier terms?

How was a perfect stranger able to divine the very words crossing their minds? It was almost as though their innermost thoughts were being flashed in some magical way on the wall in the rear of the building and the preacher was reading them back to the whole congregation. How disturbing! How eerie! This was no ordinary man; this was no ordinary service.

Changing the interrogative and somewhat theatrical style of his introduction, the speaker soon shifted into a more conventional mode of address. In a very solemn, but compassionate fashion, he proceeded to speak to the now raptly attentive audience about their need for sincere repentance and the danger of delay.

"Nothing short of immediate submission to God will relieve your distress and bring you peace with God," he said.

They knew he was right. Pastor Tyler had said essentially the same thing, though not in quite so stunning a style.

No clairvoyance or mental telepathy had been at work. The young guest simply had a thorough acquaintance with the human heart, for he himself had once been right where many of them were now. Conviction of sin was written plainly across many faces that day and the preacher needed no psychic powers to know what was going on in their minds. Thought processes of awakened sinners in those days followed a familiar pattern and an articulate preacher needed only to put them into words.

Many of those in the congregation on that Sunday in 1812 not only listened with attention but responded to the message in the appropriate manner. Those who had been under conviction had those convictions deepened. It was a meeting that no one present would ever forget. "Thrilling" was the word used by Bennet Tyler in describing the effect of Asahel Nettleton's first sermon in his church.

But if that meeting had proved to be unusual to the people of that town, it was no less so to the preacher himself. It was different from anything he himself had ever experienced. Although he had been preaching for about a year now, he had never spoken with such power. He certainly had not discovered such power to influence the minds of a congregation before.

This meeting was only the beginning, however. For the remainder of the week Bennet and Asahel were kept busy visiting in the homes of the people in the community, discussing with them the way of salvation, praying, conducting special meetings, and conversing with each other about the glorious work of God which was going on in their midst. What a delightful time it was!

This initial contact between these two men was the beginning of a lifelong friendship. A bond of fellowship and love was cemented during this week which was not severed until a spring morning in 1844. With Nettleton when he died was his friend, Bennet Tyler.

The pastor at South Britain, to whom eventually fell the task of writing Nettleton's life story, was always aware that this brief visit was a turning point in his friend's life. It was here that he had experienced his first real taste of spiritual power in a revival. Unquestionably the career of an evangelist had been launched in the solemn stillness of that school house. The course of the preacher's life took a new turn from which it never deviated.

CHAPTER 2

THE
SECOND GREAT AWAKENING

Asahel Nettleton was born in 1783 and his life span of approximately sixty years covered an exceedingly eventful period in the history of the American Republic. It was the formative years of the American political system. Although independence had been won in 1776, the basic principles of democracy were hammered out at the Constitutional Convention eleven years later and tested for many years in the workshop of American political and social institutions.

These years were also very important in American religion. The privilege of religious freedom was not established immediately but was won slowly and painfully over five decades extending into the 19th century. Also this was the period of the great missionary movement in North America and saw the beginnings of the programmes of social reform which dominated public life later. Nettleton lived during the period when the great missionary societies which sent gospel preachers such as Judson and Rice to distant corners of the world were formed. Outstanding religious institutions were being founded, such as Andover Seminary (Presbyterian-Congregationalist), Newton Theological Institute (Baptist) and many older schools, such as Yale, were expanding their theological departments.

All these developments were influenced, and in some cases directly produced, by what has been called "The Second Great Awakening". Technically this designation is limited to the period between 1792 and 1808 when there was a tremendous surge of evangelical fervour in New England and Virginia, and in Tennessee and Kentucky as well. But the afterglow of this brilliant light shone one third of the way through the 19th century. It was not until the 1830's that one could say that the second great awakening was over.

This revival differed in several respects from its earlier counterpart, during the 1740's. For one thing it was longer. Whereas the first ended abruptly almost like switching off an electric light, the second faded gradually like the coming of the night. Furthermore, the second had no truly outstanding personalities involved in it. Whereas the first featured the intellectual giant Jonathan Edwards and the masterful orator George Whitefield, the second came about through the coordinated labours of many men of smaller stature.

Theologically and spiritually the New England phase of the awakening followed in the footsteps of Edwards. Acting in accordance with his famous call, the leaders of the second awakening gathered together for seasons of concerted prayer. They assisted one another in preaching ministries. But no great, single personality arose to unite the whole in one vocal expression.

In some respects, many felt that because the second awakening was not dominated by a few strong figures, it was a purer and sounder movement. It was carried on by "settled pastors" who lived in the communities where the revivals took place and stayed to attend to them. In fact, itinerant evangelists were looked upon with suspicion. During the first awakening some "roving evangelists", such as James Davenport, became fanatical in their methods and were instrumental in corrupting the awakening and finally bringing it to a halt. For this reason many pastors were reluctant to invite free-lance type preachers into the churches.

In the opinion of many who lived at the time, the revivals of the second awakening, though just as powerful as those under Edwards and Whitefield, were attended with fewer extravagances, such as visions, trances, and violent bodily movements (in New England at least). They had fewer superficial converts and were more lasting in their results. The universal testimony of the preachers of the period is that the overwhelming majority of converts were true to their profession and provided a framework of strength and stability in the churches and communities.

Only one preacher during this period stands out as an exception to the strong prejudice against itinerants. In New England he alone was universally beloved, respected, and honoured by his contemporaries. The reason for the high esteem in which he was held was that he seemed to embody personally all the noble principles of the awakening, and he was fully in sympathy with the methods by which it was directed. The revivals he conducted were, in other words, promoted in local churches, and were managed in conjunction with and in deference to settled pastors.

This man, the subject of this book, Asahel Nettleton, though not equipped with the pulpit talents of Whitefield, and though confined to a much smaller sphere of operation, was one of the guiding spirits of this tremendous period. Of him Lyman Beecher, who was himself a celebrity, said, "Considering the extent of his influence, I regard him as beyond comparison, the greatest benefactor which God has given to this nation; and through his influence in promoting pure and powerful revivals of religion, as destined to be one of the greatest benefactors of the world . . .".[3] This high praise seems extravagant, but one who has read the first-hand accounts of what God accomplished through him can understand why men like Beecher thought so highly of him.

From the standpoint of evangelical piety, the years between the two awakenings were years of decline and spiritual deadness. There were few revivals and wickedness seemed to be getting the upper hand. It was a day of rampant infidelity: open ungodliness in society, and apathy in the churches. Heman Humphrey, one of the foremost authorities on revivals during the first quarter of the 19th century, compared this period to the time when the children of Israel were in the wilderness "only kept alive by supplies of the heavenly manna, and of the water from the Rock".[4]

Jonathan Edwards seemed to have forebodings of this period. He regarded Braddock's defeat at Fort Duquesne in July of 1755 as evidence of God's displeasure against the colonies. In the fall of 1756 he wrote to a chaplain of a Massachusetts regiment at Lake George, "God indeed is remarkably frowning upon us everywhere; our enemies get up above us very high, and we are brought down very low. . . . What will become of us God only knows".[5] The "French and Indian" threat was eventually quelled, but while the danger lasted it caused universal alarm and absorbed the minds of virtually the entire population. The agitations of the French and Indian war seemed to quench the last embers of the Great Awakening and precipitate a decline.

Scarcely was this war over when the difficulties between the colonies and the English motherland began to increase to boiling point. The Revolutionary War itself was an occasion of much mischief spiritually. Many of the restraints of more settled communities were broken down among the Revolutionary soldiers on the battlefield and as a result flagrant sin was widespread. Intemperance, profane swearing, disregard for religious institutions, bitterness and hardness, and other forms of moral dissipation prevailed. After the war the troops carried these vices back into their communities. All in all the social and political conditions of the country were hurtful to the cause of Christ and militated against the prosperity of the churches.

As the century began to draw to a close the "French infidelity" rose to challenge the church. Destructive philosophical notions began to influence the minds of many Americans. Thomas Paine's *Age of Reason* was thought by many to herald the demise of traditional Christianity and infidels, such as Volney and Voltaire, boldly predicted that the Bible would soon become a relic of the dark ages, suitable only to bemuse the superstitious.

Clearly another awakening was sorely needed lest the colonies rise in the glory of a newly found independence only to sink in the ruins of moral desolation. Many Christians wondered if their new political institutions would be erected on the ruins of their Puritan traditions. The outbreak of revivals which began in the 1790's provided just such a relief as was needed.

CHAPTER 3

FAMILY ORIGINS, EARLY LIFE

The Nettleton family in America was founded by a gentleman named Samuel who was among the early settlers of the coast of Southern Connecticut near New Haven. About the time he arrived from the old world, negotiations were going on between the colonists at New Haven and the Indians for a small tract of land which lay between their colony and Guilford. This portion of land, called by the Indians Totoket, was to be used for the expansion of the colony.

The purchase was made in 1638 and immediately afterwards a group of men from Wethersfield approached the Court of the colony about settling in this new section. Soon permission was granted to them to move into the newly acquired territory and a portion was sold to a "Mr Swaine and others".[6] Among those who came to live in Totoket, later called Branford, was Samuel Nettleton.

There are scattered references to this first Nettleton in America in the records of the colony at New Haven. They reveal nothing unusual about him. "He was a freeman, a member of the church, and an active participant in the life of the colony."[7] His eldest son, John, settled in the town of Killingworth where he was married to Martha Hull in 1669. John and Martha had ten children, including one named Samuel after his grandfather. This Samuel was the grandfather of the evangelist Asahel Nettleton.

Asahel's grandfather married Dinah Healy on 25th March, 1737 and their fifth child, Samuel Nettleton, Jr., was born on 25th August, 1745. This man grew up to be a farmer. There is very little known about him. He and his wife, Amy, were "esteemed and respected by their neighbours", and lived in "moderate, but comfortable circumstances".[8] He was an

active participant in the Revolutionary War. Following the
outbreak of hostilities at Lexington and Concord the "call
to arms" went forth throughout the colonies and patriots
everywhere "joined in hastily organised companies".[9]
Samuel Nettleton dutifully enlisted and became a member
of the Continental Army, registering as a private on 9th May,
1775.

Samuel's first stint in Mr Washington's army was short
and his company was disbanded in December of the same
year. Nothing is known about his activities for the following
year, but on 10th January, 1777 he once again enlisted. He
served until his honourable discharge on 31st December,
1779. He no doubt returned to his farm at Killingworth. On
28th February, 1781 he married Amy Kelsey who came from
one of the oldest Killingworth families. She was a descendent
of John Kelsey who settled there in 1664. Amy was born
on 9th July, 1750.

Samuel and Amy Nettleton had a family of six children.
The oldest was a daughter named after her mother. There
were three sons, Asahel, the eldest, Ambrose and David, and
two other daughters, Lois and Polly, the last dying in
infancy. David, the youngest of the sons, died at the age of
fourteen and only he and his father had headstones in the
cemetery at Killingworth.

The parents of Asahel Nettleton were not notably religious,
though they had respect for the church and saw that their
children received religious instruction. Although Samuel
and Amy were baptised in infancy, according to Congregationalist practice, they never made a formal profession
of faith. The church records at Killingworth show that
Samuel "owned the covenant" on 25th November, 1781.
This act placed his family on the basis of the "halfway
covenant" relationship to the church. This entitled their
children to baptism, but did not give their parents full
church privileges. All the children received infant baptism
as soon as possible. Their son Asahel, who was born on
21st April, 1873, underwent the rite of infant baptism when
he was only six days old.

The Nettleton children were reared in the simple rural
atmosphere of a Connecticut farm. They all attended the
district school and evidently only Asahel got any education
beyond that. The daughters grew up learning to cook, sew
and attend to all the needs of the domestic circle. The boys

worked in the fields, cared for the livestock, and were instructed in the fundamental crafts of agriculture. It was expected that they would walk in the footsteps of their father and be farmers.

Asahel and his brothers and sisters received the basic religious instruction required of their parents' church. The children had to commit to memory the catechism of the Westminster Assembly. They learned what the ten commandments were and were encouraged to live in accordance with them. The stern truths of the orthodox Calvinism which prevailed among the Congregationalists and Presbyterians of their day were imbedded in their minds.

Asahel's early life was evidently uneventful. The Biblical precepts which he learned as a child, coupled with the strict discipline of his home, preserved him from the grosser vices. In the eyes of his parents and neighbours he was a virtuous young man, a model of moral uprightness.

Asahel did not indulge in open wickedness during his childhood and youth, but neither did he conform to the strictest Puritan standards of his day. The rural village mode of life at the time afforded few opportunities for out and out sin and dissipation, viewed in the light of modern standards, but there was some fun and frolic. There were local parties, outings, and occasional dances which were frowned upon by the church leaders. Asahel, however, was allowed to participate in them and he seemed to enjoy them.

As he grew up the solemn truths of the Westminster Catechism took hold of his heart. Often, even in the midst of his youthful play and pleasure, his thoughts turned toward God and eternity. One evening, while standing alone in a field, he watched the sun go down. The approaching night reminded him that his own life would some day fade into the darkness of the world beyond. He suddenly realised that he, like all other people, would die. For a while the thought overwhelmed him. For some time he stood and wept. But such serious thoughts usually vanished as the sun came up the next morning, so there were no permanent fruits from those momentary reflections.

CHAPTER 4

A BRAND
PLUCKED FROM THE FIRE

As the 19th century approached, the "Second Great Awakening" was at its acme. The outpouring of the Spirit of God upon virtually all evangelical denominations could be called "waves of glory" which rolled across hundreds of churches and communities. This awakening, which had come after a long spiritual drought, revived the spirits of the godly pastors and filled the ranks of the faithful with new converts. Whole communities were transformed by the gospel virtually overnight. This took place in areas where formerly infidelity had paraded its poisonous wares with little challenge and moral corruption prevailed like a deadly plague. Thousands of hardened sinners were humbled in submission to the claims of Christ. Congregations long desolate and barren became fruitful vineyards where exultant labourers gathered in a glorious harvest. Edward Griffin, the president of Williams College in Williamson, Massachusetts, described the whole scene as "one field of divine wonders".[10]

In the year 1801, the little village of Killingworth, Connecticut, just east of New Haven, was touched by the revival. An eighteen year old farm boy named Asahel Nettleton was one of the first converts in this place. His own conversion set the stage for his eventual evangelistic ministry and was a pattern for the thousands of converts he eventually saw as a result of it.

During his childhood and youth he had often thought seriously about the issues of life, death, eternity, and his own relationship to God. The experience in the field after watching the sun set, which he particularly remembered, was only one of the times when he brooded about his own unconverted state. He was never able to shake off these concerns. Though he was a moral and upright young man, he knew deep down in his heart that he had never been "born again". He knew that there was such a thing as conversion, and he knew that he had not experienced it.

In the autumn of 1800, the accumulated distresses of the past seemed to rush upon him. But there were numerous opportunities available to anesthetise his inner anxieties, such as the annual Thanksgiving celebrations now approaching. Among the events associated with the holiday was a dance, which was always spiced with intoxicating drink, tantalising female company, and general revelry. He took part in the merry-making, expecting, no doubt, that the noise of the evening would drown the voice in his conscience, now speaking ever louder and louder.

But it had the opposite effect. The next morning the stabbing reality of his lostness hurried in to fill up the vacuum left by the fleeting pleasures of the past night. The scenes of gaiety, now only a memory, seemed strangely absurd against the awful peril into which his soul seemed to be sinking. As is always the case, vain amusements and carnal delights leave no abiding peace but only the debris of misspent ambitions and frustrated hopes. If one knows he is dropping into hell, the glitter of sin somehow loses its lustre. Asahel's mind was enveloped in impenetrable gloom.

Now he was about to enter a torture chamber which can only be appreciated by others who have trodden the often dark and desolate country known as "Conviction of Sin". Bunyan's famous *Slough of Despond* has also been one way of describing it. One can safely aver that no experience in the horrors of war, or conflict with physical disease, or perils on the high seas, or any other mental or physical trial is worse than the misery of an enlightened sinner, who has come to regard the God who made him as an enemy threatening to cut him off any moment into eternal perdition. It is not that God can be blamed for torturing the sinner; it is just that some enter more poignantly into the perception of the awful realities of His wrath than others. Some saintly people have never had to experience this, but Asahel Nettleton was not one of them.

Having seen his need to be in a right relation to God, he determined to do something about it. He knew that he ought to pray, so he began to seek God as best he knew how. He admits, however, that it was "not without a great

struggle in his feelings, that he was brought to bend the
knee to Jehovah".[11] Diligently he applied himself to the
"means of grace", hoping to find peace for his troubled soul.
He attended church, read the Bible and other religious
books, and abandoned the vain amusements and sinful
companions of former days. Often he wandered for long
hours in the fields praying, or trying to pray, and at times he
stayed awake at night doing the same thing.

Nettleton's attempt to find inner serenity of soul during
these initial days of awakening ended in frustration. God
seemed to be as far away as ever. The aching void in his life
was not filled. His diligent attention to religious activities,
his self denial, his separation from worldly practices seemed
to be utterly fruitless. God apparently regarded neither his
outward conduct nor his prayers. Why God did not hearken
to his prayers was especially difficult for him to understand.
Did not the Bible say that one who asks shall receive, and
one who seeks shall find? But it did not seem to be the case
with him. He asked, he sought (so he thought), but no
answers came. Why, he wondered. Why wouldn't God save
him?

Baffled and confused Asahel began to entertain infidel
thoughts. If there were a God, he would not listen to his
prayers, so perhaps the Bible was not true. Cherishing such
doubts, he set about to disprove the Bible. He searched the
Scriptures trying to find contradictions. At this point he
even began to doubt whether there was a God at all. He tried
to tell himself that God did not exist, for surely if He did
they were not on good terms. He wished that the Bible were
false, for it obviously condemned him. But wandering about
in the bleak and trackless wilds of atheism did him no good.
In fact, he could never fully convince himself that there was
no reality in religion. In his innermost being he knew the
Bible was true, whether he liked it or not.

Now God began, it seems, to uncover the very fountains
of iniquity in his soul. Formerly he had seen himself as
merely a lost soul, now he discovered that he was a rebel
against God, totally depraved. The glaring light of gospel
truth exposed all his former religious activities as merely the
cleansing of the outside of the cup. His self-induced reformation was only an attempt to establish his own righteousness
by the works of the law. The reason that God had not heard
his prayers was that he had not sought salvation by God's

grace through the blood of Christ. He had been, in short, nothing but a self-righteous pharisee who prided himself on his religious devotions and thought God was under obligation to him.

The wound in his spirit was deepened through a discussion in the community on the doctrine of election. Some said that it was true, others repudiated it. After much examination of the Scriptures, he determined that though he did not like it, the Bible taught this truth. This meant that he lay helpless and hopeless at the feet of a sovereign God. He felt that it was his duty to repent, but was aware that his heart was so in love with sin and full of pride that he was not willing to do so. He was conscious now that if God did not subdue his heart by an act of almighty power, he would never be converted.

Under an awareness of these awful realities, his distress became almost unbearable. He walked about like a condemned criminal soon to be taken to the gallows. During the day the storm clouds of God's wrath hovered over him. Even at night no sweet repose soothed his weary limbs, for he feared that he would awake in "a miserable eternity". "Could it be that I have committed the unpardonable sin?" he would ask himself. That possibility extinguished the last spark of hope in his darkened mind. At one time he considered himself in the throes of death, and felt that he was about ready to enter the realms of the damned. "An unusual tremor seized all my limbs," he said, "and death appeared to have taken hold upon me." For several hours, the horror of his mind was inexpressible.

There was, however, an unseen hand guiding the trembling sinner, a hand that was as gentle as it was powerful. Horrible as it was, this brush with despair was necessary for the training of a man for whom the great God designed nothing but abundant mercies. He little knew at the time that having learned the "terrors of the Lord" in the school of conviction, he would someday be able all the better to "persuade men" to flee to the arms of Christ.

Those who have studied the inner conflicts of the heirs of salvation know that the Saviour of men has a way, in His appointed hour, of breaking through the iron prison in which the captive soul is held. He knows how to rout Satan and his legions of helpers, setting the prisoners at liberty. The blessed hour of deliverance came for Asahel just when it seemed that the infernal spirits were about to drag their victim off into the pits of perdition. But a cross barred the way.

Peace did not dawn in his soul with dramatic suddenness. Somewhat gradually the nightmare of terror passed away and some stability was restored in a rational domain where King Reason was nearly driven from his seat. Asahel detected a decided change in his attitude toward God and the great themes of the gospel. "The character of God now appeared lovely. The Saviour was exceedingly precious; and the doctrines of grace, towards which he had felt such bitter opposition, he contemplated with delight."[12] He had learned the hard way that salvation is by grace – now he relished this truth. "He now felt a peculiar love for the people of God, and a delight in the duties of religion, to which before he was a total stranger."[13] Such a fundamental change in one's view of the Deity, the way of salvation, and ordinary Christian responsibilities, we can safely declare to be marks of regeneration.

Asahel had been converted. An unseen hand had snatched him from the yawning gulf of destruction. He was now a child of God and peace filled his heart. He was always shy about dogmatically stating in public that he was a genuine subject of grace. This can be accounted for on two grounds. For one thing, the theology of his day asserted that the glory of God is more important than one's own personal salvation. Secondly, much emphasis was put on the danger of deception. Even the most godly were not presumptuous about being Christians. They candidly faced the possibility of being deceived themselves. But Asahel did believe in assurance of salvation, and few doubted that he possessed it.

CHAPTER 5

A "USEFUL MAN" IN TRAINING

During the latter part of Nettleton's traumatic struggle to find salvation, which took the better part of ten months, the pulpit at Killingworth was supplied by a worker from the Missionary Society of Connecticut, Josiah B. Andrews. He came to the church during the spring of 1801 and stayed till the autumn, when he left for a few months. Andrews' preaching no doubt aided the young farmer in his pursuit of God.

We learn from Andrews that a revival broke out in Killingworth shortly after he came. Nettleton's conversion in September was one manifestation of this phenomenon. Andrews wrote the details of this revival in an article printed in *The Connecticut Evangelical Magazine* (T.C.E.M.), a periodical which gave a running account of the awakenings taking place in Connecticut. On the tenth of May some of his parishioners requested "a conference". In the language of the day, this meant an "inquiry meeting" in which the pastor was expected to give special counsel to awakened sinners. Andrews was astounded when fifty people came to this meeting. This response caught the preacher off his guard and he was at a loss as to what to do. Though new to such business, he brought a message in which he counselled the seekers as best he could.

The rising tide of interest in his congregation convinced Andrews that "the Spirit of the Lord was working" in Killingworth. Greatly encouraged, he set about promoting the revival and began a series of weekly conferences. These meetings were enthusiastically attended and as the summer wore on, more and more began to seek God. Some of the chronic problems in the church, such as factional quarrels

33

and doctrinal disputes, began to subside. There was no doubt about it, the second great awakening had touched the home town of Asahel Nettleton.

Before Andrews left in October, a number of people had made professions of faith, or as they expressed it then, they were "rejoicing in hope". By December thirty-two converts had joined the church. He returned in January and threw himself again into the work which had gone along remarkably well during his absence. By March 1802, the congregation had been swelled by ninety-one professions. Among these were Asahel Nettleton and a very close friend, Philander Parmele.

Prior to his conversion, Asahel's ambitions had been modest. To train for a military, legal, or academic profession had never entered his mind. He had grown up on a farm and his father still depended heavily upon him to assist in providing for their growing family. He had expected to "spend his days in agricultural pursuits". But the situation had changed radically by the autumn of 1801. He was a different person with new thoughts and aspirations. He went back to the fields with the same attention to his duties, but in the midst of harvesting the crops for that year a more noble harvest field came into his mind. Soon he became aware of the need for labourers to gather souls into God's kingdom. He often thought, "If I might be the means of saving one soul, I should prefer it to all the riches and honours of this world".[14]

Christian periodicals, especially *T.C.E.M.*, were now aglow, not only with reports of the great revival at home, but also with exciting news about events transpiring in the area of foreign missions. Nettleton read these with great interest. He eagerly studied the work being done by the London Missionary Society, which eventually sent Robert Morrison to China, and the Baptist Missionary Society in England, which had already sponsored Carey in India for eight years. His heart was stirred as he perused Horne's *Letters on Missions*. The publications awakened in his heart a strong desire to be a missionary himself. In fact he soon resolved to devote himself to the cause of foreign missions if divine providence would allow. Asahel wanted to be a bearer of the Word of Life to the heathen. All his thoughts now turned in that direction.

This would require time and preparation. He needed an

education, a *college* education, but how was this possible? He had no means of financing such an undertaking. Even as he was pondering these matters, a terrible tragedy happened. In the spring and summer of 1802 one of the periodic epidemics which swept over the country struck Killingworth. During the year over six hundred were sick in N. Killingworth alone. Many died. Unfortunately the Nettleton family was not spared. Before the siege was over, Samuel, Asahel's father, and David, his younger brother had died. They, along with others, were buried in the little village cemetery.

This epidemic may well have been yellow fever, a mosquito-borne disease which devastated the eastern seaboard of America during this period. In peak times yellow fever was known to decimate not only cities but armies as well. Philadelphia alone suffered twenty epidemics and in 1793 the disease sent twelve thousand of the city's fifty-five thousand inhabitants, including President Washington, into flight. The national government was in turmoil. The rest of the city simply stopped. Many people stayed indoors, others lit bonfires in the street to dispel the poisonous vapours they thought caused the disease. Philip Freneau, the contemporary poet, lamented:

> Nature's poisons here collected,
> Water, earth, and air infected . . .,
> O, what pity,
> Such a City
> Was in such a place erected![15]

The true cause of this disease was not known until the turn of the twentieth century and the United States was not rid of its ravages until 1905.

The untimely death of his father threw the entire family responsibilities upon the shoulders of the oldest son. This increased burden made the thought of a college career even more difficult for Asahel. His presence at home was indispensable. Nevertheless he thought it best to do everything possible to prepare himself for college if the door of opportunity should open. He dreamed of the day when he could pack his belongings and go to New Haven and become a student at Yale. He secured books however he could and studied under Andrews, who by then had been installed permanently as pastor at Killingworth. After long days of labour in the fields during the summer, he went to the parsonage where, under the tutelage of the pastor, he investigated Biblical truths.

The winters afforded more leisure from his farm tasks, so he got a job as a teacher. This enabled him to establish some financial independence other than that which came from his work on the farm. He was employed as a school-teacher for several winters, "probably in the 'Blue School House', where his cousin Titus Coan, later missionary to the Sandwich Islands, also taught".[16] In this way he was able to lay aside some money for college. By the autumn of 1805, four years after his conversion, Nettleton had mastered the preparatory studies for college. In the middle of the autumn term he entered the freshman class at Yale.

What Asahel's thoughts were when first his eyes gazed upon the chapel building with its tall, weather-vane capped spire and the rectangular, colonial styled South Middle College adjacent to it, we can only surmise. Perhaps a flood of emotion surged in his soul, borne up by his reflection upon the glorious history of this institution. He certainly felt honoured to study in a school which had produced such men as Jonathan Edwards, David Brainerd, and Joseph Bellamy. There was no place in the world Asahel would have rather been then than there at Yale, third oldest college in the United States.

He soon met the president, Timothy Dwight, the redoubtable grandson of the illustrious Jonathan Edwards. A remarkably versatile man, Dwight had spent twelve years as a pastor, wrote poetry, dabbled in politics, and was rapidly establishing himself as one of the foremost theologians and educators of the country. When he came to Yale in 1795 he found that the school was a hotbed of infidelity and immorality. The intellectual idols of the undergraduates were Voltaire, Rousseau and other antagonists of Christianity. The lives of the students reflected the libertine views they espoused. "Wine and liquors were kept in many rooms; intemperance, profanity, gambling and licentiousness were common."[17]

Timothy Dwight was appalled. No such situation would be tolerated if he could help it. For a while there was a spiritual conflict between the president, the stalwart champion of the old orthodoxy, and the young infidels with whom the college swarmed. As soon as Dwight arrived the agnostical students handed him a list of subjects for class discussion.

Previously the faculty had avoided head on debate with the students, who surmised that Dwight would do the same. To their astonishment he chose the subject, "Is the Bible the Word of God?" He encouraged those who were of the negative position to do their best. After their efforts, Dwight gave a series of lectures in which the inspiration of the Scriptures was triumphantly defended and after this, as Lyman Beecher (who witnessed the whole thing) said, "all infidelity skulked and hid its head".[18]

When Nettleton arrived on the campus, in 1805, the moral climate had changed, thanks largely to Dwight, and the institution had regained much of the prestige it had enjoyed in the pre-revolutionary war days. Yale provided just the kind of atmosphere Nettleton needed to study theology and develop his intellectual resources.

Although the school was vastly different from what it had been ten years previously, still Nettleton did not find many people there who shared his spiritual interests. In fact, in the freshman class he was "the only professor of religion". The new generation offered a fresh challenge to Dwight. There was no scepticism, swearing, or gambling, but few, like Asahel, had made the pursuit of God and truth the all-consuming object of life. Many of them had merely academic aspirations. For this reason, he was, during his college years, somewhat of a loner. His few close friends were those who, like him, were wholly dedicated to God.

Yale was the most prestigious school in Connecticut at the time and certainly many of the students came from the higher classes of society. To many of them probably Asahel seemed like a country bumpkin. His plain clothing and unpolished manners betrayed his rural background. He was quiet, shy, modest and psychologically an introvert. But one thing was evident to all, this young man was serious about his faith. He gave abundant evidence of an unquenchable thirst for God. He took great delight in "spiritual exercises". The Bible was his favourite book, the Sabbath was his favourite day, and the chapel was his favourite place. Here the young would-be missionary listened rapturously as Dwight expounded the Word of God and challenged the students to go forth in God's service. The dedication and sincerity of Asahel did not escape the notice of the college president. Once he remarked of him, "He will make one of the most useful men this country has ever seen".[19] The

descendant of Jonathan and Sarah Edwards was no fool in
analysing character.

Academically Asahel's college career was not distinguished. He was considered to be an average scholar. A close
friend and room-mate, Jonathan Lee, gives three reasons for
this. For one thing his inherent shyness and diffidence
worked against him. He was modest to a fault, and seemed
to be somewhat embarrassed when called upon to recite in
class. For another thing he was almost totally absorbed in
the study of Biblical subjects and theology. He had, frankly,
little interest in the sciences and secular literature. Also
during his junior year he had some severe mental problems,
which would be diagnosed today as depression. It was a
period of self-doubt in which he wondered whether he were
a true Christian. Such an experience would have had an
understandably distracting effect upon his studies.

We might also add to these the fact that he had heavy
outside responsibilities. He was often away, being required
at times to help on the farm at Killingworth. He continued
to labour under financial difficulties and during his first
years in college he taught in a school at New Haven. Putting
all these factors together, we can see that Asahel had more
than ordinary difficulties to surmount in getting a college
education. But he plodded on and concluded his studies in
1809.

During the winter of 1807-1808 he was involved in the
second revival of his life. It took place at Yale and in the
outlying region in New Haven. Nettleton took a great
interest in this movement and frequently counselled with
those who were awakened. Often he would be seen in the
late evening hours walking arm in arm with some fellow
student who was seeking peace for his soul. The revival
"seemed almost to absorb his mind by day and by night".[20]
Once he stayed up all night by the bedside of one who was
just coming out of a prolonged period of anxiety.

The pattern of Asahel's intellectual interests and activities
during the years at Yale would seem peculiar if we did not
look at the future work God had designed for him. All of his
experiences thus far, on the farm, in the college class room,
and as a teacher in an academy, were preparing him to be
a winner of souls.

CHAPTER 6

A KINDRED SPIRIT

Certain great movements in history are symbolised by seemingly insignificant objects. A piece of paper nailed to the door of a church in Wittenberg by an Augustinian monk is, more than anything else, remembered as an indication of the tradition-defying daring of the leaders of the Protestant Reformation. A cracked, cast iron bell hanging in a hall in Philadelphia has been gazed upon, photographed, copied, and emblazoned upon millions of walls, because two hundred years ago it pealed forth the news of a nation's birth.

Nothing is, perhaps, associated with the great missionary movement of America in the 19th century more than a haystack in a remote meadow on the Hoosic river in Massachusetts. It was beneath the shade of this haystack that a group of students at Williams College met on Saturday afternoons to pray about their duty to evangelise heathen nations. These men were praying by the haystack at the same time that Asahel Nettleton was struggling to get his B.A. degree at Yale.

All of those in this famous prayer group would make their mark in the world. There was Luther Rice, who was destined to become one of the most famous promoters of missions among Baptists. There was James Richards, on his way to becoming a Presbyterian theologian. Also in this group was the man who, in a large measure, was the real moving spirit behind the modern American missionary movement, Samuel J. Mills. There is an absolutely amazing similarity between Asahel Nettleton, the modest farm boy from Killingworth, and Samuel Mills the missionary visionary in Williams College. They were born on the same day, 21st April, 1773. They were converted at approximately

the same time, the autumn of 1801. Both pursued the
vocation of farming, and both "while toiling at the plough"
were "touched with compassion for the heathen world".[21]
Yet remarkably, and here the analogy continues, neither of
these two men was permitted to carry out his ambition in the
missionary cause. Mills died at sea in 1817, after an explora-
tory trip to Western Africa, and Nettleton became an
itinerant evangelist.

Samuel and Asahel became intimately acquainted with
each other during the latter's junior year at college. They
were brought together by a classmate and close friend of
Asahel, Simeon Woodruff. Woodruff was himself devoted to
the cause of missions and "although he never became a
foreign missionary, he spent his life in the newly opened
Western Reserve, for the Missionary Society of Connecticut".[22] On one of his vacations, Woodruff came into contact
with Mills, whose mind at the time was absorbed completely
with the thought of taking the gospel to foreign fields.
Woodruff overheard him talking about this and immediately
saw a parallel with his own intimate at Yale, Nettleton.
"You talk," said Woodruff to Mills, "just like one of my
classmates. He says, he intends never to be settled, but to be
a missionary to the heathen."[23] Ever eager to join forces with
any and all who shared his burden for missions, Mills soon
set out for New Haven to meet Nettleton.

The meeting of these two kindred spirits was most natural.
Their personal similarities and identical motivations were
readily apparent. Mills told Nettleton of his friends at
Williams who had formed with himself a partnership to
pray about missions and to begin, if possible, a society for
the propagation of the gospel in foreign lands. No doubt he
related, with glowing enthusiasm, the details of their
meetings by the haystack, and of other delightful experiences
these students had shared. Asahel revealed his own burning
desire to preach to the heathen. The conversation of these
two reminds one of the two disciples on the road to Emmaus.
As they "talked of all these things which had happened",
and shared future hopes of labours among those who had
never heard the gospel, their "hearts burned" with fervent
devotion.

The year after Mills graduated from Williams, he came
back to Yale for graduate work, ostensibly to study theology,
but his real intention was to seek out more kindred spirits

whom he wished to interest in missions. He and Nettleton
entered into a solemn covenant to "avoid all entangling
alliances, and to hold themselves in readiness to go to the
heathen, whenever God, in His providence, should prepare
the way".[24] They also agreed to meet at Andover Seminary
the following year to pursue their theological studies and to
plan future action.

Nettleton graduated from Yale in the spring of 1809,
anxious to join Mills in his rapidly developing missionary
plans. But a problem had arisen to delay his own participa-
tion in such endeavours. During his college studies he had
accumulated some debts which he felt should be dissolved
before he attended to anything else. Mills encouraged him to
seek the assistance of some friends in this matter, but
Nettleton felt that he should take care of it himself. President
Dwight offered the position of Butler in the college to
Nettleton, and, after considerable solicitation on Dwight's
part, he accepted. "The Butler acted as a sort of commissary
for the students, and, if one had any business ability at all,
it was an opportunity to make money."[25] Asahel felt that he
could not turn this offer down. He held this post for a year,
during which time he was able to liquidate his debts and
continue his theological studies under Dwight.

The extra year at Yale, though necessary, caused Asahel
to miss missionary consultations at Andover. It was in the
year 1810 that the petition by the Andover associates to the
General Association of Massachusetts led to the organisation
of the American Board (for missions). Both Samuel and
Asahel were deeply disappointed that the latter was unable
to attend these historic deliberations. The circumstance of
Asahel's absence probably changed the course of his life,
though as future events proved, it was providential. It was
one of the first indications that God had chosen him for a
work other than that which he himself had designed. In the
years following, Mills and Nettleton lost contact with one
another. Neither ever became a missionary, though Mills
was instrumental in recruiting many pioneer missionaries.

Having now graduated from college and paid his debts,
Asahel was ready to pursue his intention to be a gospel
minister, hopefully on foreign fields. In spite of the many
difficulties that had arisen, his financial problems, the death
of his father, the mental depression he had experienced in
college, and the unexpected hindrances in his missionary

aspirations, he had succeeded thus far. But another shock awaited him, for in June of 1810 his mother died. This did not divert him from his goal, however. He turned the farm responsibilities over to his brother Ambrose, and continued to seek God's leading for his own life.

The next phase of his training for the ministry was to be a sort of apprentice in training with an established pastor. It was the custom in the days following the first great awakening, before the theological seminaries were founded, for young candidates for the ministry to live in the home of a parish minister and study under his supervision. Such "parsonage schools" were conducted by Jonathan Edwards, and his own pupil Joseph Bellamy. Even after the seminary at Andover had been established in 1807, the old system of sending a young college graduate to the care and assistance of an older minister was common.

After his extra year at Yale, Asahel arranged to be an assistant to the Rev. Bezaleel Pinneo, who served as pastor of a church at Milford, Connecticut, just a few miles southwest of New Haven on Long Island Sound. Pinneo had come to the first Church in Milford in 1796 and continued there till 1849, five years after Nettleton's death. Asahel remained with Pinneo until May 1811.

Many years later, in a letter to Bennet Tyler, Pinneo commented somewhat on his impression of Nettleton at this time. He acknowledged that he could recall nothing really unusual as far as his "piety" was concerned, though he could recall that he was a man of robust physique and vigorous mind. He also remembered that the young student was exceedingly fond of theology, though not merely in an abstract speculative sense, but as the basis of a true experience of grace and a zealous Christian life.

Asahel remained in the parsonage at Milford only a short time. Plans were then made to license him to preach. The New Haven West Association performed this function on 28th May, 1811. Having been licensed he was able to preach as opportunity afforded, and ordination would follow as soon as a definite course of ministry was chosen. At the time he still devoutly looked to "the regions beyond", the mission field.

CHAPTER 7

THE LONG SHADOW OF
EDWARDS

As the summer of 1811 approached, there were many uncertainties for Asahel. Many of his past relationships had become meaningless; in fact domestic ties had been greatly weakened by death. He had already seen four of his family members buried: his mother, father, one sister and a brother. But what of the future?

At twenty-eight he was beginning his ministry somewhat later than usual. When David Brainerd (whose Memoirs he had studied shortly after his conversion) was this age his missionary work was largely done and he was soon to enter into his eternal reward. Asahel wanted to hear the "Macedonian Call" to embark for a foreign mission field, but no signs of such a call were forthcoming. He wondered what significance there could be in the fact that he had missed the important conference on missions at Andover the previous year. Did this mean that he would be left stranded on shore while the great missionary ship was being launched so auspiciously in America?

There were no inner uncertainties, of course, as far as his faith and doctrinal convictions were concerned. His theological system was built squarely upon the evangelical heritage of the Protestant Reformation. Such orthodox doctrines as the Trinity, the inspiration of the Scriptures, justification by faith, Christ's divinity, atonement and second coming, he never questioned in the least. The Unitarian and Universalist speculations, which posed an increasing threat, especially at Harvard and in the larger eastern cities, he never entertained for a moment. As far as Asahel was concerned, a literal, eternal heaven was the hope of the righteous and a fearful hell was the prospect of the wicked.

In addition to the broad evangelical traditions of the Reformation, Asahel adhered to the Calvinistic convictions which characterised the "Presbygationalists"* of New England. His theological training under Josiah Andrews, Timothy Dwight, and Bezalel Pinneo, made him a legitimate heir of the Puritans of England and the Pilgrim Fathers of America. Asahel also fell within the influence of the towering figure who dominated the theology of New England for several generations, Jonathan Edwards. Most of the educational institutions of the East, and the overwhelming majority of the pastors, adhered, with whatever minor modifications, to his teachings. Two men who studied directly under Edwards, and who were his main interpreters, Joseph Bellamy (1719-1790) and Samuel Hopkins (1721-1803) were also very influential.

Long before he walked in the academic halls at New Haven, Asahel buried himself in the writings of the great master Edwards, and his most brilliant pupils, Bellamy and Hopkins. The Edwardian school of theology held that the *glory of God* was the supreme purpose of the Deity Himself in creation, and should be the goal of all mankind. Conversion was viewed as a vision and perception of the essential beauty of God and piety or godliness was considered to be an unselfish devotion to that vision. Hopkins particularly stressed that selfishness or self-interest is the essence of sin and any religion that had *personal benefit* at its root was regarded as spurious. Hopkins went so far as to state that the godly are willing to be damned if the glory of God required it. Nettleton never went along with Hopkins in this respect, but throughout his ministry he frowned upon "selfish" conversions, that is, professions of faith based on a desire to receive some benefit from God, rather than on surrender to Him.

Great emphasis was put by advocates of the Edwardian school on the sovereignty of God. Salvation was an act of God's unmerited grace, rooted originally in His elective purpose. But it was, in reality, the fact of human freedom and responsibility that most occupied their studies. Edwards' classic treatise *The Freedom of the Will* sparked off an intense

---

*The Presbyterians and Congregationalists of this period worked together according to what was known as "The Plan of Union". Individual churches could call men of either persuasion and there was complete ecclesiastical interchange between the two groups. This amalgamation has been called "Presbygationalism". Later on differences arose and this arrangement was terminated.

and exhaustive investigation among the ministers of the
next century on the nature of man's will and its place in
redemption. Edwards' pioneer studies, some of which were
largely philosophical and speculative in nature, gave birth
to the New England position that man's depravity is *moral*,
not physical or mental. In other words, the only handicap
that natural or unsaved men have in serving God is their
own blindness and perverse unwillingness to bend the knee
to the claims of the gospel. The "deadness" of the sinner is
not that of a stump or stone, but separation from God –
rebellion against the creator. Men have the natural ability
to turn to Christ, that is, they have the mental faculties,
soul, mind and power of choosing. But they do not have the
will or desire to serve God. They believed that human
responsibility is founded on this distinction, for if man is not
endowed with the natural or psychological faculties for doing
God's will he can no more be culpable than a brute beast.

The "New England Calvinism", with its innovations in
the area of moral responsibility, placed the Edwardians
somewhat at odds with the "old School" position of which
Princeton College was the intellectual centre. Those who
moved in the Princeton orbit followed the stricter inter-
pretations of the canons of Dort, and men such as Turretin
and Witsius. These "covenant" theologians based imputation of sin and righteousness on the respective covenants
made between God on the one hand, and Adam and Christ
on the other. They were strong advocates of limited atonement. Many of the English Puritans were of the covenant
school and most of the earlier New England Puritans had
not arrived at the distinction Edwards made between moral
and natural or physical inability. Post-Edwardian divines
insisted that they did not modify fundamental Calvinism
but were merely explaining it and bringing it in line with
sound philosophical principles and thus vindicating it from
its opponents.

There were, of course, variations of interpretation even
among the followers of Edwards. One of the most hotly
contested subjects during the days of Nettleton's college
studies was the place of "means" for the unconverted. Some,
such as Hopkins, held that all the acts of the unsaved, even
in his use of the means of grace, such as church attendance,
Bible reading, and prayer, were inherently wicked since they
had not the true love of God in their hearts. For this reason

he felt that it was wrong and dangerous to tell the unsaved to "use the means" as a hope of securing salvation. Since sinners only "abuse" and never "use" properly the means, this only confirms the lost in their sinful state.

Timothy Dwight, and others, thought that while salvation could not be attained absolutely by merely the use of means, they can be a helpful "aid" in coming to repentance and faith. Dwight encouraged the awakened sinners to pray, seek God, go to church, and read the Bible. He taught that no one actually sins in doing these things, and that even the unconverted are helped by such activities.

Nettleton disagreed with his mentor on this question. Like Hopkins, he felt that the promises of salvation go out only to those who perform the ultimate spiritual acts of repentance and faith, not to users of the means. To exhort men to do anything but repent and submit to God is only to encourage carnal security and confirm men in an un-converted state. While at college this subject was hotly debated and Asahel boldly stood against Dwight and the students who took the anti-Hopkinsian position.* To our generation some of these issues seem like hair splitting, and no doubt these men were at times only looking at the same truth from two different perspectives, but at that time they were considered to be grave issues and men became quite polarised on these matters.

If the views of Edwards on the way of salvation prevailed in the colleges and parishes of New England at the beginning of the 19th century, his concept of revival was just as domi-nant. The ultimate goal of every New England pastor was to see the "Great Awakening" at Northampton duplicated in his own church. These men, like Edwards, looked upon awakenings within the church as a *work of God*, just as they attributed the salvation of an individual sinner to sovereign mercy. Their views on the depravity of human nature led them to expect nothing fruitful in their ministries short of a special and sovereign intervention from heaven. This is not to say that they were fatalistic or dilatory as far as their responsibilities were concerned. Far from it. The Edwardian pastors were diligent preachers and zealous prayer warriors.

---

*Nettleton has been falsely accused of being completely Hopkinsian in outlook. But he avoided the glaring errors of this system, namely that men should be willing to be damned for the glory of God, and that God is in some sense the author of sin.

Even in the midst of the "forty years wilderness" period, pastors and laymen alike gathered for times of united prayer. They preached the Word in season and out of season, hoping that God would "rend the heavens and come down" with revival blessings.

Asahel Nettleton was thoroughly in sympathy with such theocentric notions of salvation and revival. His own conversion experience and the revivals he had seen at Killingworth and New Haven all confirmed in his own mind that spiritual awakenings were *miracles* sent down from God. This placed him in a harmonious position with the Presbygationalist pastors of New England and thus made him acceptable to them. No itinerant preacher would ever have been invited into their pulpits who did not hold to the New England Calvinism.

So, in the middle of the year 1811, Asahel was firmly established in theology as he started down the now somewhat hazy path of life as a preacher. He possessed what he believed were the proper tools for his trade. He was "hopefully converted", he believed in sound doctrine, he had a B.A. degree from Yale, and he was now licensed to preach. But where would he put these tools into action? He was ready to proclaim the gospel anywhere, he only waited for an open door.

Chapter 8

WASTE PLACES

Asahel was looking for a mission field and at the beginning of the 19th century the closest thing to a mission field in Connecticut was the south-eastern corner of the state. This section was known among the Congregationalists at the time as one of the "waste places". This expression meant that the churches were small in membership, spiritually inert, and often unable to afford a full-time minister. It was generally known that the low state of religion here was attributable to events which took place in this region some sixty years previously.

The churches here had been "wasted" or damaged by recklessness on the part of "itinerant" evangelists, particularly one named James Davenport. He had visited some of the churches in the area around Stonington during the closing days of the great awakening. Fierce controversy had attended the ministry of Davenport and many churches had been divided because of him.

The parish in North Stonington had once contained a strong and flourishing church. The pastor during the period of the great awakening was Joseph Fish; in fact he had arrived just before that movement. Under his leadership a tremendous revival took place and there were large accessions to the church. The minutes of the church recorded, in Fish's own handwriting, this entry: "In this great and glorious day of grace were admitted in one day the following persons. . . ."[26] The names of the eighty persons who had joined the church on one day are listed. In the midst of the revival, Davenport came to Stonington. Born in 1716, he had graduated from Yale in 1732, one of the youngest ever to take a degree from that institution. In 1838, at the age of twenty-two he was ordained as minister of the Presbyterian church in Southold, Long Island. It was while pastoring on Long Island that he became acquainted with George Whitefield, who was then on a preaching tour in America. Davenport was greatly influenced by Whitefield and a warm friendship developed between them. Whitefield seems to have regarded Davenport highly, and is reported to have remarked of him, "Of all men living he knew of none who kept a closer walk with God".[27]

Davenport was very enthusiastic about the revivals generated by Whitefield and his coadjutors at the time, and threw himself with great energy into evangelism. He began in his own church, seeking to promote an awakening there. From the first his methods seemed extravagant and un-orthodox. On one occasion he gathered his church together and preached to them for a twenty-four hour period without stopping. He was so exhausted after this marathon meeting that he secluded himself for several days. Following this, however, some made professions of faith. Immediately, Davenport formed a special attachment to the new converts, addressing them as "brother" or "sister", while dubbing the other church members as "Mr" and "Mrs".

Having tasted the heady wine of revival power, Davenport began to move outside his own parish for preaching activi-ties. In 1741 he held a series of meetings in southern Connecticut, at Stonington and further west. When he came to North Stonington he met the pastor of the church, Joseph Fish, but was not satisfied with the pastor's level of enthusiasm. Although Fish had personally witnessed an awakening in his own congregation, Davenport analysed Fish as being spiritually dead. On the other hand Fish resented Davenport's coming into his parish uninvited. Thus a rivalry soon began between the two men. Davenport denounced Fish as being antagonistic to revivals, and the pastor resisted the over-charged attitude of the intruder.

Soon the people in Stonington began to polarise about the two men. Davenport's converts and others, even in Fish's congregation, attached themselves to the evangelist, while others were loyal to the pastor. Davenport soon began to encourage outright revolt on the part of his followers and urged them to leave their church. He seems to have had more influence than Fish, as seen by the number whom he had infected with the seditious spirit. Ninety-two members

of the church withdrew and, along with their families and
friends, helped to organise a new congregation of four
hundred. A minority remained in sympathy with Fish and
held together the greatly weakened older church. Other
malcontents drifted into other denominations and doubtless
some stopped going to church altogether. All in all it was a
most unfortunate schism, as unnecessary as it was hurtful.

The rift created by Davenport's intrusions at Stonington
brought an end to the revival. Not long after the division
in the congregation, Davenport left the community and
went to another town, leaving the separate group to fend
for itself. Unfortunately the trouble at Stonington was duplicated many times under the rash conduct of Davenport.
He became notorious as a divider of churches and eventually
was branded a fanatic. He came to set great store by visions,
trances, inward impressions upon the mind and direct
impressions from texts of scripture. He regarded these
experiences as infallible evidences of a work of the Spirit.
Before his stormy career had come to an end, many a good
pastor had felt the heat of his denunciations and had suffered
similarly to Fish. Those who did not give an unqualified
endorsement to his ministry were labelled as "rabbis",
"pharisees", and "letter-learned", but spiritually dead enemies of God. Eventually Davenport came to his senses and
tearfully confessed that he had been wrong in sowing such
discord among the churches, but the deed had been done.

When Nettleton came to Stonington he found the results
of the division still much in evidence. The wreckage left by
Davenport's indiscretions could be seen in both the congregations. Bitterness and antagonism still prevailed between
the two groups, and neither showed signs of spiritual life.
The old original church had very few members and had not
supported a resident minister since 1781. The separatist
congregation, which had been founded by Davenport, was
also in a run-down condition.

The situation at Stonington intrigued Asahel and he
began to make an independent investigation of the situation.
He talked to some of the people who had lived during the
time of the conflict. He found a number of pamphlets and
books which dealt with the controversy and studied them
carefully. He observed first hand the spiritual desolation in
this vicinity and it was uniformly believed that it had all
been caused by the explosive problems of the Davenport era.

Asahel found it virtually impossible to stop the long-standing feud and heal the breach. The two groups did not wish to unite. As a result, the cause of Christ was suffering drastically. As long as the two churches were at swords drawn a minister could do little good. The very name "revival" had become a reproach.

Interestingly, while at Stonington Asahel made the acquaintance of a man who was remarkably similar to Davenport in his outlook. His name was James Davis, a native of Woodstock, Connecticut. He had begun his ministry as a missionary to the Indians but also he did some evangelistic work among the white population. An ode written for the bicentennial of the Stonington church refers to him as "an odd but godly man", who "conceived and carried out a mission plan, of preaching through the land from day to day".[28]

Nettleton had opportunity to find how "odd" and "godly" he was, for he spent considerable time with Davis reviewing the situation at Stonington and discussing how revivals should be promoted. Asahel soon found that Davis had little use for "settled pastors" and, much like Davenport, he regarded them as being opposed to revivals. He sought to convince the wary preacher from Killingworth that no revival could be conducted unless the local pastor was discredited and "broken down" or humiliated in the eyes of his people. With the tragic example of Fish's congregation before him, Nettleton was not tempted to adopt this point of view. It was, as he saw it, just such a course as Davis advocated which had ruined the church in North Stonington. He was quickly coming to the conclusion that the methods of Davis were not only erroneous but dangerous in a high degree.

At this very time, Davis and others like him were causing great consternation among the Congregationalist leaders of the area. The pastors in the outlying districts were alarmed when Davis carried his banner into their parishes and did everything possible to deter him. They protested to the Congregationalist association, hoping to have him censored. But Davis was defiant. To him, this was only the "reproach" one had to bear for standing for the truth. It was more proof that the only course for a true revivalist is "all out war" on the sluggish and obtuse parish ministers.

Asahel was learning some important lessons. His views

on evangelism and the proper mode of conduct for itinerant
ministers were taking shape. If this visit to the Stonington
area accomplished anything, it was to teach him that great
wisdom is required in carrying on revival activities, particularly on the part of the visiting evangelists. Itinerants, he
concluded from what he had observed, were not to intrude
into parishes without the explicit invitation of the local
pastors, and any attempts at reaching the people of the
community should be carried on in harmony with them.
Any other approach is destined to destroy, not promote, the
work of the kingdom. The methods of Davenport and Davis
serve to bring temporary notoriety and success to their
contrivers, but the long range results would be devastating.
This was now Asahel's conviction.

The importance of his ministry in south-eastern Connecticut was in the training that this unique period afforded him.
As far as his preaching was concerned, there were few
visible results. Though there were some conversions, he
never saw anything close to a revival in this place. In fact,
he was unable to do much to repair the damage which had
been done in the previous century. But the education process
for the future evangelist was going on. He had seen real
revival at Killingworth and at New Haven, and he had cut
out for himself the path he wanted to follow doctrinally.
But one thing else was needed; the proper methods in
evangelism must be determined. The wild-fire brand of
evangelism of Davenport was a good example of what an
evangelist was not to do. Thus, by a negative model, Asahel's
concepts on how to promote a revival were being formed.
This experience would stand him in good stead in his career
as an itinerant evangelist, which was, unbeknown to him,
just around the corner. Also it would give him the background to face the "new measures" conflict which would
burst upon him fifteen years later.

The year Asahel spent in the region about Stonington set
the stage for his famous visit to South Britain. It was in the
autumn of 1812 that he received an invitation to preach in
South Salem, New York. While on his way to New York,
he stopped over for a week in the parish of Bennet Tyler.
Here he moved out of the arid "waste place" into the golden,
waving fields of spiritual harvest. In the school house
meetings at South Britain he gained the momentum for his
illustrious course of soul winning.

There were two things during his stay at South Britain which contributed to the change in direction of his life-work. First, it was here that he himself was able to have a leadership role in a revival. He found that revivals were his native clime. Second, here the gifts for which he would become famous came to the surface. His preaching always featured the piercing eye, the analytical knowledge of human nature, the serious demeanor and the dramatic style. And then, the audience reaction: the solemn stillness, the hypnotic attention, and deep convictions which were manifested at the first service at South Britain, characterised his entire ministry. As the frustrated missionary aspirant drove his carriage across the woodlands of Connecticut to meet Tyler and preach for him, he little realised that revival fires would soon be blazing behind him. He little knew what tremendous power to influence the hearts of men was now in his grasp.

---

[1] Among the helpful descriptions of Asahel Nettleton's physical appearance is that of Francis Wayland, who heard him in 1820 when he preached at Union College, Schenectady, New York (Wayland's *Memoir*, Vol. I, pp. 106-111).

[2] Nettleton's first sermon at South Britain is described by his biographer, Bennet Tyler, p. 64 of *Memoir of the Life and Character of Rev. Asahel Nettleton, D.D.*, by Bennet Tyler (Hartford, 1844).

[3] Tyler, p. vi.

[4] *Revival Sketches and Manual*, by Heman Humphrey, D.D. (New York, 1859), p. 94.

[5] Cited in *The Oxford History of the American People* by Samuel Eliot Morison (New York, 1965), p. 164.

[6] *The Life and Letters of Asahel Nettleton, 1783-1844*, Unpublished Thesis Submitted to the Faculty of the Hartford Theological Seminary, by George Hugh Birney, Jr (1943), p. 15.

[7] Birney, p. 15.

[8] Tyler, p. 13.

[9] Birney, p. 16.

[10] Humphrey, p. 115.

[11] Tyler, pp. 19, 20.

[12] *Ibid.*, p. 25.

[13] *Ibid.*, p. 25.

[14] *Ibid.*, p. 29.

[15] *Today, Supplement to The Philadelphia Inquirer*, 13th June, 1976.

[16] Birney, p. 32.

[17] *Autobiography of Lyman Beecher, D.D.*, edited by Charles Beecher (New York, 1864), Vol. I, p. 43.

[18] *Ibid.*, p. 43.

[19] Tyler, p. 36.

[20] *Ibid.*, p. 38.

[21] *Ibid.*, p. 31.

[22] Birney, p. 35.

[23] Tyler, p. 46.

[24] *Ibid.*, p. 47.

[25] Birney, p. 43.

[26] Birney, p. 51.

[27] *Ibid.*, p. 51.

[28] *Ibid.*, p. 53.

PART II

THE
HARVEST OF SOULS

(1812-1820)

I suppose no minister of his time was the means of
so many conversions. . . . He . . . would sway an
audience as the trees of the forest are moved by a
mighty wind.

Francis Wayland

CHAPTER 9

PENTECOSTAL CONVICTION

The author of *Uncle Tom's Cabin*, a literary spark which helped to ignite the greatest civil explosion in the history of the United States, was not old enough in 1813 to be troubled by the plight of the Southern Negro. As a matter of fact she was then a two year old toddler who lived at Litchfield, Connecticut, in what some later sneeringly referred to as "a Puritan penitentiary", the Congregationalist parsonage. Harriet Beecher, who in later life married Calvin E. Stowe, was the daughter of Lyman Beecher, one of the closest friends and associates of Asahel Nettleton. Between 1813 and 1821 Asahel was often in the Beecher home and he preached with great power in Lyman's church, the Congregationalist Church of Litchfield. Lyman invited Nettleton to the Litchfield area in the autumn of 1813, because, starting with his ministry in South Salem, New York, Asahel had established himself as an able and successful evangelist.

The South Salem experience had begun much like that at Stonington, but ended quite differently. The New York community was another "waste place" which was sorely in need of spiritual awakening. The church was without a pastor and in a cold and backslidden state. "Great spiritual apathy existed in the congregation."[1] Asahel preached at the church on the Sabbath following his arrival, and arranged a couple of evening meetings during the week.

His preaching began to take hold upon the minds of the people immediately. Many in the community were awakened to their spiritual needs and a great solemnity spread through the town. After one of the evening meetings a number of young people came to his room in deep distress enquiring how they could become Christians. Asahel pointed them to

57

Christ and "with affectionate earnestness", urged them to repent and believe the gospel. The next day he visited from house to house and found others under deep spiritual impressions. "The seriousness soon spread through the place, and the subject of religion became the engrossing topic of conversation."[2]

Within a couple of weeks several people had made professions of faith. Now it was time for the visiting preacher to set up a soul clinic in order to counsel those who were seeking salvation and others who had already entered the kingdom, or, as they expressed it then, were "rejoicing in hope". Converts in those days were expected to express their assurance in cautious terms lest they appear over-confident and rash. "Rejoicing in hope" meant that they felt they had been converted, based on the light they had. But they also knew that the final test of whether their conversion was real would be *time* and the scrutiny of their hearts in the light of Scripture. Nettleton and all others in the Edwardian school warned converts from the very beginning about the dangers of a false profession. In fact, according to Tyler, this was a dominant theme in the counselling of the new converts at South Salem. "He warned them of the danger of self-deception, reminded them of the deceitfulness of the human heart, and pointed out the various ways in which persons are liable to deceive themselves."[3] If converts did not enter the kingdom *boldly* under such instruction, they did so safely. Spurious conversions were not likely to occur.

Before long the church at South Salem had a different look to it from a spiritual standpoint. Over a period of several weeks the revival increased in power and soon the newly-converted formed quite a sizeable group. The people liked Asahel so well that they tried to prevail upon him to become their pastor, but he considered himself a missionary and refused even to consider such a relationship.

After his ministry in South Salem he was busy preaching at various other points in Connecticut, such as Danbury, North Lyme and Bloomfield. In all of these places he saw considerable success. In North Lyme particularly, a pattern similar to that at South Salem emerged. At first there was no interest in the gospel, but after he began preaching there were many enquirers who were eventually converted. He stayed at North Lyme most of the spring of 1813.

Lyman Beecher was the head of one of the most famous

American families in the 19th century and occupied a unique place on the religious scene during the crucial years prior to the Civil War. Eight years Nettleton's senior, Beecher was an ardent friend and promoter of revivals, a social crusader, and, ultimately, a seminary president. He pastored the church at Litchfield for fifteen years and during this period he often had occasion to enlist the preaching talents of Nettleton.

The youngest parish in the town of Litchfield, known as Milton, was without a pastor and was weakened and upset by internal divisions. The minister had left under strained circumstances and the parish treasury was depleted. Beecher was aware of the plight of the Milton congregation, so he and another pastor nearby raised funds in their churches to help support a preacher in this church. Asahel Nettleton's skills and abilities in getting run-down churches back on their feet were becoming widely known and Beecher thought he was the man to come and preach at Milton.

It was agreed that when Nettleton came he would call at the Congregationalist parsonage at Litchfield. The first meeting of these two men was, to say the least, a "scriptural" one. When Lyman met Asahel at the door he greeted his guest with a peculiar, pious flourish: "Thou hast well done that thou art come." It is hard to believe that this mode of greeting was as Puritanical and stiff as it sounds. Known as a fun-loving parson, Lyman's words may have been tongue-in-cheek. Presumably Asahel thought it safest to answer his greeting in kind. "I ask for what intent ye have sent for me?" he replied. Not to be out biblicised, the host answered, "To hear all things that are commanded thee of God". This was the beginning of a long friendship.

Beecher arranged for Asahel to take up residence on Friday night at the house of one of the members of his church who lived near Milton. On Saturday the people were notified, much to their surprise (they had not been informed of the proceedings on their behalf), that they could expect preaching on Sunday. The next morning Nettleton was there and preached to a very small group of people. Signs of spiritual death were evident. Few professed to be Christians and those who did were lukewarm. After the service, the people all filed out, unmoved thus far. For a moment there was some doubt as to whether the preacher would be entertained for the day. One gentleman, recognis-

ing the embarrassing position of the minister, extended,
somewhat reluctantly, an invitation for Nettleton to dine
with him. During his stay in their home several in this
family became Christians. They were hesitant to welcome
him into their home, but when the time came for him to
leave they were twice as "unwilling to part with their guest".

Asahel's unexpected arrival in the community of Milton
was startling. But after a few weeks of his unique preaching
the surprise gave way to excitement and great crowds
flocked to hear him. The man in their midst was a marked
individualist, as seen in a remark he made after one of the
evening meetings. He told them that he had come at the
request of others and that a revival was his goal and should
be theirs. He urged them to pray for a spiritual awakening.
"Whether you do or not," he said matter of factly, "it is
possible there may be one, for Christians in other places
have agreed to pray for you."[4] Such talk, reflecting a man
totally confident in his God, probably stunned them at first,
but eventually won their hearts.

Before long the Spirit of revival was sweeping through the
town with tremendous power. The meetings in the church
were borne along by a rising surge of interest. Many hearts
were broken up by conviction for sin, creating agony in
some quarters. Some rose up in opposition to the invasion
of godliness, but succumbed to the general spirit of inquiry
as their hearts were laid bare by the lightning thrust of the
strange visitor's sermons. Many of the unbelievers faced
their perilous state with alarm and panic. One evening, as
Nettleton was preaching, two or three experienced "horror
of mind" and had to be removed from the meeting to a
neighbouring house. Such acute distress on the part of those
under conviction was not uncommon during the second great
awakening. The solemn themes with which the preachers
dealt, such as the holiness of God, the strictness of the law,
the certainty of hell and the need for repentance, would
produce just such an effect when accompanied with the
Holy Spirit's power.

After the removal of those who had become agitated,
there was some confusion followed by quiet, reverential
attention. Asahel began to speak again, presiding now over
a spell-bound audience. "It may perhaps be new to some of
you, that there should be such distress for sin," he said. He
left no doubts in their minds as to what was going on. "But

there was great distress on the day of Pentecost, when thousands were pricked in the heart, and cried out, 'Men and brethren, what shall we do?' "[5] Thus Asahel pointed to Pentecost as a precedent for just such scenes as they had witnessed. He then proceeded to explain what conviction is. It is not "religion" which causes people to act thus, it is the lack of it. "The thousands who were pricked in their heart had found that they had no religion, and were unprepared to meet their God. They had made the discovery that they were lost sinners, and that their souls were in jeopardy every hour."[6]

The itinerant's ministry in Milton lasted three or four months. There was a large ingathering of new converts and the church came out of its slump. Before his departure some of the funds which had been collected for his support were offered to him, but he refused to accept. His only material reward for this "campaign" was some clothing which the people presented to him. Having "food and raiment" he was content.

CHAPTER 10

AN ASTONISHING WORK
OF THE SPIRIT

A number of young people from a church in the South part of Litchfield attended Nettleton's meetings at Milton and were attracted to his message. Through their initiative he visited this church at South Farms during the winter and preached there for several months with great results. One of those who witnessed the awakening at South Farms was a "teacher of youth" named James Morris. He wrote down a very careful account of what happened in the lives of some of the people there. Bennet Tyler had access to this unpublished manuscript and incorporated a good bit of the material in his biography. The names, ages, and "religious exercises" of some eighty people are related in Morris's record.

James Morris, the chronicler of the conversions at South Farms, counted it a privilege to have witnessed this revival first hand. The strong feelings he had about it are evident. He says, "The revival of religion began in South Farms in February or March, 1814. Praised be God for His glorious work of redeeming love in the ingathering of His elect. The following persons are hopefully brought out of darkness into God's marvellous light, and are made heirs of God and joint heirs of Jesus Christ, the dear Redeemer. How astonishing is the work of the Divine Spirit, the Sanctifier and Comforter, in bringing God's chosen from the bondage of sin and Satan, and prostrating them at the foot of the cross! Some have been called from among the most dissipated, thoughtless and gay; and from seventy years of age, down to school-children. Some from the haunts of sensuality, profaneness and intemperance, now apparently sing with understanding the songs of redeeming love".[7]

The converts were indeed of a wide variety of ages and backgrounds but all followed the usual path to salvation. First there was awakening, or the creation of interest, then conviction, followed usually by some resistance and opposition, then submission and peace. The following cases are characteristic.

A nineteen year old girl: ". . . after a conflict of serious impressions and opposition of heart, for about six weeks, was, apparently on the 20th of April, renewed in heart. The first evangelical exercise that she had any knowledge of, according to her own account, was benevolence to her fellow men. She would that all men might be saved, even if she was lost. The divine law appeared to her holy, just and good. She felt submissive to the divine will – a disposition to resign herself into the hands of God, feeling that the judge of all the earth would do right. She thus continued till Friday, the 22nd, when returning from a religious meeting, she felt a love to God on account of the excellency of his character. She loved holiness for holiness' sake. She then hated sin, because in its own nature, it is odious. This was the first time that she had those consolations that the world cannot give nor take away. Here she dates her hope, and rejoices in God her Saviour."[8]

This testimony is interesting as an example of the *quality* of the Nettleton-type conversions. Her experience reflects the ideal of what was expected. First, a wounding of the spirit was anticipated as the unsaved were initially exposed to the gospel. Second, the subject grasped clearly the concrete facts relating to God's character and his own need. "The law appeared holy, just and good." As an ambassador of God, Nettleton expected the awakened to take sides with God against himself, or receive the truth of the holiness of God and the law with approval or approbation. Furthermore, as a rule, peace did not come through a knowledge that the subject had received any benefit from God, but as a by-product of his perception of the inherent beauty of God and justness of His cause. This young lady loved her fellow men and wished they would be saved, even if she were lost. Self interest, in other words, was pushed into the background. The interests of true religion, that is the glory of God and the happiness of other men, were paramount. This type of attitude was rooted in Edwards' writings on *Religious Affections* and *The Nature of True Virtue*. In the latter treatise

he taught that true religion or virtue consisted in benevolence to being, the infinite and the finite.

There is undoubtedly a strain of Hopkinsianism in her
statement that "she felt submissive to the divine will – a
disposition to resign herself into the hands of God". Nettleton
followed Hopkins to this extent, that he viewed conversion
as primarily *submission*. This meant not only repentance and
faith, but something beyond that: resignation to the just
disposal of a sovereign. She felt "that the judge of all the
earth would do right", that is, she felt no claim on God's
mercy and knew that were God to leave her to perish He
would be just. To modern readers this may seem dreadfully
morbid, but Hopkinsianism was only an exaggerated
emphasis on self-denial and self-abnegation, which admittedly is at the basis of all evangelical piety.

The traits of humility and fervent devotion to the glory of
God come out in the other testimonies supplied by Morris.
The spiritual change of *a thirty-seven year old man* is thus
related: "He lived in open sin and profaneness, from his
youth. He hated to read the Bible, and to attend meeting on
the Sabbath. He hated to hear religious conversation, and
avoided religious instruction. He was of an independent
spirit and impiously heaven-daring. Yet the religious
instruction he had received from his mother could not be
wholly effaced from his memory. He often had chidings of
conscience, and was often filled with remorse; but to drive
all this from his mind, he would throw himself into vain,
sensual and dissipated company. He never offered a prayer
in his family. His mouth was often filled with profane oaths,
and the most impious imprecations on himself. His torments
of mind increasing upon him, he resolved to put an end to
his dreadfully profane and wicked life. He accordingly
procured a large dose of arsenic, and laid it up for that
purpose. In the meantime, he had a dreadful struggle in his
mind. His purpose, he thought, must be put to execution;
and it seemed to him that the torments of a future world for
sin, could not exceed the pain of mind which he felt. In this
dreadful struggle, the pride of his heart was subdued, and
he was made to bow at the footstool of sovereign grace on
the 10th day of March. Traits of humility, self-abasement,
and abhorrence of sin, in no man appear more conspicuous.
He admires, and adores, that such an awful, heaven-daring,
and heaven-despising wretch, should be plucked as a brand

out of the fire. He is altogether submissive and his life is a life of prayer."[9]

Cases of the conversion of notoriously wicked men such as this were numerous in Nettleton's ministry. The fact that he was on the verge of suicide adds a touch of pathos. Such sudden transformations understandably seized the attention of the whole community.

Another case is that of a *fifty year old woman* who had her attitudes and life-style transformed. "She had long before entertained a hope, founded on her good works. She had never before believed in total depravity. She believed that to live uprightly, and deal fairly and honestly with mankind, was sufficient to entitle her to salvation. But at this time she found that all her former hopes were nothing, and that her righteousness was but filthy rags. She now feels that her hope is in Christ. She is full in her belief of all the great doctrines of grace. She places her confidence in God through Christ, relying on the promises."[10]

One can see from this that to be converted under the ministry of Nettleton was to become Calvinistic in theology. Such ideas as total depravity, the necessity of regeneration, justification through Christ alone, and the sovereignty of God in salvation, were not only believed but felt. Any notions of dependence on the merits of man's free will as a cause or ground of salvation were routed. The doctrines of grace were meat, bread, butter and milk to those who came to salvation under Nettleton's preaching.

It was expected that even the very young would undergo the same thorough heart-searching through which adults were brought to salvation. Morris describes, as follows, how a *thirteen year old boy* grappled with spiritual issues. "On the last Sabbath in May, or the first Sabbath in June, his mother went to meeting and charged him and her other child to be good children, and not to play, but read their books. His father went to a distant field to see about his cattle. Before noon, this J—— was smitten with deep conviction of sin. He continued in a distressed state about twenty-four hours, without food or sleep. His mind seemed to be overwhelmed with a sense of the dreadful nature of sin, as committed against God. Something happened to him at the end of twenty-four hours, which caused him to wipe away his tears, to wash himself, and cheerfully to partake of some food. It is now about two months since this happened.

He has been, from that time to this, remarkably calm and serene in his mind. He answers questions rationally – says that he loves God and hates sin. He fails not of his daily devotions and reading the Bible, and has altogether a change of deportment. He appears to have a sense of the evil nature of sin. The duties of the Sabbath and the sanctuary appear to be his delight. It is apparent to all who know this youth, that a great change has taken place in him. From being passionate, petulant, perverse, and stubborn, he is now humble, meek, patient, forbearing, and forgiving."[11]

These are typical samples of the conversions which occurred under Nettleton's ministry. One can at the least say that they were not superficial. Young and old alike had profound views of the character of God, the nature of the gospel and their own sinfulness. The radical change in their views was reflected in their lives.

CHAPTER 11

BREAKING UP
THE FOUNTAINS OF THE DEEP

Worn out by a year and a half of incessant labour, in the
middle of 1814 Asahel went back to Killingworth, hoping to
find repose in the peaceful and secluded environs of the
farm. His mother and father had gone to their rest, but
Ambrose was there, as was his unmarried sister, Amy. In a
short time, however, the news of his presence in Killingworth
had spread among the local citizens. Among these were the
members of the church at Chester, near his home. Soon a
representative of the church was at the door importuning
him to come and preach. He refused at first, pleading
exhaustion. So determined was the visitor to secure Asahel's
services, that he continued to insist, even weeping openly at
the thought that his mission would fail. At length, in spite of
his weariness, Nettleton yielded and visited the church. He
remained for some time among these people, during which
time "the special presence of God" was manifested, and the
people witnessed "a very interesting work of divine grace".

In the autumn, he began a period of evangelistic work at
East Granby, Connecticut. When he arrived, the church
was in a deplorable condition; the situation was somewhat
like that in the eastern area of the state where he first started
his public preaching. An "erroneous ministry" had precipi-
tated a spiritual decline; the congregation had lost all its fervour and "the community was buried in sinful indifference".
When Nettleton arrived the church awoke. According to
Tyler, "The effect of his entrance to the place was electric.
The school-house and private rooms were filled with
trembling worshippers. A solemnity and seriousness pervaded
the community, which had not been experienced for years
before. There was no bustle – no *array* of means. All was

orderly, quiet, and scriptural. There seems to have been an *increasing* solemnity while the work continued".[12]

In 1843, twenty-nine years after Nettleton's ministry in this community, the pastor of the church at East Granby was J. B. Clark. He testified that the salutary effects of Nettleton's ministry were still abundantly in evidence. "Most of those who were connected with the church, as the result of that revival, have worn remarkably well, so far as is or can be known. Many of them have been, and are still, bright and shining lights in the church of Christ. One of the subjects, Miss C. Thrall, died as a missionary among the western Indians."[13]

Clark questioned the people as to the style and content of Asahel's preaching during that period, now over a quarter of a century removed. "I am told," he said, "that his sermons were in a high degree practical. Doctrinal sermons were frequent, but these had a practical turn. They were eminently scriptural, and plain, and made men feel that *they* were the men addressed, and not their neighbours. He sometimes preached on the severer doctrines with great power and apparent good effect. At this day we can hardly imagine the effect which his visit had upon this waste place. This seems to have been Satan's chief seat. Infidelity had been infused into the very bosom of the church. Of course sin in every form abounded."[14]

Those who could recall the ministry of the evangelist (they were now generally advanced in years) held fond recollections of his stay in that place. "When I have been speaking of him in my pastoral visits," Clark continues, "the most intense interest is excited. From many expressions used as the old people speak of him, one may know that his labours are still remembered with affection."[15]

J. B. Clark found that the faces of people still lit up at the mention of Asahel Nettleton, and that the years had not dimmed pleasant recollections. It was evidently a pleasure to labour among a people whose spiritual roots went back to a Nettletonian revival. His ministry had stood the test of time.

Asahel's preaching circuit in the spring of 1815 took him to the Connecticut towns of Bolton, Manchester, and back again to Granby. Blessings attended his labours in every instance. At Bolton he preached with "signal success". At Manchester, a revival already in progress was "greatly promoted and extended". At Granby, "many souls were savingly benefited by his labours". The church at Bolton had been without a pastor for some time, and extended to him a call to settle among them permanently as their minister. He declined, and instead was able to place his old childhood companion and classmate at Yale, Philander Parmele, in the pastorate there.

Later in the spring of 1815, some pastors in the city of his Alma Mater, New Haven, requested that he come and preach there. Soon after his arrival he was invited to visit a school for young ladies. Here he had occasion to bear witness to "what God had done" in preceding months. Those who heard this report were deeply moved. In a few days large numbers of these students were themselves enquiring about salvation. Before long this "seriousness" had spread throughout the city, touching also the students at Yale. Asahel stayed in New Haven for two or three months, preaching in the churches "with the same success which had crowned his labours in country parishes".

In the summer, autumn, and winter of 1815-1816 he preached in Salisbury, Connecticut, where a revival occurred, which was in some respects more remarkable than any which he had witnessed thus far. One of the residents of that town was Jonathan Lee, who was another of Asahel's acquaintances at Yale. Lee had first-hand knowledge of what happened under his preaching here. The church, it seems, was without a minister and had declined greatly in numerical strength, having at the time only seventeen male members. But the few who were still active were deeply anxious for a work of the Holy Spirit in their midst, and had been persistent in praying for a revival. They requested that he come.

The circumstances in which he accepted this invitation serve to illustrate what could be regarded as a *singularity* in Asahel's outlook, a commendable but rare quality. He was of the opinion that there could be no revival in a community unless the people depended upon God alone. If he suspected that a church was relying on him to bring about a spiritual awakening, they stood a good chance of not getting his assistance at all. The situation at Salisbury is a case in point. Something about the way he was approached made him suspect that the people there believed he was able to produce revivals, and that these phenomena followed him as automatically as the sun brings the light.

His initial contacts in Salisbury justified these suspicions. Quite unexpectedly, he arrived at the house of one of the deacons of the church, where his lodging had been arranged. He discovered that another deacon had been frantically riding about trying to find him. This seems to have convinced him that they were indeed placing undue confidence in himself instead of looking to God. We can perhaps pardon the people for this mistake, since his coming into a community did seem to be a certain precursor of a great spiritual stir. But Asahel could not operate in such a climate. Too many times he had learned in the valley of humiliation that "the flesh profiteth nothing", and he was not about to tolerate excessive praise for himself. He believed that he was only an earthen vessel carrying the priceless treasure of the gospel. "I can do no good here," he calmly announced, and made plans to depart. Surprised, but humbled, the people tried to change his mind. They literally begged him to stay at least till the following Sabbath and give them a second chance. He agreed to do so.

Thus, persuaded to stay, he entered into a time of prayer and discussion with the host family, who were joined by some labourers who were called in from the fields. A meeting was set for the following day, to which any interested people were invited to come. Later he conducted a meeting in the home of another deacon, where several young people were assembled. As was his custom, he began talking to them, in a simple and straightforward manner, on truths calculated to awaken their minds. Lee says, "There was no dilation of thought, but one weighty idea, such as the worth of the soul, or the necessity of true religion, dwelt upon and reiterated, and left in its naked reality and solemnity of each individual's mind".[16]

After this quiet beginning he started visiting some of the families of professing Christians and preached at the regular Sunday services. At length he was satisfied that the Lord had led him to this place, so he went to work in earnest. He urged the people to plead with God for a revival, warning them firmly against trusting in the arm of man. He instructed them in the proper manner of dealing with sinners under conviction. This was necessary, for the emotions of some had got out of hand. In one particular village, some began to groan and scream, spreading alarm throughout the village. Asahel rushed to the place and with kindness but "severity" called them to order. His method seemed rough and daring to some, but he felt that such excesses would hinder the revival.

In a short period of time, people from all over the town, of all classes and ages, began to be aroused. The revival fell like rain, gradually increasing in intensity. To the people of Salisbury, it seemed somewhat like the deluge of Noah's day, when the "fountains of the great deep were broken up". Soon he was preaching to crowded meetings, where people sat in the death-like stillness which was becoming the hallmark of his revivals. His own house was thronged with inquirers wanting counsel about their spiritual state. Sometimes he spoke to them privately and at other times he held special meetings for those who were wanting to be saved.

The harvest of souls in this place was considerable. About three hundred proclaimed their new life in Christ, and most of them joined the Congregational Church. Most of the converts were from among the young. The experience of one man in his fifties was so remarkable that it created quite a sensation in town. He was a very prominent citizen and was an obstinate and outspoken enemy of the gospel. Like Saul of Tarsus, he was "exceeding mad against the church". Suddenly, he displayed a radical change, and became broken in spirit. He became a devout Christian and an ardent supporter of Nettleton's ministry. This man's testimony was so bold and convincing, that many of his friends and associates, who had been sceptics, were won to Christ.

During this revival, religion became the common topic of conversation everywhere in the town. Nettleton became a sort of celebrity. Large groups of people followed him about wherever he went. "Whenever Mr Nettleton was seen to enter a house, almost the whole neighbourhood would immediately assemble to hear from his lips the Word of Life. Husbandmen would leave their fields, mechanics their shops, and females their domestic concerns, to inquire the way to eternal life."[17]

Twenty-seven years later, Jonathan Lee reminisced about these memorable days. He recalled the unobtrusive manner of his old friend Asahel Nettleton. "This favoured servant of Christ came, with no trumpet sounded before him, in the meekness of his master, and the Lord was with him in very deed."[18]

He still remembered well how powerful yet subdued the

feelings were, and how plain the preaching was. "This revival was distinguished for its stillness and solemnity, for deep conviction of conscience, for discriminating views of divine truth."[19]

He was aware that the converts of this revival had been the backbone of the church through the years. "Not a few, in the twenty-seven years since elapsed, have died in the Lord. Those remaining still constitute the strength of the church; for although some other favoured seasons of in-gathering have been enjoyed, none has borne comparison with this for permanent influence upon the state of the community, for enlightened piety, and for steadfastness of Christian principle and character. Many still look back to that date with the deepest interest, and liveliest gratitude, as the blest period of their espousal to Christ – as the memorable year of the right hand of the Lord. The name of Asahel Nettleton, the humble, skillful labourer in this field, at that season, employed in directing so many to Christ, is embalmed in many a heart. It stands associated with their dearest hopes, and purest joys, and will call forth praises never ending to the Chief Shepherd, Who employed him in leading so many of this flock into his spiritual fold, to stand at his right hand at the great decisive day, to the praise of his own unfathomable grace."[20]

Thus, it seems that the people of Salisbury had the last word. Try as he might to hide behind the cross and avoid adulation, fame seemed determined to knock at the modest evangelist's door.

Chapter 12

THE CASE OF
THE MISSING PREACHER

From the early colonial days, the Congregational Church was the established ecclesiastical system in Connecticut. Throughout the eighteenth and early nineteenth centuries, the "dissident" status of other religious groups was a source of friction and unrest. In 1791, the right of free incorporation was granted to all sects, but it was not until 1818 that the constitution granting total religious freedom was adopted.

The traditional Puritan concept that the state is the protector of the true religion was still a powerful influence in Nettleton's day. This is seen in the fact that the Connecticut state government set aside various days during the year for special religious activities. In the spring of 1816, the government proclaimed a certain day as the *Annual State Fast*, to be sanctified by prayer and fasting. The churches naturally participated by conducting special services. Asahel was in Bridgewater at the time, where he was labouring in a pastorless church.

The annual fast day was a very important day in Bridgewater. The programme was to include a sermon by the celebrated guest minister in their midst, Asahel Nettleton. At the appointed time the people assembled expecting to hear him. But when the meeting time arrived, nothing was seen of the preacher. Tensions mounted as the congregation anxiously awaited his appearance. It was soon apparent that there would be no preacher that day, so the people left the meeting house disappointed and went home. Asahel had in fact already left the community, having informed only the family who had been providing living quarters for him.

His departure from Bridgewater provides some insight into his character and reveals a good deal about his unusual style. All of his life he was a determined enemy of anything like sensationalism in the pulpit, and his methods in evangelism were considered very conservative. But he did unquestionably have a flair for the dramatic and, in order to make a point in the minds of some to whom he was ministering, he occasionally used a sort of shock treatment. The stranded church at Bridgewater was one of the more glaring cases of this method.

From the time when he first came into the community Asahel fought a running battle with some of the people. The Congregationalist church had been, for several years, a hornets' nest of strife and animosity. The moral condition of the congregation was described by Bennet Tyler, whose own church was only ten miles away, as one of destitution and "great stupidity".[21] Asahel saw immediately there could not be a revival here until the people had settled their differences and a better spirit prevailed. He set about dealing with the festering wounds hurting the church's harmony and influence. Pointedly and plainly he preached to them about the importance of unity and brotherly love as a means of successfully promoting God's kingdom. These exhortations had little effect. The people gave no evidence of contrition over their quarrels, and seemingly could not be persuaded to confess their sins to God. Like the church at Salisbury, this group seemed to feel that the mere coming of the evangelist to the community, like some magical charm, would solve their problems and bring a revival. It was after a night of fruitless discussion with the people about their need of reconciliation that he decided that something drastic had to be done. The annual fast day revealed just how drastic his plan was.

The "thundering silence" of the vacant pulpit worked beautifully. If there was any irritation about his startling conduct it was soon forgotten and heart searching began in earnest among the people of this community. Several of the young people in particular, who had been awakened when Nettleton was among them, became very distressed at his departure. The church, now aware that the evangelist had only chosen this dramatic way of rebuking them as a last resort, were deeply smitten and organised a day of prayer and confession. In a short time the difficulties were healed and brotherly love was restored. It was a day of "deep repentance and humiliation before God".[22]

The canny evangelist's radar screen was fully operational as the people were on their knees in repentance. He was only a few miles away, keeping in close contact with the situation through those in a position to inform him. He was spending a day "with a brother in the ministry" in a neighbouring town. Almost certainly this was Bennet Tyler, who pastored at South Britain, which was only about ten miles away. Asahel suggested that "this brother" go and spend the Sabbath in Bridgewater while he in turn stayed and preached in his pulpit. The pastor, whom we presume was Bennet, agreed and found the situation quite different from the way Nettleton had left it. He discovered that the congregation was pervaded by a "deep solemnity" and many were seeking the way of salvation. When Nettleton heard of this state of affairs, he immediately returned to Bridgewater, where he laboured for several months in a spiritual awakening.

The most outstanding conversion in this town was that of a man whom Tyler anonymously calls "Mr C.". He was a true blue infidel, and fought the gospel tooth and nail. When Asahel came to town, he had not been to church in many years and had no intention of amending this record. But the excitement generated while the itinerant was in town was something he could not ignore. His curiosity soon got the better of him. He had to get at least a glimpse of the "fanatic" who was attracting so much attention.

The meetings were in the school house, this made it feasible to Mr C. to get some exposure to the revival atmosphere. He had no intention of going inside, for his reputation as an infidel would be ruined were the people to see him seated listening to the evangelist. So he ventured to stand at the door. This seemed like a comfortable and safe position, but in fact it was a hazardous one, for it left him exposed to the same dynamic preaching which had already shaken Bridgewater from end to end. As he stood in the door, Mr C. could hear Asahel preaching very clearly. What he heard pierced his soul like "an arrow from the Almighty's quiver". He went home a shaken man.

Before long Mr C. realised that he was a sinner and was courting disaster by his way of living. Desperately he struggled against the hook which had caught him. He tried to get his mind off the subject of religion. A voice within his soul said, "You must repent – you must pray, or you will perish". This was only the echo of the fearless prophet he had heard at the school house. Indignant, he resisted. "*I pray! – no, never. I'll perish first*," his heart replied to the voice within.

The struggle continued till the once proud rebel wilted into a heap of contrition. His mental agony became such that no longer could it be hidden from the townsfolk that he was under conviction. One night he reached a stage curiously like that which the evangelist himself had once experienced. He was in such misery that he thought he would die. Neighbours and acquantances came to his house to sympathise; others watched in amazement. "To see this bold blasphemer, bewailing his sinfulness and crying for mercy, in distress and anguish which seemed too great for human nature to sustain, was a most affecting sight."[23]

The next day he received the assurance of salvation and "seemed to be in a new world". The old blasphemer became a preacher to his former associates. The following Sunday morning he was on the steps of the church house, telling all who would listen about his conversion, and pointing unsaved people to the Saviour whom he had found. Even the most sceptical in town could hardly deny that something inexplicable had happened to Mr C. "It must be the finger of God" was the opinion of many.

Up until the summer of 1816 most of Asahel's preaching was in "waste" churches which did not have a pastor. But as the second great awakening rolled along these barren spots became scarcer. Increasingly, pastors began to invite him into their parishes to do evangelistic work. In the summer of 1816 Alexander Gillett, pastor of the church in Torrington, Connecticut, invited him to spend some time there. Asahel spent three very profitable months with Gillett.

A thorough analysis of the ministry of Nettleton at Torrington was made by John A. McKinstry, who was pastor there in 1844. Signs of former harvest days still abounded. A great movement had taken place in the summer of 1816, known as "The Revival in Torrington". It was regarded by the people as "a glorious and blessed period", and nothing like this had ever happened since. McKinstry discovered that there were about seventy conversions as a result of the meetings conducted by Nettleton. Those who remembered said that it was a "powerful" revival. With few exceptions, those who came to Christ during those days still adorned their profession and some were "pillars in the church". The influence of the awakening on the church was extensive and favourable. The doctrines preached there were the same as elsewhere: the true character of God, the condition of the sinner, and "the sovereign mercy of God through a crucified Saviour".[24]

The methods used by the evangelist in this revival were also the usual ones. These were, preaching on Sunday, frequent visitation, "connected with personal conversation on the subject of religion", and prayer meetings during the week. These were characteristic of his ministry as a whole. Nettleton's "fundamentals" as a revivalist tactician were: public preaching, private counselling, and prayer. The time would come when Nettleton, Tyler and their friends would find it necessary to defend these simple tools, which had become the stock and trade of the Edwardian revivalist school.

CHAPTER 13

THE FRONT LINE OF BATTLE

By the summer of 1816 the pattern of Asahel's evangelistic endeavours had been fairly well established. He provides a most comprehensive picture of the revival activity which was common during the New England phase of the second great awakening. As the only itinerant of any consequence in this phenomenon, he held a unique position. He was in no sense a coordinator or supervisor of even the Connecticut phase of the awakening, but he unquestionably knew more about what was going on around the state than any other man. He became not only one of the most well-known preachers of the period, but perhaps the most authoritative student of revivalism during the first quarter of the nineteenth century.

Certainly, his style was vastly different than that which, in general, characterised the later evangelists of America. For example, the great length of time he spent in a community is very strange by modern standards. But the peculiar circumstances in which he began his ministry caused this pattern to develop. He started his public ministry as a "missionary" in "waste places", and very soon he gained a reputation as a sort of spiritual surgeon, who was called upon to operate upon congregations which were nearly dead. His success in this is phenomenal by any standards.

Most of the parishes in which he first ministered did not have pastors. He himself fulfilled a sort of interim pastoral role in these situations. This made anything like haste in his movements unnecessary. Being unmarried, it was easy for him to remain three or four months, or even longer, in a community. From a strategic standpoint this also had many advantages. For one thing it enabled him to determine the real spiritual needs of a community, which a brief visit could not possibly do. When he visited a church he studied the symptoms of the local problems as thoroughly as the most skilled physician trying to make a diagnosis. Within a short time he knew exactly what remedy was needed. His semi-permanent residence in a community also enabled him to do effective follow-up work. Normally he did not remain long after a revival commenced, but he was there long enough to give initial counsel to the new converts. Very early in his ministry he discovered that the babes in Christ should not be left too quickly. The local churches provided, of course, a natural nursery where the new born souls could be nourished.

Nettleton's credibility as an evangelist is immeasurably enhanced by the method through which his revival activities have been recorded on the pages of history. Many of the revival accounts came through the testimonies of eye-witnesses, who gave detailed reports in current periodicals such as *The Connecticut Evangelical Magazine* and *The Religious Intelligencer*. Asahel himself occasionally kept brief diary notations and wrote letters to his friends explaining his experiences as an evangelist. But a significant portion of the record comes from the recollections of the subjects of the revivals, who were interviewed many years afterwards. Bennet Tyler corresponded at length with pastors whose churches had been visited with great revivals under Asahel's preaching twenty-five or thirty years previously. In some cases these pastors had been on the scene themselves. In other cases the information came from ministers who laboured in the next generation. All of these pastors discussed in detail the basic thrust of Nettleton's ministry: his doctrines, his manner of life, his methods in evangelism, and the history of the converts.

Perhaps the most striking and important thing about these testimonies is the *continuance* of the converts under Asahel's ministry, and the durability of the results of these revivals. The superficiality and transience, which stigmatises modern evangelism, was an unknown quality in Asahel's track, unless we attribute dishonesty to this "cloud of witnesses". Due allowance has always been made for the tendency of the adoring Bennet Tyler to gloss over Asahel's mistakes and idiosyncrasies. It was a loving hand that wrote letters, collected manuscripts, and finally pieced together the famous *Memoir* of the departed evangelist. But the authenticity of Nettletonian revivals rests on solid pillars. The testimonies as to the purity, power, and permanence of these revivals come from a great variety of sources.

Between 1816 and 1819 he held important revivals in such Connecticut towns as Waterbury, Bolton, Upper Middleton, Cromwell, Rocky Hill, Ashford, and Eastford. His visit to Bolton was occasioned by a nervous breakdown on the part of the pastor of the church, Philander Parmele, who was the most cherished of all his many close personal friends. They were childhood companions and also class-mates at Yale. There were one hundred and eighteen converts at Waterbury, and eighty-four at Rocky Hill. There is no statistical record of the revival at Cromwell, but only a report of "many souls"[25] having been saved.

The pastor of the church at Rocky Hill, whom Tyler identifies as "Mr Chapin", was one of the men still living when the memoirs of Asahel were being put together. He represents the itinerant in an unusual light. "In an impor-tant sense, brother Nettleton's talent was *one*. In the cultiva-tion and improvement of that *one*, he was unwearied."[26] What Chapin has in mind here was Asahel's tactical skill in "practical piety". This could be summed up as a thorough knowledge of basic Biblical truth and its bearing on human experience. By those who knew him, the evangelist was considered an expert in bringing forth from the cabinet of divine doctrine those things which were pertinent to men in their various stages of religious progress. His specialty was dealing with awakened sinners.

Of all Nettleton's intellectual equipment, none seems to have impressed his contemporaries more than his perception of the workings of the human heart when confronted with the claims of the gospel. This talent seemed intuitive, but in fact it was developed through his own experience and a life-time of studying the human soul. When he interviewed people who were seeking salvation, he seemed to discern the precise stage of their spiritual development and to know exactly what part of the law or gospel should be presented to lead them to God. His old teacher, Bezaleel Pinneo, saw this ability early in his life. He had, said Pinneo, "uncommon insight into the human character", and was able "to place the naked truth upon the conscience, and to demolish with a few heavy strokes, all the vain excuses and refuges of lies to which sinners resort to screen themselves from the force

of the truth".[27] Chapin speaks of his "quickness of discernment relative to the specific instruction, and the manner of
imparting instruction, that every mind needed with which
he came in contact".[28]

This "intuitive discernment" of Asahel was never more
evident than when he was preaching. His knowledge of the
ground sinners traverse in their return to God was often
reflected in unusual ways. Occasionally he impersonated the
sinners, as he did at South Britain. Bringing out the feelings
and thoughts of the unsaved at various stages of conviction
was often as disturbing as it was shocking. Soon Asahel got
the reputation of being somewhat of a mind reader. So
penetrating and accurate was his analysis of the thought processes of the awakened that many fully expected to have their
very souls unveiled when they went to hear him preach.
Tyler did not exaggerate when he said, "It often seemed to
individuals while listening to his preaching, that he must
know their thoughts".[29] Yet his manner was so gracious and
winsome that saints and sinners alike were usually attracted
to this man, who had the apparent ability to see into their
very souls.

Asahel Nettleton was unquestionably a spiritual psycholo-
gist of no ordinary mettle. In other words, he *knew the
human heart.* "Such was his knowledge of the human heart,
and of the feelings which divine truth excites when presented
to the minds of unsanctified men, that he was able to anticipate objections, and to follow the sinner through his various
refuges of lies, and strip him of all his excuses."[30] He was
experimentally trained in this area, for he himself had gone
through a protracted experience of "law work" prior to his
conversion. Even after his conversion he continually probed
into the spiritual state of his own soul, and at times, evidently,
with some fear and trepidation.

His adeptness in curing the ailments of men in the throes
of conviction of sin could be compared to that of a physician
who diagnoses the case symptoms of his patients and pre-
scribes the proper medicine. But he was also a kind of
soldier in combat and, like any military genius, he studied
the tactics of his enemy. He seemed to have special wisdom
relative to the devices of Satan, and he was ever ready with
both offensive and defensive strategy. He was aware that
many of the doctrines that he preached were unpopular,
and he knew beforehand what objections would be raised

against the truth. Though polemics was not his field, and he shunned debate, when any point of Biblical doctrine was challenged he usually silenced his opponents with pungent thrusts of logic that left the objectors confused. As Chapin said, "He had a quick and precise perception of the sources whence objectors and cavillers draw their difficulties. In replies, showing the true answer, and the only remedy, he was ready, appropriate, generally silencing, and not rarely convincing".[31]

Nettleton's engagements in the war against evil were, of course, in the *front line* of battle. He looked upon the problems of mankind as primarily spiritual, rather than intellectual. Asahel was not interested in the discussion of theology merely as abstract points of speculation. He viewed the world of ideas as an armed camp, where hostile forces continually vie, not only for the minds, but for the souls of men. He saw sinners, not as victims of intellectual kidnap, but as willing slaves and friends of Satan. Content to leave the cerebral discussions of philosophy to the musty halls of rationalism, he sallied forth into the heat and fury of spiritual combat and won men to the cause of Jesus Christ by art and by force. His favourite authors were those who continually showed the practical application of Biblical truth, such as Andrew Fuller, John Bunyan, Edwards and Bellamy.

Because of his burning desire to lead men to Christ, Asahel was, of necessity, a student of theology in its practical, or experimental, aspects. Religious errors were not only contradictions of the Word of God, but the shackles which held men in spiritual bondage. Any doctrine which tended to secure men in their sins, or delay their laying hold of the gospel, he stiffly resisted. He opposed Arminianism, because it caused men to rely on themselves rather than God. But he also stood against hyper-Calvinism, because it tended to take away the urgency of sinners to submit immediately to the claims of Christ.

Nettleton's views on the nature of conversion were very dogmatic and carried him at times into debate, even with Calvinistic divines. He objected, for example, to the famous work of Walter Marshall, *The Gospel Mystery of Sanctification*, because it appeared to foster a false and presumptuous assurance. Marshall's position seemed to Asahel to encourage men to believe they were converted "while they had no evidence of a change of heart".[32] Marshall's book was highly praised by such outstanding divines as the Erskines of Scotland, James Hervey, and Thomas Chalmers. The burden of this book was professedly to lead men to renounce any form of works for salvation and to exhort sinners to rely upon Jesus for salvation. It made faith to consist of the belief that one's sins are pardoned. Joseph Bellamy took issue with the thesis of this book and sought to refute it in his *Theron, Paulious, and Aspasio*, because it seemed to leave no room for evangelical humiliation as a condition of salvation and had antinomian tendencies. Of course Nettleton studied Bellamy and was influenced by this treatise.

The fact is that there was enough Hopkinsianism in Asahel to cause him to view Marshall's concept that faith is trust in Christ, as having too much self interest in it. It failed to meet the vital Edwardian test of a view of the essential glory of the Redeemer. He met a lady at Upper Middleton, who was reading Marshall's book, and she remarked, "If I dared believe that book, I should think I was a Christian". Asahel answered forthrightly, "I am glad you dare not believe it".[33]

Marshall was a sort of Puritan forerunner of the Keswick movement, with its position that the life of the Christian is one of blissful, cloudless trust in Christ and repose in God's mercy. Bellamy, Hopkins, and Nettleton were of the old rugged New England school, who believed that assurance does not normally come easily. No one, in their view, had any right to claim salvation unless he sees in himself positive evidence of a change of heart. The debate between these two camps has a modern counterpart in the controversy over whether conversion includes submission to the Lordship of Christ, and whether repentance, as distinguished from faith, is a condition of salvation. Men of distinction are on either side.

Whatever one may think about Asahel's ideas on conversion, none can deny that he had the interests of the souls of men in mind. If he wounded the unconverted too deeply and held too high a standard of conversion, which is debatable, many would say that modern evangelists tend to go too far in the other direction, in rushing to give relief to the sinner at the expense of sound principles of counsel. Rough as they seem, Nettleton's strict views on conversion are hard to challenge in the light of the permanence of his converts.

CHAPTER 14

SLANDERS OF THE ENEMY

The infidel speculations and libertine morals, which were so triumphantly introduced in the last decades of the eighteenth century, met a stiff challenge in the great revivals of New England. The upsurge of evangelical activity, exemplified in the highly successful preaching of Asahel Nettleton, changed the moral climate in many communities, and rescued many educational institutions and churches from spiritual disaster. It is doubtful that this movement was anticipated by the votaries of infidelity, and it certainly was not appreciated.

The cause of unbelief, however, was far from dead. The opponents of Christianity were still very active in many quarters, and in other places they were patiently waiting for an opportunity to counter attack. Everywhere there was an unrelenting attack upon friends of the gospel. The fearless preacher, Asahel Nettleton, was one of the special targets of hostility. Not only was he the constant object of ridicule and scorn, but, like many other evangelical leaders, he was the victim of slander and verbal abuse. The infidel crowd was ever anxious to seize upon any opportunity to vilify a Christian character, and, like the wolves that prowl at night, they pounced vengefully upon any friend of Christ when he displayed a momentary weakness or made a mistake.

Such an opportunity came to Nettleton's enemies in the autumn of 1818. It was occasioned by an unorthodox and unwise method used by Asahel and Bennet Tyler in dealing with some young people at South Britain. Tyler was greatly concerned over the worldliness of some of the young people in his town, a concern he revealed to Asahel while he was visiting him in September. On the evening of 18th September, some of the young people were at a dance. The two ministers conceived a plan to startle the youths into a consciousness of the sinfulness and danger of their conduct.[34] They proposed to write them a letter as if it had come from Jesus Christ. They knew this method was novel and dramatic, but felt that this should shock them into serious thought and make them think about their need of salvation.

Accordingly, the letter was put together by the two men at Tyler's house, addressed to the young people as a message from Christ. The letter contained a solemn warning in the words of Proverbs, in which God rebuked those who despised his counsels and reproof. They used such expressions as, "Because I have called and ye have refused, I have stretched out my hand and no man regarded", and "Then shall they call me early but they shall not find me". The letter was signed, "I am, dear youth, Your much grieved friend, Jesus Christ". At the bottom of the page a note was added: "N.B. If the youth will agree to turn their meeting into a religious conference this evening please send back word and I will come and see you. If not, I will go into my closet and, with the help of God, will pray for you while you dance." The postscript was signed, "Asahel Nettleton".[35]

Asahel's proclivity toward the dramatic has already been seen in his pulpit style, and occasionally in his conduct with people. As a rule he stayed well within the rules of propriety, and generally a good result came from his method. At Bridgewater, his departure from the community caused the people to examine their conduct and lead them to repentance. He thought that perhaps a similar tactic would work with the youth at South Britain. But the letter backfired. There is no evidence that it had any effect upon the playful young people, and it became a dangerous weapon of his enemies. Tyler makes no mention whatsoever of the letter to the young people, which probably indicates that he regarded this letter, for which he was partly responsible, as a mistake.[36]

South Britain was one of the many New England towns which had a club of atheists at the time. Lyman Beecher called them "Infidels or nothingarians".[37] They were, of course, thoroughly opposed to revivals and revival ministers. They missed no opportunity to discredit the religion of the churches. The organisation at South Britain seized on the incident of Nettleton's letter and claimed that he had

"passed off himself as Jesus Christ".[38] The author had
certainly not passed off himself as Jesus Christ; his signature
at the end of the postscript identified him as responsible for
the letter.

Having taken advantage of the well-intentioned, but
over zealous preacher in one instance, they proceeded to
initiate a much more nefarious scheme. They soon fabricated
a report that he had been indiscreet in his conduct with
women. There are few outstanding preachers who have not
at one time or another faced slander on this ground. The
charge was so totally unfounded and ridiculous that it was
countenanced only by the infidels and their friends. Bennet
Tyler did not specifically identify this charge against his
friend, but only quotes Chapin's comment that "Satan's
followers attempted the propagation of injurious reports",
which were "false and infernally malicious".[39] The *Nettleton
Manuscript Collection* at Hartford Seminary Foundation
documents the problem.

The morals charge against Asahel was that he had been
guilty of "seducing a young woman in Waterbury". As
George Hugh Birney says, "The whole thing had the ring of
falseness and no one ever really seemed to believe the
slanders".[40] Nevertheless, the lie was widely circulated, and
caused Asahel no little pain.

He and his friends were, of course, alarmed about the
slanderous gossip, and were at a loss, for a while, about what
to do. Lawsuit was considered, but eventually ruled out.
They finally decided that the safest course was to ignore
the whole matter, believing that if the evangelist jumped to
defend himself it might give more colour to the accusation
than if he left the matter alone.

Nettleton's strategy to be silent and allow his life to be
its own vindication worked well. The whole matter was
soon largely forgotten. Not one of the leading ministers of
New England gave credence to the allegations; on the
contrary, all rallied to affirm their complete confidence in
him. But the perpetrators of the lie never rested in their
mischief, and even ten years later, while the itinerant was
preaching in Virginia, they continued to try to undermine
his ministry through the fabricated story.

The slanders against Asahel's character had no effect
whatsoever upon his usefulness as an evangelist. In fact, his
power and influence as a preacher seemed to rise con-

tinually. In Ashford, Connecticut, where he preached in the autumn of 1818, there were eighty-two conversions, and in Eastford, where his labours began in December, there were fifty-nine. In the spring of 1819 he was once again at Parmele's church, where there were fifty-nine professions. A graphic description of the revival at Bolton was printed in *The Religious Intelligencer* (*T.R.I.*). In this town there were a large number of teenagers converted.

Philander Parmele, in correspondence with *T.R.I.*, related how the young people came to salvation. "At one of these meetings, eight or ten of the youth were alarmed with a sense of their sins. Their convictions deepened until they became overwhelming; and within a few days they were brought to rejoice in hope. This spread conviction like an electric shock, through the society of young people, until it was evident that the Lord had appeared in His glory to build up Zion. The volatile youth could no longer resist the influences of the Holy Spirit, but in deep solemnity were daily inquiring what they should do to be saved. Vain amusements were entirely suspended. Scenes of pleasure were forsaken and the trifles of time were lost in the awful concerns of eternity. No object could divert the anxious mind from inquiring the way to life.

"The convictions of the subjects of this work were deep, increased rapidly, and were of short continuance. Unconditional submission was urged, as the only ground of acceptance with God. And as soon as this was exercised, in most instances, the sinner was filled with joy. One expressed herself thus, 'I attempted to pray for mercy while in my sins, but my conscience flashed conviction in my face. What! Will such a sinner as you attempt to pray? You are so vile, your prayers will not be heard. I then felt the reasonableness of my condemnation so forcibly, that I took up on the side of justice, and pleaded the cause of God against myself. In this condition, I soon found relief'."[41]

The Congregationalist church greatly benefited from this ingathering of believers, but also the local Baptist Church was increased by five families.

Parmele expressed his appreciation to his life-long friend, Asahel, but gave the credit for the revival at Bolton to God. "We would express our gratitude to those brethren in the ministry, who occasionally preached for us, during this revival; and especially to Mr Nettleton, whose labours were signally blessed. We trust the Lord will reward them for their labours of love. But we desire to look beyond all instruments, to the great first cause, and as a church and people, to express our unfeigned gratitude to the Father of all mercies, for this work of His grace. *This is the Lord's work, and it is marvellous in our eyes*; and to His great name be ascribed the *kingdom, the power, and the glory forever.*"[42]

Yale Coll 1809 —

Dear Friend,

It is now almost nine o'clock in evening, & I shall scribble a line in utmost hurry & this shall be on one single subject. Stone has just gone from my room, he told me a little of your dispute at Mr Meigs & but a little. Write 1 very next opportunity & give me all particulars. Stone guesses that Mr Eliott, through policy agrees with his parishioners on that subject. What particulars of your dispute were I cannot tell, but if it was respecting 1 question "What shall I do to be saved?" Without any books by me, I will give you 1 sentiment of a few celebrated authors; this I do from memory only. ————

"When a sinner does all that he can in an unrenewed state, it is no more than when a wind-mill does all it can. (President Edwards on 1 Will)

"God promises salvation to sinners on condition of faith & repentance; but he does not promise faith & repentance on any condition whatever." "The new heart as it respects 1 sinner to whom it is given, is an unconditional gift. For no covenant subsists between G. & impenitent sinners. (& then he goes on to explain 1 meaning of an important passage of scripture, one that is much plied in favour of 1 doings of 1 unregenerate) "There is a covenant between G. & his people, not only as it respects themselves, but as it respects others, When, therefore, G. promises a new heart to sinners; "He will be enquired of by 1 house of Israel to do it for them." (Mr Whitman of Goshen) This is in his own words, & he says much more. Query, Would it not be a contradiction to say that a new heart was given to 1 sinner, & then say that it was in consequence or on conditions of his doing something.

"Were some of our ministers present & heard the Apostles directions to 1 question "What shall I do to be saved!" would they not say, No, you are wrong, they can't repent, tell them to pray for a new heart— wait Gods time?&c. "To tell sinners that it is their immediate duty to repent, & at the same time to tell them that they are required to do something before they repent, is a plain contradiction." (Doctor West) This he shows to be a flat contradiction.

A copy of a letter in Nettleton's own handwriting addressed to Philander Parmele at E. Guilford. The letter concerns some important issues relative to the doctrine of conversion.

"If the sinner in asking 1 question, "what shall I do to be saved? means what act of the body he shall perform; the answer is, Nothing." (Mr Dutton of G.) This he said to me. The sentiments of Hopkins of Spring & of Hines on this subject, I suppose you know. Read Booth, particularly what he say on 1 conversion of St Paul – the Thief on 1 cross & & let Mr Elliott read it, & then tell him, that Mr Mervin has it read in his conferences & it is very highly applauded – that 1 Mr Stevert very highly recommends it. I suppose you have Mr Stevert's sermon on this subject, let him read that, I mean 1 one I coppied. But why do I quote authers, let him read the bible.

My Friend. You know that the question is asked "Are not sinners more likely to receive faith if they continue asking with their unbelieving hearts than if they did not? I have in mind one passage of scripture which, I apprehend, was designed to answer this very question, or rather, it anticipated this question, & therefore intended to prevent 1 folly of asking it. The question is plain and fairly stated. "May the impenitent sinner, even "think" that he shall be more likely to "receive any thing of the Lord," if he continue ever so long, asking without faith, any more than if he had never asked at all? The answer is "Let not that man think that he shall receive any thing of the Lord." Now I would ask, can the Christian – can the sinner or any other intelligent being believe, that those who ask in this manner are in any fairer way, or any more likely situation or circumstances to receive any thing now – tomorrow or next year or ever, than if they had never asked at all, without believing a lie? No one can deny that the expression, "Let not that man think "&c. is a command for something, or some body; & it is a command in some way respecting one who might be inclined to think of asking without faith. If it is a command to christians not to let "that man even that man, (not merely to practice in this manner of asking) but not even so much as think that he shall receive (not merely a new heart) but even any thing of the lord, I say if this is a command to christians, &

they brake it, they do it at their own hazzard. Again, if it be a command to the sinner not even to "think" in that he shall recieve &c. and yet, if christians or an Angel from heaven should pesuade that man, even that man, that he should be more likely to recieve any thing of 1 Lord. I say, in my humble opinion, should any one pesuade this man, he would not only oppose G. but would pesuade him to brake the command & believe a lie.

You will over look r. & incoherent sentences &c. for I write just as the thoughts come to my mind. You will please to give your ideas on this passage or the above passage "Let not &c" & I cannot excuse you without demanding a. of Mr Eliott an expla-nation of it, & ask him if it is not direct to 1 point; that is, if you think what I have said is correct. Ask him this plain question, that if you in any way or in any manner encourage 1 sinner to pray without faith, or even if you do not endeavour to correct his mistake if he himself thinks to recieve any thing in this manner, if you should do this, ask him if you should not brake a plain command of G. for certainly it is a command to some body.

He may, perhaps, say that the passage means that christians must not think to recieve without they ask in faith; but grant it, if so, then sinners who are acknowledged enemies to G. certainly cannot expect to recieve before christians, granting that both are to ask without faith.

Tell Mr E. that he is requested to give & his opin-ion on this text, though you need not tell by whom

Write the first opportunity.

Yours with esteem A. Nettleton

CHAPTER 15

ON THE VERGE OF ETERNITY

The scene of Asahel's ministry shifted in the summer of 1819 from Connecticut to eastern New York, where he was engaged in the first extensive preaching tour outside his native state. Several unusual revivals took place under his preaching near Saratoga Springs, New York, where he had gone on vacation. From Indian times this place had been famous for its medicinal mineral springs, and for this reason it was a favourite resort of health-seekers. The principal industry here is still the distribution of mineral waters to all parts of the world. After drinking from the springs one day, Asahel wrote to his friend Parmele that "the waters are powerful".[43]

He hoped to visit the area anonymously, but was soon discovered and called upon to preach. Revivals were unknown in this vicinity prior to his coming. But beginning at Saratoga Springs, the evangelist from Connecticut brought a shaking of the bones. About forty professed salvation here, including "some of the most respectable characters in the village".[44] This awakening spread to the town of Malta, just to the south, where there formerly had been no Presbyterian church. At this place crowds of as many as fourteen hundred came to hear him. There were soon one hundred and five converts who organised themselves into a church. This revival created great excitement in the region, and, as a result, invitations from other churches poured in. He remained in the vicinity of Saratoga till February of 1820, preaching in such towns as Stillwater, Amsterdam, Tripes Hill, and Galway. In a letter to *T.R.I.*, Nettleton gave a statistical report indicating that there were over six hundred converts in this region.

The most far reaching impact of the revivals in this area was due to its proximity to Schenectady and Union College. Some of the students and faculty caught the revival spirit and were profoundly influenced. Union College was founded in 1785 and had a notable history. Among its more famous presidents was Jonathan Edwards, son of the New England philosopher of the same name. The President of Union in 1819 was the distinguished clergyman, Eliphalet Nott, who remained in that position an incredible sixty-two years, from 1804 to 1866. He was a man of immense influence and was considered one of the most eloquent orators of his day. Among his varied accomplishments was a famous sermon on the death of Alexander Hamilton, and successful experimentation in the use of anthracite coal.

Nettleton mentions Nott in his account of the revival at Calway, near Saratoga Springs, asserting that it was he who supervised the admission of ninety-five converts into the church there one Sabbath.

There were other outstanding faculty members, including Andrew Yates, a member of a very prominent New York family, and Thomas McAuley, "one of the founders of Union Seminary in New York City",[45] who became associated with Nettleton.

Perhaps even more important, there was at this time a cluster of remarkably talented young tutors at Union who were destined to rise to great eminence. Here was Benjamin Wisner, afterwards pastor of Old South Church in Boston and later Secretary of the American Board of Commissioners (for foreign missions). Another tutor was Alonzo Potter, who eventually became bishop of the diocese of Pennsylvania. And last, but not least, there was a brilliant young Baptist tutor, Francis Wayland, who later became president of Brown University and one of the leading lights in his denomination. The lives and careers of all these men were touched by Asahel Nettleton.

Nettleton's ministry at the college actually came about through an acquaintance with McAuley. They met while the former was at Saratoga Springs. When he was preaching at Malta, McAuley visited there and assisted in the revival by preaching, attending meetings of enquirers, and counselling those attending the meetings. One Sunday, when several were to be admitted into the church at Malta, McAuley brought a group of the students to the service. What they heard and saw brought some of them under conviction and they became concerned about their souls. Suddenly one of the students died. Thus the thoughts of all were fixed on the world beyond. The corpse of the student lay in McAuley's study, and the professor saw this tragedy as a golden opportunity to drive home gospel truths to the minds of the students.

In a letter to *T.R.I.*, Asahel gave a description of a meeting which McAuley conducted for the students around the dead body of their classmate. Ironically, the letter was written from the very room where the meeting took place, for Asahel was residing in McAuley's home at the time. The picture is a grim one at first, almost ghastly, but McAuley's meeting with the students had beneficial results. Asahel wrote, "He assembled the students around the lifeless remains of their departed friend, and conversed and prayed with them in the most solemn manner. A number of them engaged to attend to the subject of religion in earnest. . . . From that time, many of the students became deeply impressed with a sense of their lost condition. For them were appointed meetings of inquiry. And in this very room, where they lately beheld the breathless corpse of their young companion, and where I am now writing, was witnessed a scene of deep and awful distress. About thirty of the students are brought to rejoice in hope".[46]

Following this initial meeting at McAuley's home, the revival spread rapidly throughout the college and the city. Nothing like this had ever been seen before. Anxious sinners now began to come to meetings of inquiry by the dozen, seeking peace for their souls. Nettleton gives this description of one such meeting in the Masonic Hall. "The room was so crowded that we were obliged to request all who had recently found relief to retire below, and spend their time in prayer for those above. This evening will never be forgotten. The scene is beyond description. Did you ever witness two hundred sinners, with one accord in one place, weeping for their sins? Until you have seen this, you have no adequate conceptions of the solemn scene. I felt as though I was standing on the verge of the eternal world; while the floor under my feet was shaken by the trembling of anxious souls in view of a judgment to come. The solemnity was still heightened, when every knee was bent at the throne of grace, and the intervening silence of the voice of prayer was

interrupted only by the sighs and sobs of anxious souls. I
have no time to relate interesting particulars. I only add that
some of the most stout, hard-hearted, heaven-daring rebels
have been in the most awful distress. Within a circle whose
diameter would be twenty-four miles, not less than eight
hundred souls have been hopefully born into the kingdom
of Christ, since last September. The same glorious work is
fast spreading into other towns and congregations."[47]

One of the students at Union College, who was an eye-
witness of the revival phenomenon, gives his impressions in a
letter to *T.R.I.* dated 6th March, 1820. "It commenced . . .
in Malta . . . and with such displays of the power of God's
Spirit in crushing the opposition of the natural heart to
every thing holy, as are very seldom seen. The *Deist* and
Universalist, the *Drunkard*, the *Gambler*, and the *Swearer*, were
alike made the subjects of this heart-breaking work. Four
months ago, Christ had no Church there. It was a place of
great spiritual dearth – and like the top of Gilboa had never
been wet by rain or dew. But the Lord has now converted
that wilderness into a fruitful field. They have an organised
church of eighty-five members, and the work of conviction
is going on."[48]

None was more deeply moved or influenced by the revival,
or impressed with Nettleton's preaching, than Francis
Wayland. As the president of Brown University from 1827
to 1855, he was "Mr Baptist" in the United States, from the
standpoint of his influence as an educator and writer. Brown
was the oldest and most prestigious Baptist college in
America, and an intellectual fountain from which flowed
a never-ending stream of ministers and Christian workers
to nourish the moral and spiritual climate in the American
church. Wayland's position gave him a highly effective
platform from which to promote his views, and brought him
into contact with the leading church leaders of the United
States and Europe. His *Moral Science*, which sold 150,000
copies, was reprinted in England and Scotland and was
translated into several foreign languages.

The Baptist tutor was twenty-three when the revival came
to the college and it came at an opportune time in his life.
Wayland's interests at the time were almost wholly academic, and religion was "a matter of small and distant
reality".[49] He thus describes how the surge of evangelical
power touched his own soul. "About this time all that region

was overspread by a revival of religion, especially through the labours of the Rev. Asahel Nettleton. It extended to Schenectady, and entered the college. There was a powerful impression made upon the students, and many of them were converted. The occasion was blessed to me in awakening my conscience and recalling me to my duty. I laboured as well as I knew how in the promotion of the work, and saw with delight a great change in the moral character of the young men."[50] One of the results of the awakening was the establishment, under Wayland's direction, of daily evening prayer meetings at the college.

Wayland's biographers, his sons H. L. and Francis, affirm that it was divine providence which had wisely and graciously so ordered circumstances that their father should be exposed to the great revival and Nettleton's preaching. They counted it a special privilege that he "should form the acquaintance and enjoy the counsels of Mr Nettleton". Wayland had stated, seemingly with great relish, "I became intimately acquainted with Mr Nettleton, and my conversations with him were of great use to me".[51] Said his sons, "His spirit received a quickening impulse, whose influence never ceased to be felt, and he gained lessons never to be forgotten in the mode of addressing men on religious subjects".[52]

Wayland heard the great preachers of his day, and he gave very high marks to two of them. One was the Scottish orator Thomas Chalmers, whom he heard while touring Europe in 1840. The other was the evangelist Asahel Nettleton, whose preaching turned his life around in the spring of 1820. Dr Wayland gave the following description of Asahel's pulpit style: "He was among the most effective preachers I have ever known. I never heard logic assume so attractive a form, or produce so decisive an effect. When reasoning on any of the great doctrines in Romans, for instance, election, the utter depravity of man, the necessity of regneration, or the necessity of atonement, his manner was often Socratic. He would commence with what must be conceded by every one present; then, by a series of questions, each deliberately considered, and not suffered to pass away until the speaker and hearer gave the same answer, his opponents would find themselves face to face with an absurdity so glaring, that notwithstanding the solemnity of the scene, the hearer could hardly escape the disposition to laugh at himself for holding a belief that appeared so utterly untenable.

"In other styles of address he was equally successful. The doom of the sinner, the danger of delay, the condition of the thoughtless, the vicious, and the blasphemer; the exercises of the soul from the first moments of conviction, the subterfuges of the human heart, and the final act of submission to God, were portrayed by him with a power of eloquence that I have rarely heard. I suppose no minister of his time was the means of so many conversions."[53]

Wayland was aware of the current slanders on Nettleton's character and his analysis of the source of these attacks adds support to the united vindication of his peers. "Notwithstanding all this, I have rarely known a man who was, for a great part of the time, more thoroughly abused. It was generally admitted that his appearance in a town was the precursor of a revival. This fact aroused all the virulence of men at enmity with God. His mode of conducting meetings was somewhat peculiar, and his preaching singularly bold and uncompromising. Thus he greatly excited against him those professors of religion who did not like anything new in the mode of preaching. Hence, at first, good men would frequently turn aside from him, and too readily give heed to the slanders of wicked men. I knew very well a physician of eminence, a pleasant, kind man, though utterly destitute of religion, residing in a village where Mr N. was labouring, who circulated a falsehood about him, retailing a conversation, which, he said, Mr N. had had with him in his office, when the fact was, that Mr N. had never been in his office; and it subsequently appeared that the doctor was wholly ignorant of his person. To such attacks Mr N. never deigned to make a word of reply, nor did he ever intimate that he knew of their existence. He considered that a man's character is the best defence of his reputation, and he left it to time and to the providence of God to refute the slanders."[54]

CHAPTER 16

FROM AGONY TO ECSTASY

When Nettleton preached at Salisbury in the latter part of 1815, a lady heard him and became "anxious" about the state of her soul. She lived, however, in an ungodly family, and the hostile influences helped to push thoughts of salvation from her mind. They evidently moved to Nassau, New York, for they were living there when Asahel visited that little village, a few miles southeast of Albany, in April of 1820.

This lady probably never suspected that she would encounter again the preacher who had wounded her spirit at Salisbury, at least her family members hoped she would not. But when she heard that the evangelist was in Nassau, she could not resist going to hear him. During this second encounter, she came under such violent conviction of sin that she nearly died.

She came home from a meeting one night with an overpowering feeling of distress. For three days and nights she writhed in uninterrupted misery. Asahel took a special interest in her case. Her depression became so acute that she was unable to attend meetings and was confined to her house. The unfortunate soul became a sort of public spectacle. Neighbours came and watched her, staying sometimes till late at night, while the members of her household looked on in shock. She was so absorbed in her own despair that she was oblivious to the curious spectators. She believed that there was no hope for her, and that the day of grace was over. Continually she groaned and cried out with such expressions as, "Lord have mercy on my soul. I am lost – Oh, forever lost".

In this pit of despair she called for Asahel. She wished to

ask for pardon for a remark she had made (possibly in criticism of the revival) fully expecting to expire after her apology. When he arrived, her agony was such that she could not remain in one position. Now she sat, now she kneeled, all the while wailing piteously, "Young people take warning from me! Young people take warning from me!" It was felt by those present that her constitution could not endure this torment much longer. A doctor was summoned, but he could only stand by watching helplessly. Recognising that the illness was out of his field, the physician looked at Asahel and asked if he thought she would die. After three days the nightmare ended; she received the assurance of complete salvation in Christ and was rejoicing in her Saviour.

This young lady illustrates the traumatic struggle through which many of Asahel's converts went before they came to Christ. These pre-conversion experiences, dubbed in modern times as "ancient mysteries", were referred to by the Nettleton school of evangelists as "law work", or "Holy Spirit conviction". While varying greatly in intensity and duration, virtually all of those saved in the second great awakening had some such heart wounds before being cured by the gospel balm. Asahel cited the cases of Paul in Romans seven, who speaks of being "slain by the law", the converts on the day of Pentecost and the Philippian jailer, as Biblical precedents for these experiences.*

Asahel was invited to Nassau by some people who had heard him preach in Malta, near Saratoga Springs. They were aware of the blessings which were falling on that community and longed for their own village to receive a similar benefit. There was one house of public worship in Nassau, shared by a Presbyterian and a Dutch Reformed congregation. Baptists also met there occasionally. There

---

*Nettleton had very decided opinions about the pre-conversion experiences. He sets forth his views in private correspondence and such sermons as "Slain by the Law" (Memoirs, pp. 116-118, Remains, pp. 328-331). In brief, he teaches that "Holy Spirit Conviction" or "Being slain by the law", is an outward or external work of the Holy Spirit which can be resisted by the sinner. While this is the normal method of God in leading men to salvation, the experience itself is not gracious or evangelical. Many who undergo this conviction work fall short of regeneration. He also believed, from many years of observation and experience, that the extreme cases in which people had acute agony could be attributed to something peculiar in the individuals. It was primarily those who were extremely self-righteous or who had openly opposed revivals who were subject to such traumatic fits of mental depression.

had been no regular ministry there for years and the churches were virtually dead. Asahel arrived on 19th April and began preaching in the school-house to a group of fifty. The following day another meeting was held, at which, it was later revealed, twelve or fifteen people received "their first serious impressions". One gentleman who attended that meeting later gave this as his initial reaction: "I went to that meeting full of prejudice. You began to tell me the feelings of my heart, and I began to be vexed and angry at one or two of my neighbours for informing you what I had said. I thought you was a man of great brass. On returning from meeting, I asked—how she liked it. She burst into tears, and we both wept."[55]

Nettleton's preaching struck this community like a hurricane. Revival in Nassau was not "the still small voice", but the fire, the thunder, and the earthquake. Some of the scenes of distress involving these people before they were converted seem incredible, and certainly defy description. On 21st April, Asahel conducted an inquiry meeting at a private home at which there were thirty present. As he was speaking, a youth sitting near a window cried out like one shot with an arrow. The people were so engrossed in the evangelist's message that it hardly caused a diversion. Several in one family were aroused at this meeting and went home weeping. The head of the house had gone to bed when they arrived. He listened as their carriage drove up and was startled by a wail of distress coming from without. He leaped from his bed, rushed outside and was met by his daughter-in-law who threw her arms around his neck and exclaimed, "My father, what shall I do? What shall I do?"[56] It was a miserable night for this young woman, but before morning all was well. She received Christ as Saviour and peace came.

On 24th April he held another inquiry meeting, this time consisting of sixty people. So many were in distress that a meeting was planned for the following evening. At this service Asahel preached on repentance, the nature of it, the reasonableness of it, and the danger of delay. There was a sense of urgency in the meeting, which Asahel describes as follows. "Never more expecting to meet my anxious hearers in this world, I urged them, by all the solemnities of the judgement, not to pass the threshold of the meeting house that night with impenitent hearts. They seemed to hear as for their lives. One, from deep distress, found relief in the midst of the discourse, and lifted up a joyful countenance. No sooner had I closed and stepped from the stage, than she came near, and taking her husband by the hand, urged him to come to Christ. It was like a two-edged sword. It pierced him to the heart. At this moment the anxious ones assembled around me, and took me, some by the hand, some by the arm, and some by the coat, exclaiming, 'Don't leave us. What shall I do? What shall I do?' Nearly the whole congregation tarried. Those who could not come near, stood, some on the seats, and some on the sides of the pews, to hear and see. From the midst of this scene of distress, I addressed the whole congregation for about five minutes." [57]

Asahel's parting discourse was short and pungent. He felt that he could tell them (till now he had hesitated to do so) that a *revival* had begun in Nassau. They were, he warned, about to witness a "solemn and trying time". He said, "You must prepare either to be taken or to be left".

After Asahel had been in Nassau for about a week, he decided to go back to Schenectady for a few days. The reaction at the meeting of 25th April, when so many hung on to him, confirmed this resolve, for the people must be taught to lean on the arm of God alone. He promised to meet with them in the school house at sunrise the next day, before his departure. The audience was told to depart quietly and retire for the night.

At the end of April Asahel was actually involved in several revivals at the same time. He had only recently left the Saratoga Springs area, where the revival had taken place during the winter. In March and the first half of April he was at Union College, where he saw the beginnings of the awakening there. During the week at Nassau the events just described took place. Still keenly interested in the revival at Union, he decided to return. There he found the situation related in the letter from McAuley's study.

After a two day visit at the College, Nettleton left again for Nassau, anxious to attend to the people there. He arrived at a house three miles from the village where he was met "with joyful countenances". He soon discovered that the Baptists were meeting in the church building that night. Hoping to advertise a meeting he had scheduled for Sunday, he drove to the meeting house, which was packed with people. When he arrived, they were standing around just ready to leave. The evangelist quietly made his way through the crowd, unobserved, so he thought, and stepped upon the stage. He calmly announced that he would be preaching on Sunday. If a visitor from the world of spirits had suddenly appeared on the scene, it could not have affected the crowd more than Asahel's entrance and announcement. He recorded, "The effect of this little circumstance was almost incredible. I could hardly say which was most prominent, the burst of joy or of grief. A number came to me with joyful countenances, while others were borne down with grief".[58]

He was not unaware that his departure from these people in their seemingly desperate situation appeared to be cruel. But from what he observed on his return, he deduced that his leaving them "in the advanced stages of conviction" was beneficial. It took them away from dependance on him, and he discovered that, after he had gone, they had repaired to the fields, groves, and their closets at home "crying for mercy". About thirty had at this time been converted.

Asahel remained in Nassau throughout May, during which time there were other unusual events. A young law student developed "law work" symptoms very much like the young lady who had gone through the valley shortly after he arrived in this village. The student had been under conviction for several days and had visited in the home where Asahel was staying. Early one morning he came to the bedside of the evangelist to discuss his problem. They were later together at the breakfast table. During the meal it was revealed that one of the young man's fellow students had come to Christ the night before. He immediately arose, obviously distraught, and went to Nettleton's room. Nettleton followed the stricken youth and found him prostrate on the floor begging God to save him. Throughout the morning his condition "waxed worse and worse", while a constant stream of visitors came to see him. These he ignored. About ten o'clock he came down the stairs and announced that he had "found the Saviour". Another law student had a very similar experience.

On 21st May Asahel preached at a "public house" outside the village, where an emotional and responsive crowd awaited him, eager to hear any word of comfort which might fall from his lips. He says, "When I arrived, the rooms were filled – doors and windows thronged. Those who seemed the most anxious, had placed themselves near the seat of the speaker. When I named the psalm, all was silence, except

the sighs and sobs of anxious souls. The moment I began to
speak, I felt that God was there. I addressed them from
Genesis 7: 1, *'Come thou and all thy house into the Ark'*. I felt
unusual freedom and satisfaction in speaking. The solemnity
of the scene will long be remembered. When I had pronounced the benediction, I know not that a foot moved. All
were standing, and still anxious to hear. I gave them an
account of what I had witnessed up in the village the week
past. Many had assembled from the surrounding regions of
desolation, doubtless from motives of curiosity, having heard
something of the wonderful movement in the village. While
giving a relation of these wonderful things, every ear was
attentive. Some were sighing, and some were gazing in wild
amazement. The language of every look seemed to be, *we
never heard such things before.* In one large room, which was
crowded entirely full, nearly all were in deep distress, besides
many crowding round the doors and windows, all apparently
equally anxious, except here and there a joyful convert.
They were crowded so closely together, that I could not pass
among them to converse. So I spoke to one and another,
here and there, at a distance, as I could catch their eyes as
they lifted them streaming with tears. All were utter strangers
whom I addressed, and not a name could I call. My only
method of designation was, by pointing and saying, 'I mean
you, and you', or 'this sinner, and that sinner'. Never did I
feel a deeper compassion for sinners, than for these poor
strangers. A number, I know not how many, were awakened
this day."[59]

On the very next evening there was another meeting in
which the evangelist's voice was drowned in groans and sobs.
Some nearly fainted and had to be helped from the building.
After his message they refused to leave and he was detained
till well in the night. At length, after much persuasion, the
crowd dispersed, save one who was in "such great agony"
that he remained through the night, pleading at the gate of
mercy. Others, who had come from a distance, stayed over
night in the neighbourhood.

By the end of May the stormy days of conviction were over
and joyful days of harvest began. Testimony meetings were
held in which dozens triumphantly expressed their faith in
Christ. Hearts overflowed with the thrilling assurance of
forgiveness, and beaming faces reflected the ecstasy within.
Asahel, delighted at what his eyes had seen in this village,

led them in services of "united thanks to God". If the night of awakening was dark for these converts, the morning of faith was all the more beautiful. It was, all in all, a blessed season for the guest minister and the people alike.

There were over one hundred conversions at Nassau by the end of June. Many revivals produced more converts than at Nassau, but few came with greater power and interest. There had been much distress under Asahel's preaching here, but it did not last. Nettletonian evangelism did not leave men in this state, but brought them all the way to the triumph of faith. Broken hearts were eventually healed.

[1] Tyler, p. 65.
[2] Ibid., p. 65.
[3] Ibid., p. 65.
[4] Ibid., p. 68.
[5] Ibid., p. 69.
[6] Ibid., p. 69.
[7] Ibid., pp. 70, 71.
[8] Ibid., pp. 71, 72.
[9] Ibid., p. 73.
[10] Ibid., p. 75.
[11] Ibid., pp. 76, 77.
[12] Ibid., p. 78.
[13] Ibid., p. 78.
[14] Ibid., pp. 78, 79.
[15] Ibid., p. 79.
[16] Ibid., p. 83.
[17] Ibid., p. 86.
[18] Ibid., p. 84.
[19] Ibid., p. 84.
[20] Ibid., pp. 84, 85.
[21] Ibid., p. 87.
[22] Ibid., p. 87.
[23] Ibid., p. 88.
[24] Ibid., p. 90.
[25] Ibid., p. 96.
[26] Ibid., p. 98.
[27] Ibid., pp. 205, 206.
[28] Ibid., p. 98.
[29] Ibid., p. 211.
[30] Tyler, pp. 210, 211.
[31] Ibid., p. 98.
[32] From a letter to Leonard Woods, Tyler, p. 287.
[33] Tyler, p. 95.
[34] See Birney, p. 78.
[35] Ibid., p. 79.

[36] The record of this problem is in the Nettleton Manuscript Collection at Hartford Seminary Foundation. Birney identifies this source as "Mss. Report of Committee investigating charges against the character of Asahel Nettleton". Ibid., p. 227.
[37] Ibid., p. 79.
[38] Ibid., p. 79.
[39] Tyler, p. 98.
[40] Birney, p. 80.
[41] Tyler, pp. 102, 103.
[42] Ibid., p. 103.
[43] Birney, p. 69.
[44] Tyler, p. 106.
[45] Birney, p. 70.
[46] Tyler, p. 108.
[47] Ibid., pp. 108, 109.
[48] Ibid., p. 109.
[49] Memoir of the Life and Labours of Francis Wayland, D.D., LL.D., by his sons, Francis Wayland and H. L. Wayland (New York, 1867), Vol. I, p. 106.
[50] Ibid., p. 106.
[51] Ibid., p. 111.
[52] Ibid., p. 111.
[53] Ibid., pp. 108, 109.
[54] Ibid., p. 110.
[55] Tyler, p. 111.
[56] Ibid., p. 112.
[57] Ibid., pp. 113, 114.
[58] Ibid., p. 115.
[59] Ibid., pp. 119, 120.

PART III

REVIVALIST TACTICIAN

(1820-1824)

I verily believe that no great warrior ever studied military tactics with more enthusiasm, or better understood the art of *killing* men with the sword of war, than Nettleton did how to wield the sword of the Spirit, to deliver them from captivity to sin and Satan, and *save* their souls.

Heman Humphrey.

CHAPTER 17

THE GREATEST SINCE WHITEFIELD

Not since George Whitefield barnstormed the American colonies had New England seen the likes of Asahel Nettleton. In 1820, at the age of thirty-seven, he was the leading evangelist of the East, in demand everywhere as a speaker. Admiring young people swarmed about him, beleaguered pastors vied for his counsel, erudite college people sat at his feet and ordinary lay people revelled in his expositions of Scripture. More importantly, legions of new born souls all over New England rose in rank after rank to call him their spiritual father.

With true Biblical modesty Asahel refused to claim any superior talents or take credit for what was taking place under his ministry. If praise became excessive, or if there was evidence of too much confidence in him, he would occasionally do his patented disappearing act. Even his biographer, Tyler, who, if anyone, would have been prone to put him on a pedestal, was jealous to give God all the glory for Asahel's achievements. In response to the question of the secret of his success, Bennet answered, "We must not overlook the fact that God acts as a sovereign, and pours out His Spirit when, where, and in what measure, He pleases. . . . He knew that he was an earthen vessel, and that when any success attended his labours, the excellency of the power was of God and not of him".[1] This comment was made after the evangelist had been laid in his final resting-place on earth. One can almost imagine Asahel shouting, "Amen!" from his tomb.

How great was Asahel as a preacher? What positive qualities as a speaker did he possess? Obviously he had many of the physical and intellectual attributes which distinguish

all great platform personalities. His voice has been variously
described, as "grave and deep-toned",[2] "clear and melo-
dious",[3] and "of more than ordinary compass and power".[4]
The tone of his voice was definitely bass, though it modulated
greatly in the course of a message. There was something
unusually captivating about his facial expression while
preaching, especially his large and deep-set eyes, which
Heman Humphrey described as "piercing".[5] Humphrey
gives the following view: "But his eye, after all, was the
master power in his delivery. Full and clear and sharp, its
glances, in the most animated parts of his discourses, were
quick and penetrating, beyond almost anything I recollect
ever to have witnessed. He seemed to look every hearer in
the face, or rather to look into his soul, almost at one and
the same moment."[6]

Asahel began his messages in a quiet, subdued manner
with a conversational tone. But, as he progressed, "his heart
grew warm, and his conceptions vivid, his voice caught the
inspiration; his lips seemed to be 'touched with a live coal
from off the altar'; his face shone; every muscle and feature
spoke; his tones were deep and awfully solemn; his gestures,
though he never flourished off a prettiness in his life, were
natural, and at times exceedingly forcible".[7] His diction was
not "splendid" but his enunciation was very distinct so "as
to be heard without difficulty in the remotest parts of the
house".[8]

Good preaching is, after all, a form of mind control. Its
goal is first to capture and then conquer the heart for the
service of God. In this regard Nettleton was a master, and
those who heard him usually felt carried along almost
irresistibly by the power of his reasoning. Wayland said he
"would sway an audience as the trees of the forest are moved
by a mighty wind".[9] This ability is sometimes hard to
analyse, and Humphrey, in commenting on Asahel's power
to seize and rivet the attention of his hearers, acknowledges
that it was mysterious and "undefinable". Perhaps it was,
after all, due to a consciousness on the part of the people
that the man before them was sent from God and that he
wielded the sword of truth. It was, in short, supernatural
ability, the result of the infilling of the Holy Spirit.

Was Asahel eloquent? There seems to have been a divided
opinion on this matter. His preaching was extemporaneous,
and because he never wrote down his sermons one must rely

on the opinion of contemporaries and the brief notes collected and printed by Tyler in his *Remains*. They reveal a simple and unadorned style, void of colourful illustrations and elegant phraseology. Asahel was not eloquent, if one is thinking in terms of the studied floridity which embellishes the speech of those with a reputation for oratory.

But there is another definition of eloquence which encompasses the preaching of Nettleton. This is sometimes defined as simple, earnest, and heart-felt speech which moves the minds and souls of men. By this standard, Asahel's command of forceful language made him one of the giants of the pulpit. If his preaching was not polished, it was vigorous and bold; if it was not grandiose, it was warm, pungent and awakening. Tyler said, "If power to arrest and chain the attention of large auditories for hours together, and to stir up the fountains of deep feeling in the soul, is proof of eloquence, then surely Dr N. was eloquent".[10]

Asahel was not considered a "graceful" preacher. His style of delivery was not such as to evoke admiration for his own brilliance. His hearers tended to forget about the speaker and become engrossed in his message. Although radiating deep concern for the souls of men and devoid of anything like coarseness or vulgarity, he was admittedly a plain-spoken man, always lucid, sometimes blunt. He usually aroused the animosity of inveterate enemies of Christ and sometimes offended men of taste. But he won the respect of all and was nearly idolised by those who loved his gospel, particularly the souls who were personally converted through his preaching.

In the accounts and descriptions of the great revivals in which Nettleton laboured, one thing comes across very powerfully, and that is that he was able to bring the awesome realities of the eternal world home to the souls of men. When he talked about the heinousness of sin, they felt its sting. When he portrayed the sufferings of Christ, they felt the trauma of Calvary. When he proclaimed the holy character of God, they trembled at the vision. When he thundered forth the judgements of hell, men were moved to escape that place.

Lyman Beecher gave the following graphic description of a service Asahel conducted near Albany, New York. Although written a quarter of a century later, he could remember in vivid detail the atmosphere and the response of the people.

The evangelist was preaching about Noah's flood. "It was in a very large and crowded hall, and the house was filled with consternation, as if they heard the falling of the rain, the roaring of the waves, the cries of the drowning, the bellowing of cattle, and neighing of horses, amid the darkness and desolation. The emotion rose to such a pitch that the floor seemed to tremble under the tones of his deep voice. He would say, pointing with his finger, 'Will you take up the subject immediately?' and each would reply, 'Yes, sir!' 'Yes, sir!' as if Christ was speaking and the day of judgement had come."[11]

An examination of Nettleton's sermons shows that they were highly scriptural in content, logical, discriminating, and always full of practical application. Some of his better messages were on such subjects as *Death, The Rich Man and Lazarus, Mortification of Sin, The Government of God, Matter of Rejoicing, The Perseverance of the Saints, Christ Standing at the Door* and *The Backslider Restored*. In *Christians Urged to Awake out of Sleep*, he challenges believers to pray and to go to work for Christ. In a message entitled *Self-Examination* his main points are that "A person may be a Christian, without certainly knowing it", and "He who is a true Christian may know it". He methodically sets about showing why doubts arise in the minds of true believers and how they may be removed.

His messages to the lost are full of pathos and tender appeal. In many of them he scarcely sounds like the Calvinist he was reputed to be. He says, "Christ still retains his compassion for sinners. He still pleads with them by His ambassadors, who are to stand and plead – beseeching hard-hearted rebels to be reconciled to God".[12] After describing Christ's sufferings, he concludes, "There He yielded up the ghost. But He arose from the dead, and ascended to His throne of glory, from which He now invites you to His arms, and beseeches you to accept the salvation which He has purchased with His blood – and is He unworthy of your love?"[13] He pours forth his heart in earnest, passionate invitations for the sinner to yield to Christ. "By the mercies of God, and by the terrors of His wrath – by the joys of heaven and the pains of hell – by the merits of a Saviour's blood, and by the worth of your immortal souls, I beseech you, lay down the arms of your rebellion; bow and submit to your rightful Sovereign."[14] The "Free Offer of the Gospel" was not just a theory to Asahel, but a conviction that had full expression in his preaching.

It is interesting how he answers an anticipated objection of the sinner on the ground of *inability*. "What! Cannot be reconciled to God? Cannot feel sorrow for sin? Cannot cease to rebel against the king of heaven? What an acknowledgement is this? Out of thine own mouth, wilt thou be condemned? If, indeed, you are so opposed to God, that you cannot feel sorrow for sin, this is the very reason why you ought to be condemned. The harder it is for you to repent and love God, the more wicked you are, and the greater will be your condemnation."[13]

Some of his addresses were designed to establish theological points and contradict current errors. In a sermon *The Government of God, Matter of Rejoicing*, he defends the view that God has "absolute control over both the natural and moral world", and has power to influence men's hearts and determine their actions. His argument against the notion that God cannot change men's hearts is devastating. "It is a doctrine clearly taught in the scriptures, that a change of heart is absolutely necessary to prepare sinners for heaven. . . . But if God cannot operate on the hearts of men without destroying their freedom, then we ought not to pray that God would renew the hearts of sinners. Surely we ought not to pray that God would convert men into machines. However wicked mankind may be, we cannot pray that God would stop them in their career of sin, because He cannot do it without destroying their freedom. . . . Sinners are then in awful condition. They will not come to Christ, and God cannot make them willing without destroying their freedom. What shall be done? It will be of no use to pray for them. Nor is it proper to pray for them; for surely we ought not to pray that God would do what He is unable to do."[16]

Many who heard Asahel made the inevitable comparison between him and George Whitefield. The two had, obviously, many similarities. Their theology was much alike and both were instruments in great revivals and the conversion of thousands. Humphrey says, "They had 'one Lord and one faith' – the same love for souls, and the same irrepressible desire to win as many of them as possible to Christ. Each was fitted for the age in which he lived, and for the work to which he was called – Whitefield, to blow the trumpet over the dead and buried formalism of the churches both in Great Britain and America; Nettleton to 'strengthen the things that remained and were ready to die' in destitute churches of Connecticut, Massachusetts, New York, and Virginia; and to help the brethren in gathering their spiritual harvest".[17]

Their dissimilarities were perhaps as pronounced as their likenesses. Tyler draws the following contrast, "The success of Dr Nettleton was not in every respect like that of Whitefield. Whitefield's power was chiefly in the pulpit. His eloquence was overpowering, and great multitudes were sometimes awakened by a single sermon. Dr Nettleton did not expect such effects from a single effort in the pulpit. His success was the combined effect of preaching in the church and in the lecture room, and of private conversation. His preaching was always solemn and impressive, and sometimes in a high degree eloquent. It was more instructive, and addressed to the conscience, and less to the passions than that of Whitefield. As a natural consequence, the revivals which occurred under his preaching were more pure – attended with less fanaticism, and a smaller proportion of temporary converts".[18]

In sheer elocutionary abilities, Nettleton was not in the same class as Whitefield. But in effectiveness, in his own way, and in the context in which he preached, he may have equalled or excelled him. Whitefield's genius found expression in a very wide sphere of operation. He held forth in the open fields where mammoth throngs were spell-bound by the power of his voice and the forcefulness of his delivery of the gospel. Nettleton's arena was the small church, the school house, the private dwelling where every eye would fasten upon his own, and all listened in breathless silence as he brought forth out of the treasure of Scripture, "things old and new". But after all, comparison of these two eminent servants of God is probably useless, if not altogether vain. The mere fact that Nettleton was compared to the great Methodist evangelist puts him in a special class, and few would deny that he was more like Whitefield than any American evangelist since. They were not cast in the same mould, but they were cut out of the same timber, and what a timber it was!

CHAPTER 18

INQUIRY MEETINGS

Nettleton's gifts were such that close contact with people was necessary for their full utilisation. With all his talents as a pulpiteer, it was as a counsellor in personal encounters and small group sessions that he excelled. It is safe to say that as many, if not more, people were won to Christ through his ministry out of the pulpit as in it. Tyler notes that his success was the "combined effect" of his "preaching in the church, and in the lecture room, and of private conversation".[19] Beecher goes so far as to say that the influence of his sermons would have been "comparatively feeble" had it not been for the "power of his personal attention where exigencies called for it, and the little *circles* which he met daily, when many were interested, to instruct and guide, and often to press submission with a success unsurpassed anywhere".[20]

The public church services were only a very small part of his work during a typical revival. An ordinary week included numerous sessions in private homes and his own room, in which he was constantly explaining and applying the truths he proclaimed from the pulpit. The many hundreds who thronged the church on Sunday were, as a rule, no strangers to Asahel. He had, in many cases, already seen them individually, and his Spirit-filled preaching only served to enforce the personal exhortations they had received from his lips. Asahel's stirring preaching and pointed private counsel became a two-pronged thrust which closed in the sinner – a double net, coming from above and beneath, from which it was difficult to escape.

He followed the apostolic pattern of visiting people from house to house. This did not necessarily mean that he chose a street or highway and knocked successively on each door.

Rather his personal calls were in response to the many
invitations from people to come and help them, or else he
was sent to deal with a particular individual who needed
attention.

It was in these intimate circles of dialogue that Asahel's
extraordinary analytical powers were exercised. The "religious exercises" or personal experiences of each person were
carefully heard and examined. Counsel and instruction
suitable to each case was given, all designed to hasten the
seeker to the point of conversion. "Immediate submission"
was ever set forth as the imperative duty, but it was presumed
that certain moral or spiritual obstacles obstructed that
goal. He sought to detect, as quickly as possible, what that
barrier was and to remove it. The particular obstacle,
whether pride, shame, indecision, or love of some secret sin,
was uncovered and rebuked. The blood of Christ was offered
as the only remedy for these problems, and repentance and
faith declared to be the only highway to that fountain of
mercy.

Like all great evangelists, Asahel divided mankind into
the two great categories of saved and lost, believers and
unbelievers. But he knew that the soul in its process of
turning either to or from God normally goes through stages.
He once said, "I do not pretend that every awakened
sinner goes over precisely the same ground".[21] But he
hastened to add that there are very "common grounds"
awakened sinners cover and he made it his business to
discover how far along the road each person he counselled
had come. Here he was at his best. Said Beecher, "Nettleton's
personal attention to the critical state of individuals in the
progress of a revival was wonderful. This is a field in which
the greatness of his vigilance, wisdom, promptness, and
efficacy lay, the wonders of which, though much may be
told, can never be recorded. His eye was open on every side
so far as to see if any danger betided, and his solicitude was
intense and his adaptations wonderful and efficacious. He
no doubt, by timely special interpositions to avert danger
and continue the unbroken associations of seriousness, has
been the means of plucking thousands as brands from the
burning and bringing them into the kingdom of God."[22]

Asahel preached that the upward path to God is "strait
and narrow", but he believed that the descent to hell is a
series of side roads and detours winding through an entangled

intellectual wilderness. He had charted this jungle remarkably well. He was trained to track the sinners through the
swamps of unbelief and he knew every cavern, bush, and
thicket in which they tried to hide. Many an inveterate
rebel, bent on escaping evangelistic pursuit, was hunted
down by this great winner of souls and startled from his
refuge. Often they were persuaded to turn from the haunts
of wickedness and hasten to the arms of Christ.

Nettleton's instructions to the awakened were brief,
tactful, and remarkably candid. He was very skillful at
introducing the subject of religion without being rude or
offensive. Bennet Tyler comments, "He had a talent which
few possess of introducing religious conversation with
individuals of every description. He was rarely abrupt,
never harsh, but always kind and affectionate. His first
object was to secure the confidence of the individual with
whom he was conversing, and to lead him on gradually to a
consideration of the importance of religion in general, and
then to a more particular consideration of his own spiritual
state. When he perceived that an impression had been
made, he would follow it up and watch its progress with
intense assiduity. He could easily introduce religious conversation with persons of every grade in society, from the
highest to the lowest. To a lawyer he once said, 'I have often
thought that persons in your situation – persons of liberal
education and high standing in society, are in peculiar
danger of losing their souls; and for this among other reasons,
that everybody is afraid to converse with them'. This remark
opened the way for a perfectly free conversation, in which
he was as faithful as he would have been to any individual
in the humblest walks of life".[23]

Asahel encouraged seekers to spend much time alone. He
felt that self-examination, Bible reading, and prayer were
healthy exercises for those who wished to obtain clear
evidence that they had been born again. As a matter of fact,
he considered it a bad sign when those who were troubled
over their spiritual state would run to and fro discussing
the subject of religion with any and everybody. He often
warned people against weeping and talking away their
impressions.

During the great revival stir he customarily called the
anxious together for special instruction. These sessions were
known as "inquiry meetings". Such gatherings were not

brief encounters after a regular church service, but periods
of concentrated and detailed teaching, set aside specifically
for the purpose of assisting those under conviction. Persons
"rejoicing in hope", or the saved, were not invited; only
awakened sinners were expected to come. Those of this class
were considered to be special cases and in need of a special-
ised and often individualised type of counsel.

If one is searching for anything unique about Nettleton's
"methods" or measures in evangelism, the "inquiry meeting"
comes as close as anything. While he did not invent this
technique, it was more central in his ministry than in any
well known evangelist in American Church history. He
certainly stamped his own style and personality on the
inquiry meetings he conducted. It was at such meetings that
some of the terrific scenes, which were so characteristic of
the revivals of the second great awakening, unfolded.

Inquiry meetings were not automatically or mechanically
organised when Asahel came to visit a community. Rather,
he waited till there was evidence of concern or awakening
among the people. Inquiry meetings were arranged when
there were *inquirers*. They were not so much means of
promoting a revival, as a sign that a revival had begun. In
times of prevailing apathy in a church or community he
had other tools. If the church was asleep or indifferent he
simply preached at the regular services of the church and
called upon the believers to repent, confess their sins and
pray for revival. Then, when the Spirit began to move
among the Christian people, and outsiders or unconverted
started seeking his help in finding salvation (the two phenomena usually went together), he announced that there
would be an inquiry meeting on a given night during the
week. As a rule they were not held in the church, but in
some public or private dwelling.

When inquiry meetings started, this was an almost
certain indication that there were "goings in the mulberry
trees". By this time the emotions and aspirations of the
church members had reached a high pitch and there was an
air of excitement and expectancy in the community. One
could predict that before long the ranks of the saints would
be swelled with new converts and the church would be
aflame with love and zeal. And, as usual, the infidels would
be up in arms.

The atmosphere in the inquiry meeting was one of hushed

stillness and subdued reverence. Normally the quiet was broken only by an occasional sob, sigh, or groan: the birth pangs
of souls in travail. Now and then the pent-up emotions of
the awakened would burst forth into a torrent of anguish,
and some would fall like the slain in battle. Asahel did not
encourage such demonstrations, however, and he insisted
on order and quiet as he dealt with the heart-wounds of the
many who were pressing into the kingdom.

A typical inquiry meeting was characterised by some
personal conversation between the evangelist and those
present, followed by a message or exhortation. Tyler describes how Asahel "managed" an inquiry meeting; most
would have followed this pattern. "After a short address,
suited to produce solemnity, and to make all who were
present feel that they were in the presence of a holy and
heart-searching God, he would offer prayer. Then, he would
speak to each individual present in a low voice, unless the
number was so large as to render it impossible. When that
was the case, he would sometimes have one or two brethren
in the ministry to assist him. He would converse with each
one but a short time. The particular object of this conversation was to ascertain the state of each one's mind. He
would then make a solemn address, giving them such counsel
as he perceived to be suited to their condition; after which
he closed the meeting with prayer. He usually advised them
to retire with stillness and to go directly to their closets."[24]
The last sentence reflects Asahel's view that it was not his
business to extract a commitment from any persons but to
let them settle their souls' interests directly with God.

Inquiry meetings were simply clinics for those in spiritual
trouble. Nettleton was the doctor, his scalpel was the law
and his medicine was the gospel. Thousands came out of
those clinics cured.

CHAPTER 19

THE TIE THAT BINDS

Nettleton established a close personal relationship with those who were converted during his revival campaigns. Although his spiritual children numbered thousands, he took a special interest in each one and tried to keep in contact with them as much as possible. His correspondence reveals that after he left a community he did not forget the souls he had left behind, born in travail. They were knit together by strong bonds: a paternal tenderness on the part of the evangelist and respect and affection on the part of the converts.

In August of 1820 he went to New Haven, where he spent most of the rest of the year. On 7th September he wrote to the new believers at Nassau, expressing his intense concern for their continued spiritual prosperity. The events there had made a strong impression upon him.

"The moment I take my pen to address you, I imagine myself seated in the midst of that same dear circle. Every name and every countenance appears familiar. The inquiry meeting, the crowded assembly, the heaving sigh, the solemn stillness, and the joyful countenances, awaken all the tender sensibilities of my heart. My dear friends, no friendship, no attachment in this world, is equal to that created in a revival of religion.

'The fellowship of kindred minds,
Is like to that above.'

"What is felt at such a season is an anticipation of the joys of the heavenly world. I doubt not your hearts retain the sweet recollection of what Paul hints to the Ephesian converts: 'Who hath raised us up together, and made us sit together in heavenly places in Christ Jesus.' But, my dear friends, after all, *the milk and the honey lie beyond this wilderness world*. A voice from heaven is heard, 'Arise ye, and depart, for this is not your rest'." [25]

Already a veteran of many a struggle against sin and Satan, Asahel could warn them that their conversion was just the beginning of their battles.

"By this time some of you begin to learn that you are on the field of battle. The world, the flesh and the devil are potent enemies. You will have need to buckle on the whole armour of God. But whatever may betide, never, *no never* think of dropping the subject. True, the conflict may be sharp, and the path-way to heaven steep and difficult, but brethren, *the time is short*. The conflict will soon be over. Think not so much about present enjoyment, as about present duty." [26]

As he wrote this letter, the itinerant still imagined himself in the midst of that "dear circle". He could see the tears of repentance rolling down their faces and the blissful, beaming countenances that followed. The signs and groans of the awakened still sounded in his ears, and in his mind he still could hear happy testimonies of praise to God. Asahel was in his native clime in the midst of a revival. The storm of spiritual conflict, the routing of Satan, the claiming of lives for Christ – these were the life of his soul.

He had gone to New Haven in response to the urgent invitation of his pastor friends there. In the summer there had been "unusual seriousness" and the prospects for a great revival were very good.

The face of Yale had changed considerably since his matriculation there in 1809. The school boasted a larger student body, three hundred in 1820, a medical school which Dwight had founded, and a growing divinity department. The intrepid Dwight had been dead for three years. He was succeeded by Jeremiah Day who, though not as brilliant as his predecessor, proved to be steady and resilient. The pastor of the First Congregational Church in New Haven was a friend of Asahel, N. W. Taylor, who had graduated from Yale in 1807. Taylor's influence in the town was steadily rising.

Asahel's arrival in New Haven produced a powerful impetus to the work and soon there were scenes of tremendous revival excitement. The normally cautious and conservative evangelist waxed bold and eloquent in des-

cribing the awakening to the believers at Nassau. "The
cloud of divine influence has gone rapidly over our heads,
and covered us with awful solemnity. And there is the
sound of abundance of rain. The fields have whitened
everywhere, and we are in danger of losing much of the
harvest, because we cannot reap everywhere at once."[27]
He conducted daily inquiry meetings with as many as three
hundred in attendance.

In the afternoon of 25th August, Asahel conducted an
inquiry meeting in a private home with twenty present.
This meeting equalled anything he had ever experienced in
excitement and drama, and was one of the most memorable
of his career. When he arrived they were sitting in "pensive
silence", obviously distressed about their condition. After his
usual session of instruction, he dismissed them. A few left,
but some remained "with heavy hearts". The evangelist
explained the scene that followed. "Very soon, Emily
returned exclaiming, 'Oh, I cannot go home. I dare not go.
I shall lose my concern. What shall I do?' and threw herself
down in a chair, and her head on the table, in the deepest
agony. All at once she became silent, and gently raised her
head with a placid countenance, and was heard to say in a
mild tone of voice, 'Oh, I can submit, I can love Christ.
How easy it is – why did I not do it before?' We sat in silent
amazement. Every word sank deep into our hearts. We felt
the conviction that God was there."[28]

As soon as Emily received peace she "seized her next
companion by the hand" and began to urge her to submit to
Christ. Those in the room, including Asahel, listened in
amazement as she pressed home the truths of the gospel to
those about her. "Every word became an arrow," the evangelist commented. "I felt that the work was taken out of my
hands, for I perceived that God had made her the most
powerful preacher."[29] Then, one at a time, others in the
circle began to beam with joy and express faith in Christ.
By five o'clock, nine had been delivered from their fears and
had received the hope of salvation. Asahel had seldom been
moved as he was at this fathering. "Oh, it was a delightful
circle, humble, tender, affectionate and joyful. They appeared like children of the same great family."[30]

After five weeks in New Haven there had been over a
hundred conversions, including twenty-five at the college.
Pastors in the area enthusiastically reported the results of

the revival to *T.R.I.* in the usual colourful language. "God has done great things for us"; "He works like himself, and none can hinder"; "The blindest infidel must see and acknowledge that it is the work of God."[31]

The story of the nine converts of 25th August ends on a somewhat sad note. Some of these were teenage girls. One, named Susan Marble, died shortly after her conversion and her testimony was considered so impressive that a memoir of her life was published. At a later date Asahel was in New Haven again when another of the group, Betsey Bishop, also passed away. About this time he spoke to this group of new converts, reminiscing about that "interesting afternoon" in which they had been saved. One of those present was Adeline Marble, Susan's sister, wearing at this very time the garments of mourning. Not long after this he read in the paper that she too had "gone to her long home". At this news the evangelist's soul was deeply touched. "I retired, and could not but weep – 'Child of mortality'. Thus three of these blooming youth have found an early grave. Had you seen them as I have, you too would weep, as well as rejoice."[32]

The demise of these young women illustrates the unusual events which seemed to surround Asahel continually. It also demonstrates his warmth and tenderness toward his spiritual children and how he followed their progress with deep emotional involvement.

The revival at New Haven continued for many months and eventually between fifteen hundred and two thousand were converted as a direct result of it. But the influence of Nettleton's visit was not confined to this city. Occasionally, during the summer and autumn, he preached in towns nearby with scarcely less effect than in the city of Yale. For some weeks he was in his home town of Killingworth where there were a hundred and sixty-two converts. In the latter part of December he was at Wethersfield, where the church was increased by two hundred through a revival.

These spiritual awakenings were contagious and spread from one congregation to another. Often when a pastor and his parishioners heard about a revival in a nearby town or parish they went to see for themselves and frequently caught the flame and carried it back to their own vicinity. The revival at Wethersfield, which is just south of Hartford, is an example. Jacob Brace was the pastor of a church in Newington, to the east of Wethersfield. The people in this town "heard with awe" of what was going on in their sister church, and they occasionally visited there to observe for themselves. They did not want to be "passed by".

About Christmas time, Asahel came to Newington, seemingly as "unexpectedly as a messenger from heaven". The first day of his visit, no doubt a Sunday, he preached three times. In the morning his subject was, *Being Ashamed of Christ*, in the afternoon he spoke on, *Causes of Alarm to Awakened Sinners*, and in the evening his text was, *Behold I stand at the door and knock*. After the prayer, while the people were still standing, he admonished them to go home immediately, not talk on the way, and as soon as they were home, "retire to your closets, bow before God and give yourselves to Him this night". After the benediction, he asked some privately such questions as, "Have you made your peace with God?" and "Do you calculate to attend to this subject?"

Not long after this, the church had a day of prayer and fasting, and the community was soon shaken with revival power. News of this excitement travelled into nearby towns and "multitudes came from neighbouring congregations". Newington became a "centre of divine entertainment", said Brace, "in comparison with which all the pleasures of this world are faint and feeble".[33]

CHAPTER 20

EMMANUEL'S TROPHIES

After ten years of experience and preaching, Nettleton's evangelistic gifts attained maturity in 1821. His methods had been tried and proven, and he was at the height of his intellectual powers. However, the gruelling schedule he had been keeping up was beginning to tell on his physical constitution – a portent of future trouble.

Fittingly, the New England phase of the second great awakening reached its climax about the same time. According to Noah Porter, who was pastor of the Congregational Church at Farmington, Connecticut, there were between eighty and one hundred churches in that state which were "signally blessed" with spiritual awakenings. One of these congregations was his own.

From the beginning of the year Porter could detect a "new state of feeling" among his people. Accordingly, it seemed to be a good time for him to seek Nettleton's assistance. Asahel arrived in Farmington on 18th February and preached his first message on Sunday evening, the subject being, *Causes of Alarm to Awakened Sinners*. The following evening he brought his message on, *My Spirit shall not always strive* from Genesis 6: 3. About fifty persons "dated their first decided purpose of immediately seeking their salvation from that evening".[34]

On 26th February an inquiry meeting was held with one hundred and seventy in attendance. Porter was amazed at the change which came over some of these people. "Here were persons of almost every age and class – some who, a few weeks before, had put the subject of serious piety at a scornful distance, and others who had drowned every thought of religion in giddy mirth, now bending their knees together in supplication, or waiting in silent reflection for a minister of the gospel to pass along and tell them, individually, what they must do."[35]

Within three months, two hundred and fifty had passed from death unto life, and Farmington looked like a new place. *T.R.I.* recorded, in the usual superlatives, the transformation of the town. The change in the moral aspect of things was "astonishing". Inveterate, hard-hearted sinners who "once appeared hopeless" were now "in their right minds, at the feet of Jesus". The greedy worshippers of money left their idols and "parted with all for Christ". Clashing interests, based on selfishness and pride, were reconciled and neighbourhood quarrels and much "hostility of spirit" ceased. Many who formerly would not speak to each other, joined hand in hand in the work of Christ and earned the New Testament description, "See how these Christians love one another".[36]

According to Noah Porter, the state of feeling which pervaded the town at this time was "interesting beyond description". There was no commotion, no boisterous excitement attending the revival, but serenity and solemnity everywhere, a "stillness in the streets". There was a general conviction that "God was in this place".

After the taxing revival days at New Haven, Wethersford, Newington, and Farmington, Asahel's reserve of energy was depleted. His exhausting schedule had rendered him sorely in need of relaxation and diversion. The bow had remained bent too long; it was about to break. With recuperation in mind, he went to Pittsfield, Massachusetts, to "rest awhile" in the parish of the pastor of the Congregational Church, Heman Humphrey. Pittsfield seemed at the time to be sufficiently remote from the Connecticut revivals to afford some prospect of repose.

Asahel visited Humphrey early in May and for a couple of weeks he relaxed and took no part in religious meetings. But by the middle of the month there was some "excitement" among the people of Humphrey's congregation, which raised hopes of a revival. Soon a kind of holy hush came over the church, a spirit of reverential silence. It seemed like the stillness that precedes an earthquake; there was a "quiet expectation" that God was about to visit Pittsfield.

At the end of the month inquiry meetings began and the undeniable signs of awakening started to appear. Many of the unconverted were "sinking in the deep waters of conviction". During the month of June, "the revival grew more interesting every day". Conversions began to multiply and family religion was inaugurated in many homes. In one day "five domestic altars were erected".

The influence of the revival moved outside the environs of the church into the heart of the town where, as Humphrey said, "the strong man armed, had for a long time kept his palace".[37] A surge of evangelical life threatened the domiciles of vice and unsettled the confederations of infidelity. A revival meant, in short, that there would be fewer patrons of the local tavern, fewer recruits for the atheist cult and an emptying of the coffers of the flesh traders. At Pittsfield, the ranks of the enemy continued to be thinned as scores deserted to the cause of Christ. Asahel and Heman worked hard and watched the church grow rapidly; they seemed to be getting the upper hand in the battle for the town. But the enemy was planning a counter-offensive.

On 4th July, the day when the nation was observing the 46th anniversary of the Declaration of Independence, a meeting was held at Humphrey's church which certainly must go down as one of the most bizarre of Nettleton's career. Since the spiritual interests of the community were at a high pitch at the time, it was felt that it would be appropriate to have special religious services on that day. Plans were made for a prayer meeting at sunrise and a public service at two in the afternoon. It was also a public holiday and a traditional time for political celebration, including such exercises as the parading of troops, firing of cannons and setting off firecrackers. As it turned out, the political aspect of the day became a source of mischief.

The early morning prayer meeting was well attended and uneventful. The political celebrants occupied the church in the morning. Among these there were some who were opposed to the revival which was going on and were only waiting for an opportunity to harass the preachers. In the military equipment and explosives they found a convenient way of carrying out their intentions.

In the early part of the afternoon there was obviously malicious intent afoot, for when the crowd was assembling for the two o'clock service, some along the way set off firecrackers as they passed. The service began with Mr Humphrey taking as his text John 8: 36: "If the Son therefore shall set you free, ye shall be free indeed", a suitable verse for the occasion. He had hardly begun when, from without the church, came a shout piercing the silence, "Fire!" followed by a blast of a cannon. Soon soldiers began to march back and forth before the church, while drums beat and fifes played in the background. In spite of this annoyance, which kept up through the entire service, Humphrey continued his address and the worshippers remained seated.

The noise outside Humphrey's church on this day, which would have broken up the average service, became, in a curious way, an asset to the preacher. He very skillfully alluded to the cannon blasts, drums, and music so as to make them punctuation marks for the points he was making. More than human ingenuity seemed to be in operation here. Humphrey later declared that had he showed his sermon headings to the citizens outside and asked them to shoot the cannon at a certain point, and again at another. They could not have served his purpose better! The agitators soon seemed to be aware of their folly, and left the church in shame. One actually testified that the shots of the cannon "pierced his soul" as he reflected on his own sinful conduct. Mr Nettleton was noticed to smile several times at the way the antics of the opposers were inadvertently accentuating Humphrey's message.

That evening Asahel himself was the speaker at an inquiry meeting which preceded the evening service. All were waiting to see what the effect of the afternoon's agitations would be. The evening meetings were to be a sort of thermometer to determine "the degree of warmth and feeling" in the church and community. Would the distractions of the infidels quench the revival spirit?

As the people gathered in the evening, it was soon evident that the stratagem against the revival had backfired. "The daring and outrageous attack in the day had driven many to the place in which he that appeared was always supposed to be asking, '*What must I do to be saved*!' " The largest crowd yet, assembled.

In the evening meeting Asahel was at his best. His text was Genesis 19: 14, "Up, get you out of this place". In his customary, graphic way he described Lot's admonitions to his sons-in-law, and the awful doom of Sodom. In vivid pictures he told how the fire fell from heaven had reduced the guilty city to ruins. During the discourse he spontaneously pointed toward a window as if to direct the attention of the people to the city going up in flames, and every eye "looked around to see the conflagration".

Independence Day in Pittsfield was a day of triumph for the revivalists, and defeat for the infidels. One who was in attendance at the meetings that day later wrote in the Charleston, South Carolina, *Intelligencer*, "This was an eventful and glorious day for Pittsfield. From that time forward Emmanuel spread his trophies among great and small".[39] There were one hundred and forty converts in this place as a result of the awakening. Eighty of these publicly professed their faith on the third Sunday in September. More than half of them were "heads of families".

Asahel made Pittsfield his headquarters through the summer of 1821, preaching occasionally in nearby churches. These included the church of Samuel Shepherd at Lenox, and Alvan Hyde's church at Lee. There were numerous conversions in both places. Shepherd characterises the evangelist as "eminently a man of *prayer*". "No one would readily doubt," he says, "that he entered the pulpit, or the inquiring meeting, directly from 'the mount of communion' with his Maker."[40] Herein, unquestionably, lay much of the secret of his spiritual power. The one who had so earnestly and eloquently pleaded *for* God, had already, before addressing his fellow men, pleaded *with* God for the blessings which came down so abundantly.

Dr Shepherd supplies a perhaps redundant, but nonetheless interesting, testimony as to the earnestness with which Nettleton preached and his ability to make the truths of God real to men. "The joy with which his heart seemed to be filled by a contemplation of the love of Jesus in giving His life a ransom for sinners, marked his preaching, and imparted an unction and uncommon energy to his eloquence. When he spake of the glories of heaven, it was, *almost*, as if he had been there himself. When he made his appeals to the sinner, he made them with directness which placed before him, as in a mirror, his utterly lost state. It seemed at times as if he was about to uncover the bottomless pit, and to invite the ungodly to come and listen to the groans of the damned; and then, drinking deeply of the spirit of his master when He wept over Jerusalem, to urge them to flee from the wrath to come, with an expression of countenance, which it is not in my power to describe."[41]

CHAPTER 21

TRAGEDY STRIKES

Lyman Beecher often suffered from dyspepsia, a malady which seemed to be a family trait. The symptoms he often complained of were "debility of stomach", producing indigestion, and acidity accompanied by a multitude of other "aches and pains", but especially "depression".[42] In the autumn of 1821, his nerves got in such a state that he was unable to carry on his pastoral responsibilities, so he left on a vacation to Maine. Before his departure he asked Asahel Nettleton to fill his pulpit, and conduct the affairs of the church in his absence.

Litchfield was a charming country town, seemingly endowed with every geographical and social advantage. The wide and shady streets were laid out around a village green with rows of stately colonial mansions reflecting the elegant taste of its sophisticated residents. Surrounded by beautiful hills, valleys, mountains and lakes, which teemed with all sorts of game, it was a paradise for hunters and lovers of nature. In Beecher's day the woods and lakes were frequented by snipe, quail, partridges, and wild ducks, while, within the township itself, foxes, minks, muskrats, rabbits, woodchucks, and raccoons were often trapped.[43]

The citizens of Litchfield were generally of a high class who were well known for their social and literary taste and were proud of their town's history. At the time of the Revolutionary War they could boast that three members of the state council, four members of congress, and seven captains in the army lived there. In a short time two of its citizens had become chief justices of the Supreme Court and two had been installed as governors of the state. Among those living in Litchfield when Lyman came in 1810 were

Governor Oliver Wolcott, who was a member of Washington's cabinet, John Allen, the seven foot giant who was a member of Congress, John Pierpont, the poet, Sarah Pierce, whose Female Academy drew people from as far away as Florida, Michigan, and the Indies, and Judge Tapping Reeve, the founder of the famous law school, who was married to the sister of Aaron Burr, Vice-President of the United States and grandson of Jonathan Edwards.

There were numerous growing industries such as those relating to the manufacture of paper, cotton, leather products, carriages, furniture and a host of other things. The commercial interests alone would have made it a busy, bustling town, but being the home of so many prominent people, it was a thoroughfare for visitors from all over the nation. Travellers en route between Boston and New York or Albany and Hartford often stopped briefly at its taverns and then hustled away by stage coach. All day long these "red, four-horse coaches" came and went with "whips cracking and horns blowing".[44] It was, in all probability, from just such a stage coach that Asahel Nettleton stepped down in mid-September and surveyed the challenge of the town.

The two prominent churches in town were the Congregational, which until three years previously had been "the established" church, and the Episcopal communion which had been the tolerated sect. Asahel's work was to be in the former, which he found to be torn with strife and plagued with "spiritual apathy". After a few weeks of preaching, however, "the church seemed to awake out of sleep and to mourn over their backslidings".[45] On 15th October he reported that there were more people coming to the special week night services than usually were in attendance on Sunday. Prominent residents, referred to by Asahel as "men of influence", were among those showing interest in his gospel. The absent pastor was kept informed of the stir in his congregation, and in a letter to his daughter Catherine from Boston, dated 20th October, he stated, "The revival in Litchfield is great and rapid. How good is the Lord!"[46]

Asahel was quite at home at Litchfield, though he viewed some of the "goings on" there as threats to the interests of the revival. He was afraid that a "cattle show" would divert the attention of people from their thoughts of God, and he was particularly concerned about an approaching Military

Review. Many of those who were coming to his services were officers in the army and he did not want them to be carried away by the bustle of the day or to get drunk. He called them together on the morning of the review and warned them to be on their guard against "vain and trifling conversation" and "ardent spirits". After this, he solemnly prayed for their preservation. The soldiers were impressed and did just as the evangelist told them.

Feeling that his health had sufficiently improved, Lyman returned to Litchfield in November, arriving very early in the morning of the sixth. He went to church, where he met his friends with "shaking hands and quaking nerves", and administered the sacrament. Asahel preached the morning sermon and Lyman followed with a thirty minute exhortation. He found the revival at its height and the people highly responsive both to the message of the evangelist and to his own admonitions. There were seventy conversions at Litchfield.

Beecher's health slowly improved, but he was still oppressed with "pain, and fear, and fog, and depression".[47] For this reason he wished Asahel to remain with him, though he discerned a reluctance on the part of his visitor to stay. Beecher's private correspondence of this period reveals that Asahel himself was sick and wanted to leave. Beecher complained to his son, Edward, that his guest was trying to slack up on his revival activities, the reason being that he was "becoming unwell".[48] The exact nature of this sickness cannot be determined, but the frequent references over the past year to Nettleton's weariness and need of retirement from his busy schedule point to a generally deteriorating state of health. We can conclude that he was becoming anaemic, run down, and unquestionably vulnerable to a serious infectious disease. He left Litchfield in January.

There seemed to be, however, little opportunity for rest. In the spring of 1822 he was active in building up the converts at New Haven, reminiscing with them about the "never to be forgotten" revival days of recent memory. In May he began preaching in the northern part of the state, in the vicinity of Somers, Connecticut, just southeast of Springfield, Massachusetts. His ministry in this area was among the most fruitful of his entire life. A revival began at Somers, spreading in a generally southeasterly direction to other towns such as Tolland, North Coventry, Montville and Millington. All told, the conversions in this area numbered about thirteen hundred.

October of 1822 arrived, a fateful month for Asahel Nettleton. It found him preaching, visiting, conducting inquiry meetings; his customary toil in the revival harvest fields for about ten years. That such activity put a tremendous strain upon his physical endurance cannot be doubted. The rewards he received during these incredible days of divine visitation far exceeded the heavy burdens he bore, but his schedule appeared herculean to others. As his biographer remarked, "How he could endure such accumulated labours, was a mystery to many".[49] The stage was set for a breakdown, and that disaster came on 5th October.

It was on this date that he visited a family in South Wilbraham, Massachusetts, where there was a case of typhus fever. Like yellow fever, which probably killed his father, typhus occasionally reached epidemic proportions in some communities in those days and was still an unsolved mystery. By the 16th of the month Asahel began to have the tell-tale symptoms, which included high fever, headache and rash. Suspecting that he had contracted the disease, he went to the closest place to a home he had, the parsonage at Bolton, residence of his life long friend Philander Parmele. Here he was sure to find a welcome.

He daily grew worse, and by 26th October he was completely confined to his bed, complaining of "head-ache, sore bones, difficulty in breathing, cold feet, heat sweats, and a very great degree of dullness".[50] On the 27th, his friends sent for a doctor, who diagnosed a case of typhus. The mortality rate of this disease for his age was in the neighbourhood of thirty percent about this time, so understandably he and his friends feared for his life.* He was bedridden for about forty days, desperately ill much of the time.

The typhus crisis seemed to reach its climax about 10th November when he experienced "the most trying time of my sickness",[51] finding it almost impossible to breathe. A

---

*Charles Murchison (1830-1879) estimated that the mortality rate for typhus in his day was 18% on the average, but it was much higher for older people. Though only 5% for children under fifteen it was 46% for those over fifty. Nettleton became ill a generation before Murchison's calculations so the mortality rate then would have been at least as great. Since he was thirty-seven when stricken, conservatively the death rate would have been 30% for his age group. (*Ency. Britannica*, 15th Ed. on "Typhus".)

physician was called, after which he "took brandy freely". Four days later he was well enough to dictate his will to Mrs Parmele. The worst was over.

During these critical days, in which he constantly looked death in the face, Asahel was composed and peaceful. His mind was much upon the glorious days of revival he had experienced. The pleasant scenes of the past ten years passed before his mind, especially the "countenances of young converts". Also, the hymns and tunes which had so often swelled forth from joyful congregations re-echoed through his soul and cheered his heart. Especially he thought of the oft repeated lines of the hymn "The Loving Kindness of God", which was now particularly meaningful.

> "Soon shall I pass the gloomy vale,
> Soon all my mortal powers must fail.
> O may my last expiring breath,
> His loving-kindness sing in death."

Before the seriousness of his condition became generally known, letters from far and near poured in, requesting him to come and preach. These numerous invitations were not conducive to a composed state of mind, and thus hindered his recovery. Asahel was prone to push himself back into a vigorous preaching schedule, even when really unable to do so, and these urgent pleas from his brethren for his help were unquestionably unsettling to his mind. Seeking to prevent such pressures, a pastor friend published a note in *T.R.I.*, explaining the dangerous state of his health and urging all to suspend communications with him.

Mr and Mrs Parmele faithfully and patiently nursed their guest until December, when the situation was complicated by the fact that they fell ill from typhus themselves, having caught it from Nettleton. On the 9th of December he was moved to another home. Mrs Parmele rallied and recovered, but on 27th December her husband, Nettleton's most intimate personal friend and companion, succumbed to the disease and died. This news fell heavily upon the invalid evangelist; he referred to this as the "most trying" of his afflictions. With a broken heart, he reflected upon the fact that they had been born the same year, in the same town, and were awakened and converted in the same revival. "Often have we met, and prayed, and wept, and rejoiced together in revivals of religion," he said.[52] The feeling that he was personally responsible for Parmele's contracting this fatal illness drove the knife of grief deeply into his soul.

Asahel's friends were aware of the trials he was experiencing, and soon letters of condolence began to come in. The outpouring of sympathy was so tremendous that he counted it more than compensation for his suffering. In December a "very affectionate" letter came from Wilbraham, inviting him to go and stay there. He expressed his deep appreciation, but declined. "Had it been possible, most gladly would I have accepted your invitation; and I should almost esteem it a privilege to be sick, if surrounded by such a circle of friends."[53]

The tenderness extended to him during this difficult period lifted his spirits, and before long he slowly began to recover. He was also encouraged by reports of the continuing of the revivals which his preaching had initiated. One came from Coventry and told him that the awakening there was "still spreading, and advancing with power". This welcome news had a cheering and healing effect upon him.

Nothing, perhaps, demonstrates the high esteem in which Asahel was held, and the deep affection of Christian people for him, more than the many expressions of sympathy and friendship he received during his illness. Had he desired, he could have probably made almost any town in Connecticut his home, so numerous and widespread were his children in the faith. The letters he received were not only tokens of sympathy, but many of them contained money as well. As Birney notes, "It was known that he had no income of his own and that whatever he had received for preaching above his bare necessities had gone for benevolences".[54]

Unlike his friend Philander Parmele, Asahel's life was spared. But it was a narrow escape, and the typhus attack left behind a somewhat debilitated body, which could never muster its former strength. Ahead of Asahel Nettleton lay several more great revivals, productive intellectual pursuits, and highly publicised polemic engagements, but the Samson-like warrior, who had often smitten the enemy hip and thigh, would never go forth again as of old.

CHAPTER 22

VILLAGE HYMNS

For two years after he was stricken with typhus, Asahel preached only occasionally. After he was strong enough to get about, his friends urged him to travel, with hopes that this would be beneficial. Accordingly, on 3rd June, 1823, he sailed from New Haven on a coastal voyage to Machias, Maine, arriving on the evening of 7th June. Four days later he rode to Lubec, a distance of twenty miles, and was much fatigued by the journey. He was in Lubec for several days before returning. He preached only once in Maine.

In the summer of 1824 he went to Montreal, Quebec, with a party which included Thomas McAuley. In August they returned by steamship down the Hudson River to New York, stopping briefly at Saratoga Springs to renew acquaintances. While at the Springs he had a relapse and had to remain for two weeks. "I was quite sick," he reported, in a letter to Mrs Parmele, dated 27th August. When he returned to New York he found a letter from her with some money enclosed. He thanked her for her kindness, but returned the money saying, "My conscience will not allow me to retain the enclosed".[55]

For many years Asahel had taken great interest in hymnology and had seen the usefulness of good music in worship, particularly in revivals. We would suppose that he was a good singer, though this is not certain. Whatever his own musical talents, he knew that "the universal language" was a valuable medium in expressing devout sentiments of praise to God.

Progress in the area of hymn usage in the churches of New England had come very slowly. From the Puritan period, New Englanders had been using the Psalms of David, "sometimes set to none too good a metre".[56] During the great awakening the churches began to use the *Psalms and Hymns* of Isaac Watts, which, to some extent, helped to break the prejudice against uninspired writers. Eventually it became evident that there needed to be improvements even upon Watts, and there was a growing feeling that other poets should be incorporated. Several attempts were made at revising Watts, including an effort by Timothy Dwight, in 1801, at the request of the General Association of Connecticut. Some of the Presbygationalists were so conservative, however, that these revisions were not acceptable to them. Although everyone was aware that Watts had some deficiencies, his reputation was so prestigious that any modification of his hymn book had to be approached with great caution.

The impetus for an entirely new hymnal came at a meeting of the General Association in 1820. The purpose of the meeting was to "devise measures for the prosperity of religion within their limits". Their first recommendation was that there be a new selection of hymns made available. Asahel Nettleton took note of that suggestion, which was not acted upon immediately.

Asahel found confirmation for the need of a new hymnal in his own ministry. When preaching in Albany, New York, in 1819 and 1820, a number of people had expressed to him the opinion that orthodox Christians, particularly in the opening settlements in the West, and in the South, could use a hymnal more in keeping with the times than those currently on the market. More or less quietly, and on his own, he began to collect some material for such a project, even while he was labouring in the revivals of 1820-1822. His period of convalescence gave him an opportunity to complete this work.

Asahel sympathised with the progressives who were advocating the use of poets other than Watts. He had great respect for him, but believed that his style was somewhat too lofty and formal for the warm atmosphere which prevailed in the churches of his day. Particularly, he felt that there was a need for hymns which expressed the feelings of people during great spiritual awakenings, including those of sinners under conviction. At the same time, he believed that all hymns used in worship should be reverent and conform to high standards of poetic and literary taste. All in all, the time was ripe for some capable person, held in high esteem

by the Christian community, to put together a completely
new hymn book. He resolved to do this.

Knowing the prejudice against hymns outside the Psalms-
Watts orbit, he decided not to replace or even revise the
works that had preceded him. Instead, he proposed to
publish a *supplement*, to be used alongside the standard hymn
books already in use. The fruit of his labour was published
in 1824 at Hartford, with the title *Village Hymns for Social
Worship, Selected and Original, Designed as a Supplement to the
Psalms and Hymns of Dr Watts*. As a supplement, Nettleton's
little volume had avoided the pitfalls of past editors, and his
book was warmly received.

There had been considerable debate about what to name
the book. Since he was at Bolton during the period of its
preparation, *The Bolton Selection* was at first considered. But
this was too limiting, and besides, the author was not really
closely connected with Bolton. He also entertained the title,
The New England Selection, but he was afraid that this would
hinder its usage in other parts of the country. Thomas
McAuley suggested that it be named *Nettleton's Selection*, or as
a second choice, *The American Selection*. But Asahel was much
too modest for the former, and the second did not satisfy
him either, so finally he settled on *Village Hymns*. This stuck
and proved to be a happy choice.

When he was putting together this collection, Nettleton
consulted every hymnal he could get his hands on. He
looked over the older editions of Watts as well as Worcester's
Watts Entire. He made use of Nathan Strong's *Hartford
Selection* and also a volume recently published by Leonard
Bacon, entitled *Hymns and Sacred Songs for the Monthly
Concert*. He also secured the hymns in use among the evan-
gelicals of England, including *Rippon's Selection*, London,
1787, and John Newton's *Olney Hymns*, which was published
in 1779. This last collection had perhaps the greatest impact
upon Nettleton's work, and made up a full one-eighth of
his hymnal.

Interestingly, he was not content to limit himself to the
older writers, but also searched for new talent and new
poetry. He inquired widely among his own friends and
acquaintances for American writers whose poems had literary
merit and might be adaptable to congregational singing.
Fortunately, for him and others as well, he was able to
discover several new authors. Among these were Lydia

Sigourney of Hartford, a friend of Mrs Parmele, and Abbie
Hyde, wife of Lavius Hyde, a Congregationalist minister who
preached in several Connecticut towns. In fact, he succeeded
Philander Parmele as pastor at Bolton. Nettleton was
impressed with the poetic talents of these ladies, and included some fine pieces of theirs in his hymnal. They have,
unfortunately, passed into oblivion. Lydia Signourney
requested that her poems be printed anonymously, which
partly accounts for their failure to survive.

One of those discovered by the evangelist was not, however, destined to be forgotten. Nettleton, it is generally
thought, was the first to use the poetry of William B. Tappan
as hymns. Tappan was a Congregationalist minister and
evangelist who lived at Beverly, Massachusetts, and published in all, ten volumes of commonplace verse. In one book
of verse, which appeared in 1822, there appeared the famous
"Tis Midnight, and on Olive's Brow". Nettleton saw it and
immediately recognised its possibilities as a hymn. Although
he used five of Tappan's poems altogether, only this one
became famous.

Asahel laboured under considerable difficulty in regard
to the source and authorship of many of his hymns. As
Birney states, "The science of hymnology, then in its infancy,
furnished him no means of properly tracing some of his
selections, and the source material which was at his disposal
was often erroneous".[57] Particularly, Charles Wesley was
not credited with many of his most outstanding pieces. To
George Whitefield was attributed "Love Divine, All Love
Excelling" and to Cowper "Jesus, Lover of My Soul".
There was at this time some hesitancy among Calvinists to
use the name of Wesley, because of prejudice against his
theology, but the errors of acknowledgement in *Village Hymns*
cannot be ascribed to this. Since Wesley is correctly credited
with seven hymns, it is evident that Nettleton, the New
England Calvinist, was not averse to using the poetry of the
Methodist. The fact is that the sources from which Nettleton
drew his hymns were in error, and he simply unknowingly
perpetuated the mistakes. He was certainly not reluctant
to use the great hymns of those of other denominations, as
seen from the fact that hymns of Baptist writers such as
Henry Alline and John Leland were included.

A considerable portion of *Village Hymns* is devoted to
poetry suitable for times of revival. Over a hundred are of

this type. The revival songs are carefully divided into sections which express the moods of sinners during the stages of awakening. There are eleven for the sinner first awakened, and sixteen for the individual under conviction. Ten are for the experience of conversion itself, fifty-one are for the new convert, and twenty-one are to be used to praise God for revival.

The hymnal is also broken up into doctrinal sections with such headings as *Character of Christ*, and *Doctrines of the Gospel*. Under the latter section are such topics as *Atonement, Decrees of God, Election*, and *Sin and Misery Connected*. Part of the hymnal is devoted to *Graces of the Holy Spirit*.

Village Hymns reflects the fact that its author was himself very missionary minded, indeed he had planned to be a missionary at one time. Consequently, there were a large number of missionary hymns. The most outstanding hymn of this sort, and one which is still very popular, is Reginald Heber's, "From Greenland's Icy Mountains".

Along with the hymnal itself, Nettleton published a book of tunes called *Zion's Harp*, which was to be used in conjunction with it. At that time, hymns and words were not written together; the hymnal itself, as a rule, only indicated the metre of each hymn. *Village Hymns* not only gave the metre but also suggested a tune to go with it, all of which were found in the companion volume. The tune book *Zion's Harp* is significant in that it may have helped to prepare the way for the printing of each hymn with its own tune.

Village Hymns fully reflected the theology of Nettleton's time, and even the missionary hymns throb with the theo-centric-Calvinistic view of evangelism. This book was immediately popular, especially among the ministers and churches who had experienced revival. It is the only book that Nettleton himself published during his lifetime. But his one and only literary production was very influential and passed through many editions. It continued to pay large royalties long after its author was dead.

Nettleton's efforts represented a considerable advance in the science of hymnology in America, a fact that has not gone unrecognised. Louis F. Benson said that "Nettleton knew a good hymn when he saw it and produced the brightest evangelical hymnal yet made in America".[58] He not only brought forth Tappan's famous "Tis Midnight on Olive's Brow", but introduced the hymns of Samuel Davies, successor to Jonathan Edwards as president of The College of New Jersey. His "Great God of Wonders" is included in one of the most widely used modern hymnals, *Great Hymns of the Faith*, first published in 1968.

No study of the history of hymnology can ignore Nettleton's yeoman labours. While this effort does not place him, by any means, in the category of the great hymn writers, his collection did make a significant contribution to the total history of church music. The Word of God has, through the centuries, been scattered through the printed page and propagated from the pulpit, but it has also been borne along on wings of song. The church of Christ must include Asahel Nettleton among those who not only preached the gospel of redemption, but who passed it along through beautiful poetry and melody. As one has said, "Its (*Village Hymns*) variety and vivacity were a revelation to many accustomed to more didactic strains and gave it a long popularity. It served as a source book to numerous compilers, who spread its hymns even more widely."[59]

CHAPTER 23

THE GLORY OF REVIVALS

It was widely believed among evangelical scholars and pastors of the eighteenth and nineteenth centuries that the world would be converted to Christ by the preaching of the gospel. Particularly this is true during the period broadly encompassed between the two great awakenings in America, which spanned about a century. No doubt these phenomena nourished and fostered this opinion. If virtually whole towns could be converted and transformed by gospel power, so, many reasoned, God could bring the entire world under a similar influence.

Admittedly, the days of the revivals were a glorious period for evangelical Christianity; it may have been the golden age of the church. Rarely, if ever, since New Testament times, have gospel principles so influenced society as a whole. While no one would claim that either America or Great Britain was totally Christianised, few would deny that the social and political structure of these two countries was permeated by the Judeo-Christian world view. However far the leaders of society failed to follow its implications, the Bible formed the cultural backdrop for the English-speaking world.

When one considers the missionary and philanthropic activity which was spawned by the second great awakening, one can understand, to some degree, the buoyant optimism which prevailed among some Christians of this period. All the evangelical denominations were bursting with life. Schools were proliferating and growing, Bible and tract societies were flourishing,[60] and Christian magazines, almanacs, and children's books were sold by the million. The Sunday School movement had been initiated and was growing by leaps and bounds, and missionaries had pene-

trated the far-flung corners of the earth with the good news
of salvation.

The awakening also provided an immediate impetus to
various types of moral and social reform. Lyman Beecher,
the Congregationalist preacher, was one of the leaders of
this movement, as was the Massachusetts lawyer, Jeremiah
Evarts. Humanitarian interests, such as the abolition of
slavery, grew out of the spirit of missions and evangelism
which was arousing the churches, and some of the most
influential advocates for the freedom of negroes were
products of the second great awakening. Harriet Beecher
Stowe, author of the civil war classic, *Uncle Tom's Cabin*,
grew up in a Puritan type home and listened to such
preachers as Asahel Nettleton when she was a child. Francis
Wayland was one of the most vocal and eloquent supporters
of the abolition of slavery, and though president of the
American Peace Society, when the war between the states
broke out he justified it on the ground that "to be enslaved
was worse than war".* The increased numerical strength of
the evangelical churches, and the greater financial resources
brought in by the conversion of thousands, enabled Christians to exert greater influence in all areas of society, political, educational, and medical.

Of all the leaders of this exciting period of revival and
missionary endeavour, none was more enthusiastic and
optimistic than Edward Griffin, the silver-tongued president
of Williams College. Griffin witnessed first-hand the beginnings of the New England phase of the awakening in 1792,
and was at Williams when the famous haystack prayer
meetings were going on. His mood may be measured by a
sermon he delivered on 14th September, 1826, at Middle-
town, Connecticut, at a meeting of the American Board of
Commissioners for Foreign Missions. His attitude was not
peculiar to himself, but mirrored that of many others. The
message, *Arguments for Missions*, based on Matthew 28: 18-
20, is not only a classic model of pulpit eloquence, truly one
of the great historical sermons of America, but also one of
the most rosy forecasts of the future of the cause of Christ
ever pronounced.

*In 1816 the American Bible Society was organised and in less than four
years it had distributed nearly 100,000 Bibles. The New England Tract
Society was transmuted into the American Tract Society in 1823 and had
already printed 777,000 tracts and was publishing a bi-monthly magazine,
a Christian almanac, and a series of Children's books.

Griffin saw the awakening energies of the church of his day as one of the signs of the great approaching universal spread of the kingdom of Christ. Griffin had himself lived to see Europe and America unite in the great missionary movement which was circling the globe. He had seen "the golden limb" of gospel light spreading westward in conjunction with the expansion of the American settlers into the heart of the continent. Within his recent memory missionaries had accomplished incredible feats, preaching Christ on "the burning sands of Africa", on "the plains of the Hindostan", India, and even in China where then, as now, one quarter of the globe's population lived. As far as Griffin was concerned, this was the fulfilment of the mission of the angel of Revelation, who "having the everlasting gospel" went "to preach unto them that dwell on the earth, and to every nation, and kindred, and tongue, and people".

Griffin fully expected to see, himself, the "latter day glory" introduced on earth. It was only a matter of time until all mankind would bow to the sovereign claims of Jesus Christ. The final pulsating paragraph of this sermon is indicative of the spirit of this message.

"Countless millions are shortly to awake from the sleep and darkness of a hundred ages to hail the day that will never go down. I see the darkness rolling upon itself and passing away from a thousand lands. I see a cloudless day following and laying itself over all the earth. I see the nations coming up from the neighbourhood of the brutes to the dignity of the sons of God – from the stye in which they had wallowed, to the purity of the divine image. I see the meekness of the Gospel assuaging their ferocious passions, melting down a million contending units into one, silencing the clangor of arms, and swelling into life a thousand budding charities which had died under the long winter. I hear the voice of their joy. It swells from the valleys and echoes from the hills. I already hear on the eastern breeze the songs of new-born nations. . . . Come that blessed day. Let my eyes once behold the sight, and then give this worthless body to the worms."[61]

One cannot be absolutely certain to what extent Asahel Nettleton shared in the exuberance of the times, in so far as its long-range promise was concerned. He did believe that there would be a period of universal peace and righteousness prior to the final judgement, which he refers to as "the millennium". In a sermon on *Christ's coming to judgement*, he cites, as a basis for this belief, such texts as, "The earth shall be full of the knowledge of the Lord, as the waters cover the sea", from Isaiah 11 : 9, and Revelation 20 which speaks of the binding of Satan. "These predictions," he says, "it is evident, have not yet been fulfilled."[62]

It is also a fact that Nettleton believed that revivals were an important instrument of God in advancing His kingdom in the world. But the awakenings of the eighteenth and nineteenth centuries, which were the most characteristic religious phenomena of that period, not only had many friends but also many enemies. Among the latter were not only the infidels, whose interests were threatened by revivals, and the rationalistic Unitarians, but also the very con-servative Calvinists who focused on the extravagances which attended them, particularly the first awakening in the 1740's.

Asahel did all he could to keep the movement of his day pure and put down anything that bordered on the fanatical in the meetings he conducted. Although occasionally some fainted under the tension of conviction, he never tolerated the kind of violent bodily movements which characterised many of the frontier camp meetings. Such demonstrations as shrieking, groaning, rolling on the floor, clapping hands, jerking, or leaping were unknown under his preaching. Also he discountenanced visions, trances, and immediate impres-sions of one kind or another, as being fanatical and delusive.

But he defended real revivals and succeeded in making them acceptable to orthodox people who were wary of emotionalism. The kind of revivals he promoted were so rational, scriptural and beneficial in their effects that few pious people could really object to them. He strove to avoid criticism, except what comes against the gospel itself. For example, unlike many evangelists, he was very respectful of pastors, and all his methods in evangelism were supportive of the pastoral office. Ebenezer Porter, a teacher at Andover Seminary, says of him, "This distinguished itinerant found no difficulty to labour with stated pastors without making himself their *rival*. If, in any instance, he could not con-scientiously coincide in the views, or co-operate in the measures of a pastor, among whose charge he was invited to labour, he did not sow dissension in that church, nor seek to detach their affections from their minister, but quietly withdrew to another place. The consequence was, that the visits of this devoted servant of Christ *were always sought*, and never dreaded nor regretted by ministers of churches". Bennet Tyler adds, "An instance probably cannot be mentioned in which the influence of Mr Nettleton led to the dismission of a pastor."[63]

Asahel believed that a revival was a golden opportunity for reaping a harvest for Christ. He felt that such a time represented a "crisis" in the feelings of people which, if not profited from, would result in the loss of many souls.[64] He stated, and his whole life was living proof of it, that one sermon, in a revival, could do more good that a hundred, equally good, out of one. He also stated, "More good may be *lost*, for the want of that *one* (sermon), than can be done with it, and with a thousand like it, when the crisis is past. 'Say not ye, there are yet four months, and then' – It is now, or never."[65]

He wished to show also that the converts of revivals were real Christians, not just temporary believers. He once said, "If genuine religion is not found in revivals, I have no evidence that it exists in our world".[66] Hundreds of people, pastors especially, of his own day and a generation later, rose up to testify that this was the case as far as his own ministry was concerned. Relatively few of the conversions professed under his preaching, proved to be spurious.

Asahel Nettleton's revivals were authentic, but, unfortunately, Edward Griffin's glowing predictions were not fulfilled. What he saw was not the dawning of one grand day never to end, but the meridian splendour of a day soon to pass into history. The sanguine dream of world-wide conversion never became a reality. Missions have gone on, and many millions have come under the influence of the Christian gospel, but while Griffin was being carried away with his vision of glory on the earth, the god of this world was girding himself for a defence of his domain. Some desperate social and political problems were arising, and old heresies, garbed in a different dress, were about to make a powerful stand.

Griffin did not foresee that, within a few years, a poisonous rationalism would be imported from Germany and devastate all the great denominations. He did not take into account the seething cauldron of unrest which, within four decades, would burst forth into a bitter war, tear his country apart, and leave over six hundred thousand of its sons lying beneath the sod. Neither did he calculate that just around the corner were theological disputes which would fill the air and press, shatter the peace and unity of the Presbygationalist churches, and have repercussions throughout the religious world.

[1] Tyler, p. 203.
[2] Francis Wayland, *Memoir*, Vol. I, p. 109.
[3] Bennet Tyler, *Ibid.*, p. 337.
[4] Heman Humphrey, *Ibid.*, p. 364.
[5] *Ibid.*, p. 364.
[6] *Ibid.*, p. 365.
[7] *Ibid.*, pp. 364, 365.
[8] *Ibid.*, p. 364.
[9] *Memoir*, Vol. I, p. 110.
[10] Tyler, p. 337.
[11] *Autobiography*, Vol. II, p. 484.
[12] *Remains of the Late Rev. Asahel Nettleton, D.D.*, by Bennet Tyler (Hartford, 1845), pp. 250, 251.
[13] *Ibid.*, pp. 261, 262.
[14] *Ibid.*, pp. 262, 263.
[15] *Ibid.*, p. 258.
[16] *Ibid.*, p. 293.
[17] Tyler, *Memoirs*, pp. 366, 367.
[18] *Ibid.*, p. 207.
[19] *Ibid.*, p. 207.
[20] *Autobiography*, Vol. II, pp. 484, 485.
[21] *Remains*, p. 338.
[22] *Autobiography*, Vol. II, p. 482.
[23] *Memoir*, pp. 212, 213.
[24] *Ibid.*, pp. 220, 221.
[25] *Ibid.*, pp. 126, 127.
[26] *Ibid.*, p. 127.
[27] *Ibid.*, p. 127.
[28] *Ibid.*, p. 128.
[29] *Ibid.*, p. 128.
[30] *Ibid.*, p. 129.
[31] *Ibid.*, p. 132.
[32] *Ibid.*, pp. 131, 132.
[33] *Ibid.*, p. 140.
[34] *Ibid.*, p. 141.
[35] *Ibid.*, pp. 141, 142.
[36] *Ibid.*, pp. 144, 145.
[37] *Ibid.*, p. 148.
[38] *Ibid.*, p. 152.
[39] *Ibid.*, p. 153.
[40] *Ibid.*, p. 154.
[41] *Ibid.*, p. 155.
[42] *Autobiography*, Vol. I, p. 464.
[43] *Ibid.*, p. 205.
[44] *Unvanquished Puritan, A Portrait of Lyman Beecher*, by Stuart C. Henry (Grand Rapids, 1973), p. 71.
[45] *Memoir*, p. 157.
[46] *Autobiography*, Vol. I, p. 464.
[47] *Ibid.*, p. 466.
[48] *Ibid.*, p. 466.
[49] *Memoir*, p. 165.
[50] Cited by Birney, p. 86.
[51] Birney, p. 87.
[52] *Memoir*, p. 168.
[53] *Ibid.*, p. 167.
[54] *Op. cit.*, p. 88.
[55] *Memoir*, p. 169.
[56] Birney, p. 90.
[57] Birney, pp. 96, 97.
[58] Cited by Birney, p. 96.
[59] *Ibid.*, p. 112.
[60] *Autobiography*, Vol. II, p. 280.
[61] *Enterprise, Discourses on Missions by American Authors* (Boston, 1846), p. 36.
[62] *Remains*, p. 190.
[63] *Memoir*, p. 59.
[64] *Ibid.*, p. 207.
[65] *Ibid.*
[66] *Ibid.*, p. 224.

PART IV

CIVIL WAR IN ZION

(1824-1829)

Irregularities are prevailing so fast, and assuming
such a character, in our churches, as infinitely to
overbalance the good that is left. These evils, sooner
or later, must be corrected. Somebody must speak,
or silence will prove our ruin. Fire is an excellent
thing in its place, and I am not afraid to see it blaze
among briers and thorns; but when I see it kindling
where it will ruin fences, and gardens, and houses,
and burn up my friends, I cannot be silent.

Asahel Nettleton.

CHAPTER 24

THE WINDS OF CHANGE

The course of American religion seems to be curiously interwoven with the great political and social movements which have affected the history of the nation. As one traces the fortunes of the church, it can be seen that they closely parallel changes in the mood of the country as a whole. Generally speaking, powerful spiritual awakenings have come in times of political peace and tranquillity, while radical changes of one sort or another, such as social turmoil and major war, have signalled the beginning of spiritual decay.*

On the fiftieth anniversary of the signing of the Declaration of Independence, 4th July, 1826, something happened which seemed to symbolise the end of one era and the inauguration of another. On that day, by a curious coincidence, the two elder statesmen of the Republic, John Adams and Thomas Jefferson, both chief architects of the political system and signers of the Declaration, died. The federal period, when there was only one political party, was over and in two years the campaign for the presidency between the Whig party, led by John Quincy Adams, and the Democratic-Republican party, led by Andrew Jackson, began. That four-year contest has rarely been equalled for savagery in American history.[1]

But the famous "western movement" was the most important upheaval of the times. It had been made possible

*Dr Edward Hindson, a contemporary student of American Revivalism, points out that every major revival came during a time of peace and was followed by a war. The great awakening preceded the Revolutionary War, the second awakening was before the war of 1812, and the great prayer revival of 1857-1859 came before the Civil War. (*Glory in the Church*, New York, 1975, p. 24.)

by such events as the purchase of the Louisiana Territory in 1803 by President Jefferson, which doubled the size of the United States, the opening up of passageways to the Great Northwest by the Lewis and Clark Expedition (1804-1806), and the construction of the Erie Canal (1817-1825). The emigration of people from the industrial centres of the East across the Blue Ridge and Allegheny Mountains to the pioneer communities of Tennessee, Kentucky, Ohio, Illinois, and Missouri began as a trickle in the seventeen-nineties, but became a flood twenty-five years later. In 1811 a single month saw two hundred and thirty-six wagons move out of Robbstown, Pennsylvania, on the western highway to Pittsburg, and between March and December of 1817, two thousand westward-bound families pushed through gate number two on the Dauphin Turnpike in the same state. One traveller, watching the white tops of the covered wagons, commented, "Old America seems to be breaking up and moving westward".[2]

The frontier people were fast becoming a different breed to the folks back east. The carpenters in the long-settled coastal regions were framing federal-style houses, but in the western "raisings" they were building log cabins, with the log walls chinked and their chimneys coated with mud. In the East the gentlemen wore knee breeches and silver buckles; in the West they adopted deerskin pants and their wives donned homespun skirts. Back east there were the theatres, the concerts, and the steepled churches; in the West were gamblers, brawls that killed and maimed, and occasional religious services conducted by circuit-riding preachers.

But throughout the country, among the elegant citizens of the East and the rough frontiersmen of the West, there was a swelling spirit of national pride. After all, there had been immense progress in the first half-century of the country. They had come through two wars with Great Britain, a major one and a minor one, and there had been tremendous industrial growth, aided by such inventions as the cotton gin and the steam-ship. Although there were still religious revivals, outsiders believed that the real religion was free enterprise, and a German visitor wrote that America was "one gigantic workshop" and "business is the very soul of an American".[3]

But the primary reason for the optimism of the times was

that the day of political freedom had arrived and the implications of democracy were being felt. The ancient tyrannies had been broken and the people were in power. The ascendancy of the fiery-tempered Tennessean, Andrew Jackson, brought the spirit of the West to the heart of America's authority base, the capital at Washington, and he seemed to embody the ideals of the common man who yearned to control his own destiny. The "rights of man" were being asserted, and the "age of reason" was getting a second chance. Pride in human progress and freedom fostered confidence in man's intellectual prowess.

The two great awakenings had, in no small measure, been responsible for the social advances and political freedoms which came to the new American Republic. Both George Whitefield and Asahel Nettleton preached that one becomes a Christian by being born again, which from a human standpoint is submission to the yoke of an almighty God, Who alone can rule the conscience. If the Puritan movement in America proved anything, it was that the sons of God make bad slaves. Souls who have bowed humbly at the sceptre of the God Who rules the nations and counts them as "a drop in a bucket" and "the small dust of the balance", are notoriously unbending in the face of oppression from fellow mortals. And when they gain any liberty, whether it be spiritual, political, or economic, they are prone to give God the glory.

But, unfortunately, there is another interpretation to the origins of human liberty and progress. The blessings of this earth can not only be attributed to the beneficence of a merciful Creator, but also, through man's short-sightedness, to mere human ingenuity. And when men have made great strides in the realms of science, politics, and economics, there is always a tendency to self-congratulation, vanity and conceit. Beneficiaries of great movements, over which they really had little control, can mistakenly think that they themselves have unlimited power. And then the stage is set for the final delusion, namely that liberty is absolute and that man is his own saviour. In such a context, thanksgivings to God, let alone submission and worship, are unthinkable.

At the very same time that the American nation was basking in the light of its new found liberties and triumphing in its unprecedented material advances, certain leaders in the Christian communities were questioning the very foundations of these blessings, and flattered by their own intellectual successes, were setting sail upon the high seas of speculation. In New England the creeping cancer of Unitarianism was destroying the institutions of the founding fathers, though its friends were the elite of society. In its essence, Unitarianism is a revolt against pure *supernaturalism*, a putting down of revealed religion and a setting-up of human wisdom. It rejects a divine Saviour, an inspired Bible, and a miraculous salvation.

But Unitarianism is only an extreme and advanced form of anti-supernaturalism. It represents a total resistance to Biblical religion in the four critical areas of Christology, Anthropology, Bibliology (to coin a word) and Soteriology. Historically the front line of defence is in the last of these departments, and against it forces of rationalism, sometimes with the aid of true Christians, have initially moved. Asahel Nettleton and his school of thought stood unswervingly upon the principle that salvation is a work of God, supernatural in its origin and efficacious in its application. In this Calvinism, Biblical theism finds its fullest and most natural expression.

But in Nettleton's day there arose a powerful movement, led by some of his most cherished personal friends, which sought to modify this solid tradition, which derived ultimately from the European Reformation and had been explained and defended most successfully by one of the intellectual geniuses of Christian history and a spiritual giant of America, Jonathan Edwards. Nettleton first confronted this movement on one of its somewhat superficial, but nonetheless characteristic manifestations, that of *methods in evangelism*. This initial phase of the struggle was the famous "new measures" controversy of 1827. Later it settled on the more fundamental theological differences which separated the parties.

The second great awakening, with all its intellectual, evangelistic, and humanitarian by-products and ramifications, was connected doctrinally with the type of theology which Asahel Nettleton proclaimed so boldly. Allowing for minor differences, the influential theologians in such schools of learning as Yale and Andover, and their graduates, who took leadership places in the churches and went to the mission fields, followed in Edwards' footsteps. Pastors such as Gardiner Spring and William Sprague, educators such as

Humphrey, Griffin, and Ebenezer Porter, and missionaries such as Mills, Judson, and Rice were nurtured in the atmosphere of such traditional Calvinistic tenets as man's innate corruption by the fall, his inability to save himself, God's elective grace, and the need for substitutionary atonement. This type of God-centred theology, which had produced a successful generation of Christians and initiated many noble enterprises for the benefit of mankind, was now about to be repudiated.

Indeed, the winds of change were blowing. Even as the first great awakening was soon corrupted and finally dissipated, so the second would suffer fatally from internal contamination and modification. In the eighteen twenties, religious theories more in keeping with the swelling national spirit of self-initiative and confidence were brought to the fore. Human progress had moved to the centre of the social spectrum and must be attended by the shifting of man to the top of the theological sphere. The day of the exaltation of God was past. Along with the new theology came a new evangelism consistent with it.

It must be admitted that many of those involved in the innovations of the second and third decades of the nineteenth century never intended to water down the gospel, nor did they believe that they were altering the theology of Edwards. Professedly they followed him and marched under his banner. They even quoted him and tried to use his influence to buttress their speculations. But the debate was not very old before it was evident that the new theories represented fundamental changes in the New England orthodoxy, and the Edwards who was being expounded was really only a grotesque caricature of the theologian from Northampton.

The debate between the defenders of the old orthodoxy and the new liberalism is unquestionably one of the most significant in the history of American theology and evangelism. It signalled the beginning of a new and mighty force called usually by the name of "modern evangelism" and spotlighted a theological cleavage which remains unresolved until this day. The repercussions of some of these issues are still profoundly felt throughout the world. A development of such tremendous importance to American religion deserves careful scrutiny and evaluation. The ailing evangelist, Asahel Nettleton, played a fairly important role in this struggle. In fact, his relationship to the "new measures" controversy fills up, to a great extent, the final chapter in his life, albeit a tragic one.

CHAPTER 25

STORM CLOUDS FROM
THE WEST

Asahel's health had sufficiently improved by the autumn of 1824 for him to begin his preaching circuit once again. His first effort was at Bethlehem, Connecticut, in the former parish of one of his spiritual guides, Joseph Bellamy, who had died in 1790. There were forty professions of faith during his stay in this community. In 1825 he laboured in Brooklyn, on Long Island, and in Taunton, Massachusetts. Not much is known about the Long Island venture, except that his preaching was attended with "success". At Taunton there was a revival fully as powerful and effective as those he had experienced before his bout of typhus. It followed the old pattern of the awakening, conviction and conversion of sinners, with the normal methods of visitation being used. Due to his health, however, his schedule was less rigorous.

In February of 1826, he went to the town of Jamaica on Long Island, to preach in a church which was badly divided. As he frequently did, he went to this place unannounced. He made his first appearance on a communion Sunday. Accompanied by another preacher, he walked slowly up the aisle, taking his seat on the front pew. The bearing of the two gentlemen indicated that they were preachers, and great curiosity was excited as to their identity. Soon it was revealed that one of them was "Rev. Mr Nettleton, the great revival preacher".

One of the residents of Jamaica was an aged believer named Othniel Smith who had listened to George Whitefield preach in this community seventy years previously. He had heard of Nettleton and aroused considerable interest in him by telling one of the local residents, "This Mr Nettleton that is going to preach for us is a most wonderful man; he is said

153

to be the greatest preacher that has been among us since the days of George Whitefield". He went on to report of Nettleton's reputed ability to "almost *read a man's heart*, so wonderful was his knowledge of human nature".[4]

The church at Jamaica was without a pastor and the clergymen who had supplied the pulpit in preceding months had tried in vain to reconcile the warring factions in the congregation. They had expatiated over and over again on "brotherly love", but the people shrugged off such preaching and continued their feuding. Nettleton's approach was entirely different. He ignored the surface problems and dealt with rock bottom issues such as "the claims of God and the duty of sinners".[5] This policy was considered a tactical master stroke, and under such "judicial management" the breach was healed and conversions started multiplying.

It was while he was in Jamaica, during the summer months, that he began to receive reports of problems among the churches in the vicinity of Oneida County, New York. In former days he had often preached in the eastern sections of New York and he, of course, had many friends in that area. A considerable number of ministers wrote that the churches were being agitated by the introduction of "new measures" in revival meetings. Some became so alarmed that they travelled to Jamaica and discussed these problems with Nettleton.

At that time, great revivals were going on in this area of New York, as all acknowledged. But many of the pastors were dissatisfied with certain practices which attended these revivals. They felt that commonly accepted laws of propriety and wisdom were being violated by some of the visiting evangelists. One was that they were being exceedingly bold and harsh in their method of addressing the unconverted. Often individuals were specifically mentioned by name and called upon to change their method of living. This created a sensational atmosphere but grieved many of the Christians who felt that the unconverted should be dealt with in a more private and cautious way.

Another departure from the norm was the policy of permitting women to speak in mixed assemblies. In all the revivals among the Presbygationalists and Regular Baptists in the previous quarter of a century women had had a prominent place. In personal prayer support, in private visitation and in attendance on the preaching of the Word, they undergirded the ministry of evangelists and pastors. But the restrictions laid down by Paul in 1 Corinthians and 1 Timothy were taken literally.* It was thought to be a violation of modesty and decorum for women to pray and exhort in mixed assemblies, particularly in the public meetings in the church. But according to the report from New York, women were encouraged not only to pray but to speak as well.

The most conspicuous innovation was the practice of calling upon people to make some kind of physical movement in public meetings to assist them in securing salvation. Sometimes they were told to "rise up" from their seats. At other times an "anxious seat" was arranged in the meetings, and sinners were urged to "come forward" to the seat in order to become Christians. Such methods had been used for many years by the Methodists, but were discountenanced by most Presbygationalists.

Some of the advocates of these methods, so Nettleton was told, were not content to use them in their own circles, as a matter of private judgement and liberty, but carried them into other places and insisted that they be universally adopted. In fact, some evangelists, allegedly, came into communities without invitations from local pastors, and stirred up people against the resident ministers who were not in sympathy with the novel methods. This had always been regarded as a breach of ethics in the ministerial fraternity and was especially repugnant to Nettleton.

In addition to these complaints, a somewhat reckless and irreverent spirit was reported with regard to the manner of some in the pulpit. They were throwing aside the customary worshipful and devout mode of prayer and were addressing God with rude familiarity and presumptuous audacity.

These improprieties were, of course, objected to and resisted by many of the pastors and lay people, including some who had been actively involved in revivals themselves. But when they did not go along they were denounced with great harshness and were called "dead", "cold", and "enemies to revivals". Thus the initial efforts to check the evils were rebuffed in the same bold spirit in which the new methods had been introduced in the first place.

---

*1 Corinthians 14: 34 says, "Let your women keep silence in the churches: for it is not permitted unto them to speak" etc. 1 Timothy 2:12 says, "But I suffer not a woman to teach, nor to usurp authority over the man, but to be in silence."

As the autumn of 1826 approached, an increasing flow of people began to come to Nettleton, the acknowledged expert in the field of revivals, and complain about what was going on in New York. His opinions and advice were being urgently sought by those whose churches were being upset by "the new measures".

From the very first, when he read and heard of these problems, Nettleton's mind went back to the first great awakening in the seventeen-forties, particularly the sad manner in which it terminated. The ghost of James Davenport seemed to be rising again. It was he whose intrusion into quiet parishes and indiscreet boldness in denouncing other ministers of the gospel had hurt the ministry of more stable evangelists, and contributed materially to the decline of the revival. He also recalled the state of things in eastern Connecticut, where he began his ministry. While he was unacquainted with any of the particular individuals who were allegedly perpetrating the offensive techniques, he feared that history was about to repeat itself.

Although busily engaged in a revival in Jamaica, the thoughts of the evangelist turned increasingly to the problem area in New York. News of the disturbances in the churches of his friends and brethren in the ministry increased his concern daily. The conflict over the new methods and the agitations in the churches caused him "inexpressible pain". As an ardent friend of revivals, he was anxious that nothing be done to corrupt, hinder, or divert them. But he was exceedingly reluctant to get involved in the problem in New York. The awakening at Jamaica was at its height and demanded his constant attention, which gave him quite enough work to do without the added burden of some difficulties in a distant community.

As the events of the summer unfolded, a new stage in the "new measures" conflict was reached when he was told that the trouble-makers in New York were appealing to him in justification of their methods. They were actually pleading his own example as a defence. This was certainly a shrewd move, though unfair, for no preacher stood higher in the esteem of the churches than he. The sound and salutary influence of his ministry and the revivals that attended it had made him the premier evangelist of New England and the champion of orthodoxy. But he was naturally horrified that he, who had pleaded so earnestly for stillness, reverence, and discretion in evangelism, should be appealed to in defence of the controversial methods.

Still he hesitated. Heretofore his battles had been with infidels and out and out enemies of the gospel. Although he had been engaged in minor debates with other preachers about various points of theology, these discussions had taken little of his time and energy. Nothing had interfered with his total concentration on the winning of souls. But the uproar in New York gave every appearance of a major struggle. Obviously, should he get involved with the problems created by the new measures, it would remove him from the revival atmosphere and thrust him into the field of controversy. It also meant that he would be uprooted from his present location on Long Island where his ministry was needed. Added to these considerations was the fact that he was still in a feeble physical condition. Since beginning to preach again in 1824 his schedule had had to be carefully measured and restricted. Did he have the physical and emotional stamina for the gathering storm?

But the pressures on him to speak out continued to increase. His "friends . . . constantly urged" him to come to their aid.[6] They felt defenceless, almost overwhelmed by the juggernaut which seemed to roll irresistibly through their territory. To whom could they turn, but to him? No one else, apparently, had the stature and respect among the churches to check the rising tide of fanaticism.

At length Asahel decided that "the interests of Christ's kingdom" required him to act. More was at stake here than his own personal feelings or tranquillity. Churches near and dear to his own heart were in turmoil, and pastor friends were turning to him for a solution to the problem. Silence was becoming impossible. In the latter part of 1826, he decided that the time for confrontation had come. Nettleton crossed a sort of Rubicon when he left Jamaica and headed for Albany, to see for himself what was disturbing the churches in that vicinity.

Chapter 26

THE "NEW MEASURES"
CHAMPION

The central figure in the controversy over new methods, which began in Oneida County, New York, was a sensational young preacher named Charles Grandison Finney. He was just beginning a career which would eventually propel him into international fame as an evangelist. He was born in Warren, Connecticut, in 1792, but two years later his parents, Josiah and Rebecca, moved to the New York Frontier, in Oneida County, where he grew up. At the age of sixteen he began teaching in a school, but after four years he returned to Litchfield County, Connecticut, where he attended an academy.

He seriously considered attending Yale, but his private tutor dissuaded him and encouraged him to study privately to become a lawyer. This was one of the first major turning points in his life. After teaching in New Jersey from 1814 to 1816 he came back to New York and entered the law office of a Judge Wright in the town of Adams, which is near Lake Ontario. Here he successfully completed his studies for the bar and became Mr Wright's assistant.

Whatever exposure to religion he had received when a child had not made much impression upon him, for at the time of his legal studies, according to his own testimony, he was "almost as ignorant of religion as a heathen".[7] But through the prayers of his fiancée and the solicitations of other friends he determined to settle once and for all the matter of his own personal relationship to God. In the autumn of 1821 he went through three agonising days trying to find peace. One night "a strange feeling came over me", he says, in his *Memoirs*, "as if I was about to die. I knew that if I did I should sink down to hell".[8] Shortly thereafter, on the morning of 10th October, 1821, while engaged in prayer he had a dramatic experience. He was alone in "Squire" Wright's office at the time. Suddenly his heart "seemed to be liquid" within him, and like a geyser bursting through the surface of the earth, his feelings seemed to "rise and flow out". "I want to pour my whole soul out to God," he said. He rushed to a secluded place to pray, and the room suddenly appeared brilliantly lighted, and "it seemed as if I met the Lord Jesus Christ face to face". He fell on his knees, and what seemed like waves of electricity went through him. It was like "liquid love . . . the very breath of God".[9]

Almost immediately after this experience, Finney felt a desire to preach. "I soon sallied forth from the office," he said, "to converse with those whom I should meet about their souls."[10] He was twenty-nine at the time and ready to abandon the legal career and devote his life to the ministry. He was even involved in a lawsuit, but broke off the case, telling his client that he had a "retainer from the Lord Jesus Christ to plead his cause".[11]

Charles Finney was marvellously equipped to be a public speaker. Tall and handsome, he had hawk-like eyes which could nearly hypnotise those upon whom his gaze fell while speaking. He had a mellow, wide-ranging voice and exuded poise and self assurance. Almost from the beginning of his public ministry, all who heard him were captivated by his stage presence. As one has said, he had a "dramatic talent that made him one of the best pulpit actors of his day. He put his whole body into his preaching, and in his early years writhed, gesticulated, and groaned so in the pulpit that unfriendly observers thought him coarse, crazy, or hypocritical".[12] Many found him inspiring and instructive.

Recognising his need for preparation and training, Finney decided to study for two years under his pastor, Rev. George Gale, before seeking a licence to preach from the local Presbyterian council. While in these preparations, he preached often, and many made professions under his ministry. The St. Lawrence Presbytery licensed him on 30th December, 1823 and six months later he passed the ordination procedures.

In the examination which preceded the ordination he was required to preach an extemporaneous sermon. His eccentric style came out in this message and was a foreshadowing of future trouble. He refused to enter the high pulpit and instead delivered his exhortation from the floor of the centre aisle of the church. The examiners were annoyed, but gave him his ordination papers all the same.

A part of his ordination vows included an affirmation of his belief in the Westminster Confession of Faith, but, amazingly, he later acknowledged that at the time of his induction into the ministry he had not even read it. According to one Presbyterian historian, some Presbyterians in Western New York during this period took very lightly the affirmation of the Confession by licentiates.[13] This is evident from Finney's ordination.

Although Finney had not studied the Westminster Confession at this time, he was not totally ignorant of some of the teachings of that document. Through his association with Gale and other Presbyterian ministers of the area, he had come into contact with such teachings as man's depravity through the fall, the imputation of Adam's sin, the satisfaction theory of the atonement, and the inward and efficacious work of the Holy Spirit in regeneration. As soon as he was exposed to these ideas he rejected them as being "contrary to reason". Especially he found the notion of *human inability* distasteful, for he regarded as incredible the view that men are required to do things they are not morally capable of doing.

Finney explains why he rejected original sin and the Calvinist doctrine of regeneration in the following sentence. "If man had a sinful nature, there was no adaptation in the gospel to change his nature, and consequently no connection, in religion, between means and end."[14] He was mistaken, of course, in stating that Calvinists do not believe that there is a connection between "means" and "end" but he could not accept the idea that something in addition to *means* (the preaching of the gospel) is essential to regeneration, namely, a supernatural work of the Holy Spirit.

He also rejected the idea of the imputation of sin to Christ and of Christ's righteousness to the believer. "I insisted," said he, "that our reason was given us for the very purpose of enabling us to justify the ways of God; and that no such fiction of imputation could by any possibility be true."[15] Finney believed that religious opinions should be tested not so much by Biblical evidence as by the *human reason*. Thus the neophyte preacher began his ministry with a definite rationalistic strain in his system of epistemology.

Finney did not deny that man was a sinner or that there was a certain agency of God connected with conversion. Sin exists, but it consists simply and solely in the overt and voluntary acts of the mind. Man, he taught, has not inherited a corrupt nature, nor is there anything sinful in man's disposition or constitution, but rather sin is the positive choice of the mind for evil. These views, explained at length in his *Memoirs*, sermons, and *Systematic Theology*, were considered by the Calvinists of his day as fundamentally a revival of Pelagianism.

Since he rejected the idea of innate depravity, he believed that the work of the Holy Spirit on human nature is solely by "moral suasion". The influence of God in deterring men from an evil course of conduct is like that of a man who stands on the bank of a river and shouts to endangered friends who are drifting toward a rapids in a boat. He calls, he warns, he pleads. The access that God had to the minds of men is through the written Word or the preacher.

Finney found the commonly accepted doctrines of grace not only intellectually unacceptable but also functionally intolerable. If these views were irrational, they were false, and if false, deleterious. He believed that a vibrant and thriving Christianity could not co-exist with such concepts as inherited depravity and "constitutional" regeneration. These beliefs, though hoary with age and loved by thousands, were, according to Finney, inimical to godliness and damaging to evangelism. Successful preaching, he maintained, must be based on the proposition that men have the full ability to convert themselves. Finney viewed the theology of the Westminster Confession, as far as evangelism is concerned, somewhat as a carriage driver would a swamp; it does nothing but bog it down.

In his *Memoirs* Finney tells about his two-pronged campaign of slaying sinners on the one hand and waging war against Calvinism on the other. He discusses at length his initial debate with his pastor, George Gale, and his eventual triumph over him. Forceful and persuasive polemicist as he was, he soon prevailed upon Gale to abandon his old-fashioned notions and to take up with his own. As Finney went from place to place, building all the while a large following, he considered it essential, in moving into a community or church, to crush whatever strongholds there

might be of people who held to inherited depravity and
sovereign grace in salvation. Sinners were told everywhere
that they needed no special divine agency to convert them,
and they reacted by professing faith in thousands. Many
pastors and laymen, who had formerly held to Calvinism,
found him too formidable an adversary and yielded to his
verbal hammer strokes. Finney soon came to regard himself
as a crusader against the status quo, a prosecuting attorney
bent on convicting and sentencing systems opposed to his
own.

By the end of 1826, Finney's star was rising fast. From the
very start of his evangelistic career he was instrumental in
promoting powerful religious revivals, beginning at Antwerp,
a small village in northern New York. This was followed by
successive revivals at Gouverneur, De Kalb, Westernville,
Rome, Utica, and Auburn. During this time his ability to
dominate the minds of those who listened to him continually
increased. Finney notes in his *Memoirs* that while he was at
Westernville, called then Western, some Congregational
ministers, known as "The Oneida Association", published a
pamphlet condemning his revivals. This may well have been
the beginning of the opposition to him of which Nettleton
was soon to hear. His preaching so antagonised some of the
people at the Presbyterian Church at Auburn, that they
withdrew and formed a new congregation.

Initially the more conservative pastors took issue, not so
much with Finney's doctrine, for this did not come out so
strongly at the outset, but with his harsh, crude, sometimes
abusive style and his use of the so-called new measures.
There was, of course some connection between the measures
and the doctrines, but this was not readily apparent. It was
not long, however, before many traditionalists knew that the
old standards were being fiercely challenged.

Finney was not responsible for all the confusion going on
in New York over the new measures, for, as is always the
case, some followers of great public figures tend to emulate
the faults rather than the virtues of their leaders. But the
reports Nettleton received in 1826 fairly accurately reflected
Finneyism. He did indeed, for example, pray for people by
name, a fact that could be very embarrassing for those who
opposed him. In fact, there is a slightly amusing story about
this proclivity of Finney many years later, when he was
president of Oberlin College. At faculty meetings he called

each member by name in prayer, sometimes dressing them down in his supplications to God. On one occasion, after the president had thoroughly discussed the faculty with the Lord, one young instructor asked permission to lead in prayer. He told God that it was not right that all should be prayed for but the president, and went on to describe Finney, not excluding the critical vein in which they had been accustomed to hear him speak of them. He concluded with an earnest petition that Finney be given the spirit of meekness and charity. Reportedly, the tenure of the instructor was brief, and the president's prayers were also briefer and more general after this. In this instance, at least, he found his strong medicine rather easier to give than to take.

There was only one of the measures with which Finney, according to his *Memoirs*, was not directly associated at this time. Although in the eighteen-twenties he did call on people to stand up in response to an invitation to declare their faith, he did not use the anxious bench until several years later. It is probable, however, that others associated with him did so. All in all Asahel had received an accurate picture.

CHAPTER 27

TWO TITANS MEET

Nettleton went on his reconnaissance trip to the Albany area in November of 1826. The reason he chose Albany was that he had been invited to come there by some of the ministers who were under the gun because of their opposition to Finneyism. Some of Finney's followers had brought the new measure type of evangelism into Albany, and already there was an uproar. The Second Church, where John Chester was pastor, was divided over these issues. Among those who knew of the situation and were lined up against the Finneyites in town was Thomas McAuley of Union College. The same is true of some of the leading members of the Troy Presbytery where Finney was preaching.

Asahel was not at all interested in meeting Finney at the time, but wanted to see the spirit prevailing among his followers, especially sympathetic pastors. He soon found out that the situation was fully as bad as had been reported, if not worse, so he determined to talk to the pastors who had come under the new influences. He felt that if he could deal with Finney's disciples, he could indirectly bring pressure upon Finney himself.

Two of Finney's friends and close advisors, whom he met with while in Albany, were Alvin Coe, and John Frost, who was minister at Whitesborough, New York. Frost had obviously been carried away with Finney's type of evangelism. In his conference with Frost and Coe, Nettleton tried to convince them of the dangers of the new measures. In this attempt he was not successful, a disappointment that pointed to tough days ahead.

After Frost's session with Nettleton, he was convinced that some of Nettleton's objections to Finney were due to misunderstanding and were not too great to be removed. It is probable that he suggested a personal meeting between the two evangelists. Since Finney came to see Nettleton shortly after he came to Albany, almost certainly Frost had suggested that he make this move, or at least had indicated that such a meeting would be profitable.

Nettleton and Finney met on two occasions, both of which took place about the turn of the year (we do not know the exact dates). In order to understand these meetings, one must be aware of the older evangelist's feelings at this time. He believed that although Finney was the leader of the new measures party he was being not only supported, but actually spurred on, by many of his disciples. These young preachers were as thick as flies and were buzzing all around the Albany area and throughout New York. Their flattery of Finney and zeal to carry out his tactics (and even go further in certain extremes) were having a bad effect upon him. This support for Finney made it difficult for Nettleton to have an influence on him, or so Nettleton believed. He felt that by stopping the disciples, he could halt the leader.

Finally the two masters, both, in a sense, heads of parties in the church, got together. At the first meeting Nettleton was evidently in a somewhat dejected mood. In a letter to Frost some time later he stated that he was "already worn out with conversation".[16] The meeting was evidently a cordial and pleasant one, and the thorny points at issue between them were not discussed.

The second meeting was definitely initiated by Finney. While in Albany, Nettleton was a guest in the home of a mutual acquaintance and Finney went there to see him. Unfortunately, we only have Finney's account of this meeting, which he recorded forty years after the event. Nettleton was scheduled to preach in the evening and Finney suggested that he accompany him to the service. At this, according to Finney's account, Nettleton "manifested uneasiness, and remarked that I must not be seen with him".[17] The uneasiness which Nettleton may have felt at this time would have been based on the fact that a public appearance of the two men together would have been used to advantage by the new measures advocates. In spite of all that Nettleton had said up to this time, they still persisted in claiming that he approved of them.

A careful examination of the letters of Nettleton after these meetings with Finney makes it evident that he did not try to "mould" the younger evangelist or rebuke him for his errant methods. The reason, which has already been explained, is given in Nettleton's own words: "I have long been wishing to correct some of his peculiarities, that I might invite him into my own field and introduce him to my friends. Aside from feeble health, one consideration only has prevented me from making the attempt. Some of his particular friends are urging him on to the very things which I wish him to drop. I fear that their flattering representations will over-rule all that I can say. And having dropped these peculiarities, his labours for a while might be less successful; and then he would resort again to the same experiment."[18] These remarks are in a letter to S. C. Aiken, written after the meetings with Finney.

What this explanation means, in short, is that he had no hope of success in changing Finney's thinking by a personal discussion and so did not attempt it. Whether Nettleton was wise in this regard can only be a subject of speculation. In all probability Finney would not have changed, for as George Hugh Birney says, "Finney was not the sort of man to be led by anyone".[19] Even so, in not dealing with Finney directly about the problem, Nettleton may have made the second serious tactical mistake of his life (the first being the "Jesus Christ" letter of 1818).

Finney's record of this epochal confrontation, which was widely circulated in his *Memoir*, has gone far toward elevating him in the minds of American historians and casting Nettleton in a bad light. He claims that he had the "greatest confidence" in him and even "dreamed of visiting him" and "sitting at his feet, almost as I would at the feet of an apostle".[20] He represents himself as being as pliable as clay, and ready to be influenced in any direction by the revered New England preacher. "At that time my confidence in him was so great that I think he could have led me, almost or quite, at his discretion."[21] The fact that Nettleton did not take him by the hand and seek to lead him into sounder concepts of evangelism has not enhanced his image in the minds of many who take Finney's account without qualification.

But to say the least, it may be doubted that Finney's only or chief motive for going to Nettleton was instruction. Other men, such as his early counsellor, George Gale, who was much sounder theologically than he, had tried to influence him, but in vain. As a matter of fact, before the relationship of Gale and Finney had been concluded, their roles of teacher and pupil had been reversed, such was the forceful-ness of Finney's personality. The fact is that Finney was a totally independent spirit and there was scarcely an older minister with whom he was associated who had any in-fluence on him.

The great need of Finney and his movement at this critical point in history was justification and vindication. Although they had started a wild fire which was blazing in all directions, a number of talented and respected men were busily engaged in stamping it out. They recognised that, if they could have brought Nettleton over to their side, or even have persuaded him to countenance them in the mildest sort of way, the issue would have been settled once and for all. If Asahel Nettleton had so much as raised one little finger in approval of them, it would have been a crushing defeat for those who opposed the new measures. Finney's younger disciples even went so far as falsely to claim Nettle-ton's approval, and there can be little doubt that Finney himself longed for this when he went to Albany to see him.

If one takes into consideration all the factors in the situation at the time, it can be seen why the meetings between these two men were so unpromising and, in the end, fruitless. The two confrontations between Nettleton and Finney were not in any way formal or official meetings to discuss issues. They were not, in fact, even an attempt for the two evangelists to come to a better understanding. The men were thrown together on Finney's initiative primarily, not Nettleton's, and each had a different purpose in mind. One was trying to enhance his own image in the eyes of the public by association with the other, who was in turn really only marking time and trying to figure out how he could best counteract a religious movement which he frankly believed to border on fanaticism.

Setting aside for a moment the theological and tactical problems involved in Nettleton's meetings with Finney, it is interesting to compare the men personally. In many ways they provide a study in contrast. The older evangelist, some nine years Finney's senior, was not altogether a picture of strength at the time. His physical stamina had been partly destroyed by typhus fever and he was easily exhausted. On the other hand, Finney was in the full bloom of health, a specimen of vigorous young manhood. Nettleton was shy, cautious, and reserved, except to those in his own intimate circle. Finney was bold, restless, self-confident; a genuine extrovert. Nettleton was wary of change and a protector of tradition, while Finney was audacious and fearless of any conservative elements, no matter how deeply entrenched.

But in spite of these differences, similarities in the two men are not hard to find. They both had tremendous natural endowments as preachers, such as piercing eyes, powerful voices and dominating personalities. Both would be considered severe by modern standards in the way they preached. They put great emphasis on the sterner aspects of truth, such as the terrors of the law and the holiness of God. Both were very decided in their opinions and were not noted for compromise.

These men are rightly known in history as antagonists, as leaders of two opposing forces in the American church. Finney was the spokesman for the surging frontier religion which was both speculative and emotional. Nettleton was the defender of the old New England orthodoxy which refused to be shaken from the moorings of the past. When these two elements came together, like the collision of warm and cold air in the upper atmosphere, thunder and lightning was inevitable.

CHAPTER 28

THE ANTIDOTE

In January of 1827 Asahel Nettleton sat down, pen in hand, to give his personal, official assessment of the "new measures" movement in New York. It came in the form of a letter to S. C. Aiken of Utica, New York, for whom Finney had preached in the summer of 1826, and who was becoming sympathetic with his evangelistic methods. The letter was designed for general circulation and specifically for the perusal of Finney and his friends. It was one of the most important letters that Asahel ever wrote and was a crucial development in the controversy at hand. It contains an exposé of the objectionable elements of the "western revivals", suggestions for correcting these excesses, and a statement of his attitude toward Finney personally.

Having been in the Albany area for over a month, during which time he had seen first-hand the spirit of the new evangelism and had held personal interviews with its advocates and their chief, Asahel was in a position to speak with some authority on the matter. His attempts to deal with the problem on a face to face basis with the individuals involved had not been successful, and in spite of all he had done heretofore, some of them still claimed his approval. He hoped that a written corrective would make his own position crystal clear and change the course of things generally.

This lengthy epistle, along with other similar material, was printed in its entirety in a booklet entitled *Letters on the New Measures in Conducting Revivals of Religion*, and thus preserved for posterity. It was published in New York in 1828 and is remarkably restrained in tone, utterly devoid of rancour and invective, and, in many respects, generous toward those with whom he was at issue. "We do not," he states, "call in question the genuineness of that revival, or the purity of the motives of those who have been the most active in it. You, doubtless, are reaping and rejoicing in their happy fruits."[22] Finney was at the time preaching at Troy, New York, where Nathan Beman was pastor. Nettleton believed that there was "doubtless a work of grace" at that place.

He was quite aware that there will never be a perfect revival, and that some "irregularity" will exist in the best of them. He was not frightened about "little things" and was not about "to make a man an offender for a word".[23] But having conceded this, he was convinced that the revivals had come "at an awful expense" and the evils attending them could not be ignored.[24] "Irregularities," in this particular case, "are prevailing so fast, and assuming such a character in our churches, as infinitely to overbalance the good that is left. These evils, sooner or later, must be corrected. Somebody must speak, or silence will prove our ruin."[25] The New York revivals were not unlike a fire out of control. "Fire is an excellent thing in its place, and I am not afraid to see it blaze among briers and thorns; but when I see it kindling where it will ruin fences, and gardens, and houses, and burn up my friends, I cannot be silent."[26]

Nettleton makes reference to the fact that several of "our first ministers", had gone to Troy to see and examine for themselves the revival there. Among these were Edward Griffin, David Porter, Eliphalet Nott, and Mark Tucker. Their report was anything but flattering. He later told John Frost that "it was the universal opinion . . . that irregularities were prevailing to such an alarming extent that the *character of revivals had gone back half a century*".[27]

Getting down to specifics, he first objects to an irreverent attitude which many of the revivalists had displayed in the pulpit. He makes several references to Edward Griffin's alarm over this matter. Griffin gave specimens of what sounded to him like "the accredited language of profanity".[28] While acknowledging that "much truth" was being preached, those in his group who had been to Troy said that they had "never heard the names of God used with such irreverence".[29] Another "pious woman" of Troy had said, "I do wonder what has got into all the ministers to swear so in the pulpit".[30]

Nettleton did not like the strife and anger he saw among some of the churches as a result of the harsh and abusive

style of some of the young ministers. Certain prominent
people, including pastors, were being publicly "skinned" and
denounced with such labels as "stupid", "dead" and
"enemies of revival".[31] The natural tendency of such verbal
abuse was to provoke hard feelings and opposition.

One of the "new measures" involved a change in the order
of the churches relative to the position of women in the
church. The revivalists insisted that they be allowed to take
a more prominent role, such as praying in the public services.
This was deeply resented in many quarters. But when these
changes were resisted, the headstrong evangelists set about
to "crush" and "break down" their opponents. "And so,"
said Nettleton, "they wax hotter and hotter, until the church
is fairly split in twain."[32]

This evil was "running in all directions". Many of the
churches in the vicinity were experiencing not a true spiritual
awakening, but "a revival of anger, wrath, malice, envy, and
evil-speaking, without the knowledge of a single conversion,
merely in consequence of a desperate attempt to introduce
these new measures".[33] But the offending parties were not at
all bothered by the opposition to them, rather they thrived
on it. If the minister of a church, so they said, "gets mad, and
all the church too, no matter for that; 'the more opposition
the better' ".[34] This, so it seemed to Nettleton, was their way
of promoting a revival. They believed that only in a climate
of war and debate could a revival be conducted.

Nettleton was particularly disturbed by the fact that so
many of the pastors and other church leaders were succumb-
ing to the tremendous pressure being put upon them by the
new firebrands. Some, who did not really sympathise with
the turbulent spirit abroad, felt that they had to "go along"
or at least keep silent in order to save their own reputations.
The new measures advocates had convinced many that their
antagonists were going against God. Thus to "get rid of the
noise", and save themselves, they "broke down" and were
"crushed", which was the precise design of the revivalists.
Some who had been caught in this maelstrom, and had
yielded reluctantly, warned their brethren to stay away
from it if possible. One was reported as saying, "I have been
fairly *skinned* by the denunciations of these men, and have
ceased to oppose them, to get rid of their noise. But I warn
you not to introduce this spirit into your church and society".[35]

As far as Finney himself is concerned, Nettleton seemed

reluctant to blame him altogether for the excesses. Their interviews had evidently convinced him that he was a man of piety and talent. He continually refers to him as "Brother Finney" and considers him "a good man and wishing to do good".[36] "I have long been wishing to correct some of his peculiarities," he writes, "that I might invite him into my own field and introduce him to my friends."[37] Unquestionably, Asahel recognised in the young evangelist a genius for preaching, which, if properly trained, could be a mighty force for truth.

But "peculiarities" were also evident and Finney's connection with the controversial measures could hardly be denied. His friends gave him credit for the "crushing" and "breaking down" technique, and anyone who heard him could see that he was a prime example of the abusive and denunciatory style of preaching. He seemed to be in his natural element when there was a fight in the church.

After spotlighting the irregularities in the western revivals, Nettleton pleaded for a return to the orderly and quiet type of evangelism which he had so long promoted. He called for tact, as opposed to bombast and harshness in dealing with the unconverted, modesty and reverence in the pulpit, Biblical restrictions on women, and above all *stillness* in revivals. The noisy clamour connected with the new measures movement sounded harsh and painful to him. "Seven years ago," he said with a touch of nostalgia, "about two thousand souls were hopefully born into the kingdom, in this vicinity, in our own denomination, with comparative stillness. But the times have altered. The kingdom of God now cometh with great observation."[38]

After appealing to Aiken to forgive anything unchristian or unkind that might have inadvertently slipped into his letter, he closes with an invitation for him to use the communication in the wisest manner he could. "If, in your opinion, it can do no mischief, or will do any possible good, you are at full liberty to show it to Brother Finney, or any of the friends of Zion whom it may concern. We will lay the subject at the feet of our divine Master, and there will we leave it."[39]

Nettleton's letter was soon circulated among some of the pastors in New York and also reached Finney himself. He took it not only as a criticism of some of his followers but also as an attack upon himself which could not be ignored.

He immediately jumped to his own defence by preaching a sermon in Beman's church from Amos 3: 3: "How can two walk together except they be agreed?" In this sermon, he subjects the resistance to the "new measures" to his own critical scrutiny. He had a simple analysis: the objections being raised to the new evangelism were based on spiritual deadness. The reason professors of religion and impenitent sinners have difficulties with *means* in revivals is "their frosty hearts".[40] They are not right with God, thus they cannot appreciate white-hot revivalism. "Now, while their *hearts remain wrong*, they will, of course, cavil; and the nearer right any thing is, the more spiritual and holy, so much the more it *must* displease them, while their *affections grovel*."[41] This sermon of Finney's got a lot of attention and was printed in Philadelphia in March.

Thus the moving spirit behind the western revivals, now on the defensive, draws blood in the rebuttal. His antagonists are proud, lukewarm, carnal, and therefore unable to discern or appreciate a real revival. Christians who resist new measures are making common cause with worldly and ungodly men. This proclamation was not conducive to settling the dispute or even promoting dialogue on the issues.

Nettleton was, of course, stung by Finney's sermon. In a letter to Gardiner Spring of New York, dated 4th May, he examines some of the sentiments expressed in the sermon, and expresses strong disapproval. He finds evidences of some basic misunderstandings, by its author, of the nature of true religion.[42] Finney seems to be exalting false zeal, pride, and self-righteousness in opposition to the meekness and humility which is enjoined in the New Testament. He includes a long quotation from Jonathan Edwards' work on *Religious Affections*, which he hopes would supply this deficiency in Brother Finney's sermon.[43]

Thus began the debate over the new measures between Nettleton and Finney. Nettleton had referred to the uproar he found when he came to New York as "a civil war in Zion . . . a domestic broil in the household of faith".[44] By his letter to Aiken he joined the conflict, though he had hoped that his influence would have been great enough to put down the opposition. But such was not the case. Clearly the lines were being drawn between two opposing schools of thought on evangelism, each side headed by men of great ability and influence.

CHAPTER 29

SHOWDOWN AT NEW LEBANON

Nettleton's letter to Gardiner Spring of New York was
printed in an eastern magazine, *The New York Observer*,
which drew the attention of the entire eastern seaboard to
the new measures problem. The great excitement over
Finney's revivals was propelling him into the national spot-
light and also began to polarise pastors into the two camps
of supporters and opponents. Nettleton's stature among the
people in the East caused the more conservative traditionalists to side with him, but the Presbygationalists of New
York, who were far removed from the intellectual strongholds of Calvinism, moved into Finney's orbit. The developing division was at this stage somewhat geographical, the
easterners being proponents of the staid, orthodox evangelism of Nettleton, and the westerners backers of Finney's
fiery, audacious revivalism.

Following his letter to Aiken, which by no means quelled
the new measures uprising, but only solidified the two
camps, Nettleton moved to enlist other friends in his cause.
He turned to his old friend and revival associate, Lyman
Beecher, who had just moved to Boston to become pastor
of the Hanover Church. If Beecher's sympathies could be
secured, he certainly had much to offer in the way of
energy and influence. At the time Beecher was engaged in
a red-hot battle in Boston with the Unitarians. When he
received communication from Nettleton about the fanatical
excesses in New York, he recognised in these developments
a potential advantage for the Unitarians. They stoutly
opposed revivals and loved to brand the Calvinistic preachers as enemies to science and progress. His long friendship
with Nettleton and confidence in him gave him a sym-

pathetic ear. Beecher's *Autobiography* says, "With Mr Finney he was personally unacquainted; with Mr Nettleton he had been intimate for years, and cherished an exalted opinion of his wisdom. If but a moiety of that résumé of reports was true, too well he could anticipate the comments of the Unitarian press, and the bearing of the whole on that revival in which all his energies were absorbed."[45]

After careful consideration and consultation with respected leaders such as the Andover professors, Ebenezer Porter, Leonard Woods, and Moses Stuart, he put together a letter to Finney and Beman expressing his concern. This letter was not intended to be a critical broadside but an attempt to suggest ways for Finney to modify his style so as to avoid some of the criticisms which he was receiving. His "object" in that letter, as he afterwards told John Frost, was not to "check their ardour, and boldness, and moral momentum", but to propose "emendations" which would put Finney on ground where all the godly could defend him.[46] At the end of the letter he said, "We cannot justify his faults for the sake of his excellencies".[47]

Such was the intimacy of Beecher and Nettleton at the time that Beecher sent Asahel a copy of his letter to Finney and Beman, along with an accompanying explanation. Nettleton showed it to the moderator of the Presbytery of Troy, who, in turn, lent it to another. In this manner it was made available for general circulation. Later in life Beecher expressed some resentment toward his old colleague in this matter, for he had supposedly written the letter to Finney and Beman in confidence. But at the time he was obviously not trying to conceal his opinions, as is seen by the fact that Beecher authorised the publication of this letter in its entirety, along with Nettleton's letter to Aiken, in the pamphlet on *New Measures*.

Now, for the first time, the proponents of the new revivalism really began to feel the stiff winds of opposition. With not only Nettleton but Beecher, Griffin, and the Andover faculty against them, they could be in serious trouble. Reacting to this pressure, Nathan Beman decided that a face to face conference between the two camps might be useful in ironing out the difficulties. He felt that the Finneyites, of whom he was one, could win over some of the eastern men if they could openly discuss their objections. He went to Boston to discuss the matter with Beecher, who agreed to the plan. Beecher took this overture as an indication that the western men were open to correction. Accordingly, he called together some of his colleagues to meet with the same number of Finney's friends at New Lebanon, New York, where Finney was preaching.

Curiously, the leaders of the two factions did not seem to be excited about the proposal. Finney claimed that he had nothing to do with the arrangements for this meeting, and did not even know who was responsible for it. In his autobiography he also claims that the conference was in no sense a complaint against himself and denies that he was "any more particularly concerned in its results, than any of the members that attended".[48] Candour requires one to agree with George Hugh Birney, however, when he states, with reference to Finney's claim, that this "is hardly justified by the bulk of the evidence".[49]

When Nettleton was first approached he flatly refused to take part in this conference. He gave several reasons for his desire not to become involved in the confrontation: his "feeble health", the feeling that he had already done what he could to deal with the new measures problem, the fact that his actions had been misunderstood and misrepresented, and his ignorance of who had been invited and had accepted the invitation.[50] In the summer of 1827, Nettleton believed that the whole matter should be left to the discretion of "settled pastors", and until they really felt the evils of the new revivalism, nothing could be done. Unquestionably he had his own firm personal opinion of the Finneyites and seemed to be content to let them go their own way.

His friends, and those who sympathised with his own views, eventually persuaded him to attend. They convinced him that "great advantage would undoubtedly be taken of his absence" by the other side.[51]

When the convention met at New Lebanon, on 18th July, Finney and Nettleton were in attendance. The others present were Beecher, Beman, Asahel Norton of Clinton, New York, Moses Gillett of Rome, Dirck Lansing of Auburn, Heman Humphrey, now President of Amherst College, John Frost of Whitesborough, William R. Weeks of Paris, New York, Justin Edwards of Andover, and Henry Smith of Cambden, New York. Four others came who were not originally part of the convention: Caleb Tenney of Wethersfield, Joel Hawes of Hartford, both from New England,

George Gale, Finney's original tutor in the ministry, and Silas Churchill, a resident of New Lebanon. Three others came during the sessions and were voted seats as members of the convention: S. C. Aiken, Henry Weed of Albany, and Abner Benedict. This list shows a number who had been associated with Nettleton in revivals, and of course those who had worked with Finney.

At the first session the convention was organised with Heman Humphrey as moderator and William R. Weeks and Henry Smith as scribes. It was decided first to see where the two parties were in agreement, although the Finneyites wanted to begin by correcting misapprehensions. They were able to approve a joint resolution upholding revivals as an important instrument in the extension and preservation of religion in the land. During the rest of the convention, which lasted till 26th July, there was some free discussion, but their time was mostly spent on consideration of resolutions which focused on the differences between the two groups and which were hotly debated. Such questions, such as the proper place of women in the church, and the propriety of calling persons by name in prayer publicly were brought up. On these matters the New England delegation approved positions favourable to them and the westerners declined to vote.

One morning, Justin Edwards raised the question of whether "measures" should be introduced "to promote or conduct revivals of religion without first having obtained the approbation of said ministers".[52] The Finneyites declared that they had never been guilty of entering a parish of a minister uninvited. Hawes was satisfied that they were innocent on this point, but Beecher interrupted and asserted that while they might not go in uninvited, when people expressed a desire to have them come, they sent the people back "like hounds" to compel the minister to call them.[53] So the sessions went, with charges and countercharges, accusations and denials, discussions and debates, not always without strong feeling.

During all this, Nettleton sat back quietly listening in frustration at the apparent futility of the whole thing. At one of the final sessions he was persuaded by his colleagues to read a statement of his views. After permission was granted, Asahel stood up and read a rather lengthy paper which, in essence, explained that he and the New Englanders in general were not convinced. It was not exactly a moment of triumph for the somewhat weather-beaten warrior. To the opposition he appeared nervous and agitated, and unquestionably the convention had been extremely trying for him. Nettleton's paper marked a somewhat sombre "finis" to the convention from the standpoint of any hopes of an accommodation.

Beecher ended the conference thoroughly on Nettleton's side in his attitude toward the new revivalism. He seemed to be proud of the fact that the New England men had stood firm. "We stood out against them as having been disturbers of the churches," he later wrote.[54] At one point in the convention he got quite exasperated with Finney. He faced him and said, "Finney, I know your plan, and you know I do; you mean to come into Connecticut and carry a streak of fire to Boston. But if you attempt it, as the Lord liveth, I'll meet you at the State line, and call out all the artillery men, and fight every inch of the way to Boston, and then I'll fight you there."[55] This outburst supplies one of the more curious sidelights to this convention.

One decidely unfortunate result of the debate was the use the Unitarians made of it. *The Christian Examiner* seized on the story of the conference, the details of which had been made public by *The New York Observer*, and declared it to be evidence of "the disgraceful conduct of evangelical Trinitarians".[56] They declared that this discord in the ranks of the orthodox marked the end of revival enthusiasm.

In fact Finney came away from this conference the victor, for up to this point no one had challenged his theology; his antagonists had merely taken pot-shots at the methods he employed. It is not entirely clear why Finney's Pelagian tendencies had not come under scrutiny. Perhaps one reason is that New England theology itself was in a transition period. Modifications of the old orthodoxy were already well under way at Yale, and beneath the surface there were differences between the men who stood united at New Lebanon. In fact, the two leaders of the easterners, Beecher and Nettleton, who were old friends, were themselves gravitating to different centres theologically and were destined eventually to part company. Indeed, they stood together for the last time at New Lebanon.

Having more or less triumphed over his opponents at New Lebanon, or at least forestalled any serious movement against him, Finney gained a new notoriety and larger fields of operation opened to him. He was soon invited into the large eastern centres such as Wilmington, Delaware, and Philadelphia, which was one of the strongholds of Calvinist orthodoxy. This gave him an opportunity to carry out one of his long cherished intentions, which was to "reform the Presbyterian Church" by cutting the ground from under the feet of those who expounded the Westminster Confession of Faith.[57] But this also brought his real theological sentiments directly into the light and pitched the battle on the real ground which was at stake: orthodox theology. On the new ground and in the new battle soon to develop, Lyman Beecher sided with Finney, and Nettleton joined with the vanguard of old line Calvinists, who were now marshalling their forces for the defence.

CHAPTER 30

A VISIT TO THE SOUTHLAND

Nettleton's time and energy was by no means totally devoted to the new measures problem in 1827. In the spring he was in Durham, New York, where he continued to preach, though slowed down by great "bodily weakness". As a matter of fact, he gave a good deal of thought during this period to what seemed to be his approaching death. Bennet Tyler discovered among his private papers a letter, dated 21st April, which was addressed to the local pastor, Seth Williston. It reveals his frame of mind at the prospect of death, and was, ironically, written on his birthday. In it he said, "This day I am forty-four years old. I feel thankful that a kind providence has led me to this place, and that I have had the satisfaction of a short acquaintance with you. I cannot express my feelings now. But in view of the uncertainty of life, I would say, that I am happy in the thought of laying my bones in your burying ground. I cannot tell how it may be in the solemn hour of death – and a willingness to die, I do not think, is, in itself, any evidence of grace. But the thought of leaving the world appears rather pleasant – and above all, the thought of never sinning. I feel it to be a *great thing* to be a Christian. Such words as these appear sweet,

> O glorious hour! O blest abode!
> I shall be near and like my God;
> And flesh and sin no more control,
> The sacred pleasures of the soul!"[58]

From the standpoint of his earthly ambitions, this seems to have been a low point for Asahel. Although he felt "peculiar delight" as his mind "ranged over all the towns

and places where I have laboured in seasons of revival", he
expected soon to depart this life. His note to Williston was a
sort of "good-bye" letter. He writes of his "inexpressible
tenderness and compassion for all the young converts". He
gives his "affectionate regards" to all his relatives at Killingworth, whom he urges to "prepare to follow" him. He
admonishes the local congregation, especially the young
people, to "seek an interest in Christ without delay". Then,
thinking about a nearby burial plot, which he had no doubt
passed, he winds up his message in a touching valedictory
spirit. "When I am buried on yonder hill, tell them to
remember the evening when I preached to them from these
words, 'Seek first the kingdom of God'. Whenever they pass
my grave, tell them, they will each one remember, 'There
lies the man who talked to me about my soul'." This moving
epistle ends with the words, "I die in peace with all mankind".[59]

Asahel's "peace" was rudely disturbed while he was at
Durham by a young Finney convert who came to town and
boldly announced that there would be a revival. This young
man, a native of Oneida County, announced that "he knew
all about how to conduct a revival".[60] He began his revival
campaign with a blistering attack upon the local minister
and church. He inveighed against the "abominations which
were portrayed on the walls" of the Presbyterian meeting
house. He encouraged the people to defy the pastor, and
went about asking, "Are you afraid of him?"[61] He held
meetings at which he referred to Williston as "a liar" and
said that he "was the head Achan in the camp and that his
character was as *black as hell*".[62]

The revivalism of the intruder caused quite a stir in the
little village. Williston believed that the young man was
demented, as did evidently a majority of his church members. Nettleton was greatly disturbed and wondered whether
some of his spirit had been caught from his master, Finney.
At any rate, he used this as an illustration of the irresponsible
attitude of some of the new revivalists, and related the
details of the matter in a letter to John Frost. Such cases
hardly caused Asahel to change his mind about the new
measures movement.

He survived the weak spell at Durham, and early in the
summer went into the high elevations of the Catskill mountains, to Lexington Heights, near Tower Mountain. The

solitude and quiet of this remote wilderness area afforded much needed refreshment both for his mind and body. The small village was surrounded by forests in which "the bear and the panther, the wolf and the wild-cat", were occasionally seen and heard. Once he saw a deer leaping a fence and mound, "with a hound close to his heels".[63] This made him think of the Scripture, "And he was with the wild beasts; and the angels ministered unto him".

Nettleton stayed in a "mansion" in Lexington Heights and preached to a small church, in which there were between thirty and forty conversions. He also engaged in correspondence. He wrote to Charles E. Furman at the Auburn Theological Seminary, Auburn, New York, stating his belief that revival preachers need to have occasional periods of solitude, in which they can "review the past" and "attend" to their own hearts. Undoubtedly he had much to think about during these weeks of temporary asylum from revival activity. It was while he was in the Catskills that his brethren summoned him for the convention at New Lebanon.

Throughout 1827 Asahel was subject to spells of faintness, which seemed to be getting worse. His doctors advised him to try a southern climate, so in the autumn he decided to go to Virginia for the winter. He chose to go to Hampden-Sidney, where there is a college of that name and also Union Seminary, a Presbyterian institution.

Located in the rolling hill country of central Virginia, Hampden-Sidney College could look back to a noble past. It was founded in 1776 and named for two English patriots: John Hampden and Alcernon Sydney. Two Presidents of the United States were connected with its early history. James Madison, the fourth, along with Patrick Henry, were on the original board of trustees, and William Henry Harrison, the ninth, was a member of the class of 1791. Next to William and Mary the school was the oldest in Virginia, and was the last college to be established under the British crown. In the eighteen hundreds Hampden-Sidney was "the chief educational centre in Virginia and indeed in the south".[64]

Its spiritual heritage was no less noteworthy than its academic history. It was here, in the year 1787, when the Federal Convention drafted the Constitution in Philadelphia, that the southern phase of the second great awakening began. Archibald Alexander, one of the organisers of Princeton Seminary, was a resident of this area and was converted as a direct result of the revival. The famous evangelist, James McGready, stopped here in 1788 while travelling from Pennsylvania to North Carolina, and first caught the revival flame which he later carried into the settlements of Kentucky.[65]

Union seminary at Hampden-Sidney was under the direction of John Holt Rice, in 1828, and through his initiative it was experiencing vigorous growth and development. Born in New London, Bedford County in 1777, Rice, early in life, met Patrick Henry, who said something to him which permanently affected his life. "Be sure, my son," said the great patriot, "and remember that the best men always make themselves."[66] Rice's outlook on what preachers should be can be deduced from a letter he once wrote to a "Mr Peters" stating, "We want plain Bible preachers – men, who instead of thinking that they have wonderful discoveries which will cause the people to admire their ingenuity, will be self-denying enough to tell them just what is in the Bible, and no more, nor no less".[67]

After Asahel Nettleton arrived in Virginia, he and Rice struck up a warm friendship and became collaborators in revivals. Following a brief period of rest, Nettleton began to preach in the Hampden-Sidney area and a revival began which created a sensation throughout the whole vicinity. The first inquiry meeting was at the home of Rice, "the very mansion containing the theological students", and more than a hundred were present. The most unusual thing about this revival was that five prominent lawyers from "several adjoining counties" were converted, a "circumstance" which "attracted no little attention".[68] According to a young minister who lived nearby, "Not many gentlemen of this profession had, up to this time, been members of any church in this section of country".[69]

Nettleton preached throughout Prince Edward and nearby counties, such as Cumberland and Buckingham, with great success. Shortly after the revival began he went to Buckingham Court House where he preached at a small new Presbyterian Church, and at the County Court House. The pastor of the church when Nettleton visited the area was Jesse S. Armistead, who had just recently been inducted as pastor. His comment on Nettleton's preaching was that it "excited great attention, and was accompanied with the special blessing of heaven".[70]

The church of which Armistead was pastor is still in existence and is known now as Maysville Presbyterian Church. Although the records of the church are somewhat cloudy on the matter, it is generally believed that the present building was erected in 1828, the year Nettleton visited Buckingham Court House. If so, he preached in the same building that is currently in use. The court house is still standing, though its interior was gutted by fire in 1869 and it has often been remodelled. The architect for this building, in which Asahel preached, was the third president of the United States, Thomas Jefferson. One of the lawyer converts in the revival under Nettleton lived at Buckingham Court House, and traditions about his experience and the revival generally are still talked about among the old timers in this little town.

Rice was delighted at the great revival which had come to his region, and was impressed with Nettleton as a man and a preacher. In a letter to Archibald Alexander he said, "Mr Nettleton is a remarkable man, and chiefly, I think, remarkable for his power of producing a great excitement, without much *appearance* of feeling. The people do not either weep, or talk away their impressions. The preacher chiefly addresses *Bible truth* to their *consciences*. I have not heard him utter, as yet, a single sentiment opposed to what you and I call orthodoxy. He preaches the Bible. He derives his illustrations from the Bible."[71] He told Nettleton personally that he had reached a class of people who had never before been influenced by vital religion. "You never had such hold on any population in your life as you now have on that class in Virginia."[72] People came from as far as forty miles away in "covered carriages" to attend the revival meetings.

It had been Nettleton's intention to return north to avoid the excessive southern summer heat, but Rice prevailed upon him to take a trip into the western mountain regions of Virginia instead. Accordingly, he crossed the Blue Ridge Mountains and the Shenandoah valley to the high elevations of what is now West Virginia, stopping en route at Staunton, Virginia, where he ministered briefly. He went as far west as Lewisburg, and almost certainly stopped at White Sulphur Springs, the famous resort area.

Asahel remained in the mountain region, where he had a number of interesting meetings, till early in 1829. His generally pleasant and profitable visit to Virginia was unfortunately marred by one circumstance. A man in Carterville, Virginia, who had opposed the revival, was in correspondence with a man in South Britain, Connecticut, who revived the stories about him which had originated in 1818. While the ministers in Virginia did not believe the rumours, they sought to trace down their source and discover the truth. They sent a delegation to see the accuser, Oliver G. Wheeler, to demand proof of his claim. He produced a copy of the letter to the youth in the ball room and told them he had heard other things about Nettleton.

Rice wrote to a number of New England ministers to ask for their opinion on the rumours and on Nettleton's character. In a short time he received an avalanche of letters which left absolutely no doubt concerning Asahel's reputation in New England. Jeremiah Day, president of Yale, Lyman Beecher, Leonard Bacon, Gardiner Spring, Thomas McAuley and laymen such as the Honourable John C. Smith of Connecticut and the Honourable Jonas Platt of New York wrote vindicating him. One letter certifying Asahel's "unblemished purity of life" which was "universally" known throughout "this State" (Connecticut) was signed by six distinguished gentlemen, including Noah Webster, the famous lexicographer. Tyler wrote to explain the background of the "Jesus Christ letter".

Some of the New Englanders were not a little irritated by this investigation about one of their most famous native sons. N. W. Taylor, with whom Nettleton was soon to be in debate, wrote to Rice, not only to defend Nettleton's character, but protesting against any further discussion of the matter. At the end of a letter from Beecher he said curtly, "If such testimonials as this of Dr Beecher and others are not sufficient to give brother N. a character in Virginia, in defiance of the obloquy of his enemies and his Master's, he had better come back to Connecticut".[73]

Thus were revived the old calumnies against Nettleton, and thus they were quenched. He was wholeheartedly welcomed again by Rice and the men of Virginia and continued to be used greatly. In fact the flurry of correspondence about his character was carried on while he was in the mountains, and he knew nothing about it.

[1] See *The Growing Years*, by Margaret L. Coit and the Editors of Life, Vol. 3, of *The Life History of the United States* (New York, 1963), p. 155.

[2] *Ibid.*, p. 147.

[3] *The Sweep Westward*, Vol. 4 of above series, p. 10.

[4] This was originally reported in the *New York Observer*, included in later editions of Tyler's *Memoirs*, and also in the English edition, *Nettleton and His Labours*, by Rev. Andrew A. Bonar (Edinburgh, 1854), p. 252.

[5] *Ibid.*, p. 255.

[6] *Memoirs*, by Tyler, p. 247.

[7] *Memoirs of Rev. Charles G. Finney* (New York, 1876), p. 7.

[8] *Ibid.*, p. 13.

[9] *Ibid.*, pp. 19, 20.

[10] *Ibid.*, p. 25.

[11] *Ibid.*, p. 24.

[12] *Modern Revivalism, Charles Grandison Finney to Billy Graham*, by William G. McLoughlin, Jr (New York, 1959), p. 17.

[13] E. H. Gillet's *History of the Presbyterian Church*, cited by McLoughlin, p. 23.

[14] *Memoirs*, p. 59.

[15] *Ibid.*, p. 59.

[16] From a letter to John Frost, cited by Birney, p. 125.

[17] *Memoirs*, p. 203.

[18] *Letters of the Rev. Dr Beecher and Rev. Mr Nettleton, on The New Measures in Conducting Revivals of Religion* (New York, 1828), p. 19.

[19] Birney, p. 125.

[20] *Memoirs*, p. 202.

[21] *Ibid.*, p. 202.

[22] *Letters on the New Measures*, p. 10.

[23] *Ibid.*, p. 19.

[24] *Ibid.*, p. 9.

[25] *Ibid.*, p. 17.

[26] *Ibid.*, p. 17.

[27] Cited by Birney, p. 123.

[28] *Letters on New Measures*, p. 13.

[29] *Ibid.*, p. 9.

[30] *Ibid.*, p. 13.

[31] *Ibid.*, p. 11.

[32] *Ibid.*, p. 12.

[33] *Ibid.*, p. 11.

[34] *Ibid.*, p. 14.

[35] *Ibid.*, p. 12.

[36] *Ibid.*, p. 12.

[37] *Ibid.*, p. 19.

[38] *Ibid.*, p. 9.

[39] *Ibid.*, p. 20.

[40] *Sermons on Important Subjects*, by Rev. C. G. Finney (New York, 1836), p. 190.

[41] *Ibid.*, p. 191.

[42] *Letters on the New Measures*, p. 31.

[43] *Ibid.*, p. 38.

[44] *Ibid.*, p. 11.

[45] *Op. cit.*, Vol. II, p. 96.

[46] *Ibid.*, p. 96.

[47] *Ibid.*, p. 97.

[48] Finney, *Memoirs*, p. 210.

[49] Birney, p. 137.

[50] *Letters on the New Measures*, p. 102.

[51] *Ibid.*, p. 102.

[52] From the *Christian Examiner*, Vol. IV, p. 361, cited by Birney, p. 142.

[53] *Ibid.*, p. 142.

[54] *Autobiography*, Vol. II, p. 101.

[55] *Ibid.*, p. 101.

[56] Cited by Birney, p. 149.

[57] *Modern Revivalism*, p. 41.

[58] Tyler, *Memoir*, pp. 182, 183.

[59] *Ibid.*, pp. 183, 184.

[60] From Ms. letter to John Frost, cited by Birney, p. 133.

[61] *Ibid.*, p. 134.

[62] *Ibid.*, p. 134.

[63] Tyler, *Memoir*, p. 184.

[64] *A Miscellaneous Collection of Letters, Sketches, Articles, etc., Concerning the History of Hampden-Sidney College*, by Dr J. D. Eggleston, p. 9.

[65] See *The Great Revival*, 1787-1805, by John B. Boles (Lexington, Kentucky, 1972), p. 38.

[66] *Memoir of the Rev. John H. Rice, D.D.*, by William Maxwell (Philadelphia, 1835), p. 9.

[67] *Ibid.*, p. 349.

[68] Bonar, p. 275.

[69] *Ibid.*, p. 275.

[70] *Ibid.*, pp. 275, 276.

[71] Tyler, *Memoir*, p. 186.

[72] From Ms. Letter to Bennet Tyler, cited by Birney, p. 198.

[73] Tyler, *Memoir*, p. 355.

PART V

A SCHOOL
FOR THE PROPHETS

(1829-1844)

Nettleton believed in the old doctrines, not only
on the basis of his prejudice, but because they had
been tested by his experience. In his revival preaching he had used them without reservation and he
knew that they were "the wisdom of God, and the
power of salvation to many". He did not see any
reason why he should exchange "the weapons thus
tried for the new forgings of New Haven".

George Hugh Birney.

CHAPTER 31

NEW HAVEN THEOLOGY

While Nettleton was preaching in the mountains of western Virginia, Hampden-Sidney College was visited by a number of young students from Yale. They were disciples of one of Asahel's old friends, N. W. Taylor, who for many years had been pastor of the First Congregational Church in New Haven and was now professor of Didactic Theology in the theological department at Yale. These brash young men announced that their teacher had made a dramatic new discovery which would "make as great a revolution in the systems of theology, as was made in the science of chemistry on the discovery of the *basis of potash* by Sir Humphrey Davy". N. W. Taylor, had, so they said, discovered "the essence of sin".[1] They were referring to Taylor's theories on human depravity, which he had been developing for some time and had recently made public.

Nettleton was aware that Taylor had been indulging in speculations which were contrary to New England orthodoxy. In 1808 and 1809 when Nettleton first went to Yale, Taylor was a graduate student and a secretary to Dwight. At that time the two men became acquainted and Taylor read to Nettleton "a dissertation on the doctrine of the divine decrees, and the free agency of man". Nettleton was far from pleased with the dissertation, claiming that it represented "a virtual denial of the former and an avowal of the self-determining power of the will".[2]

N. W. Taylor was born in 1786, which made him three years Nettleton's junior. Such was his charm and intellectual acumen, that he was once known as "the pride of all Yale college".[3] In a rise to fame that, chronologically, paralleled that of Nettleton, Taylor soon captivated the elite circles of New Haven. After attaining considerable notoriety as a preacher in the town's most influential pulpit, he was offered the chair of theology in the newly enlarged theological department at Yale.

Taylor carried to a climax certain refinements in the theology of Jonathan Edwards, which had been going on at New Haven and throughout New England for many years. These changes were in areas pertaining to human depravity and moral agency. Edwards, though making a distinction between physical and moral inability, adhered to the traditional Calvinistic concept of original sin. He believed fully in infant depravity and regarded sin as both a rational act and an inherent quality in the soul. He rejected the Arminian notion that the will has a self-determining power, or in other words, that man's powers of choice are above the influence of motives. According to Edwardian orthodoxy, man's choice is determined by the ruling preferences or dispositions of the soul. Joseph Bellamy, Bennet Tyler, Asahel Nettleton, and Leonard Woods were among those who followed him in these views.

It should be noted that Samuel Hopkins, the Rhode Island pastor, prepared the way for the new views which were brought to fruition by Taylor. Although in many respects strongly Calvinistic, Hopkins propounded the theory that there is no sin but actual or overt transgressions. He denied the imputation of Adam's sin to his posterity and also rejected the idea that a corrupt nature has been passed down from the first man. Because of his strong views on God's decrees, he held that sin was a part of God's plan, being the necessary means for the greatest good of the universe as a whole. The condemnation of some men makes the salvation of the rest more precious.

Taylor took up Hopkin's denial of innate depravity, but went a step further. He not only rejected inherited and imputed sin, but attributed to man's will a total sovereignty. He taught that the freedom of the will is absolute and cannot be influenced by any external power. His view even placed man beyond the power of God to influence him, and argued that if anything could constrain the will in any given direction it would not be truly free. In *A Genetic History of New England Theology*, Frank Hugh Foster, one of the most acute students of this movement of the last century, explains Taylor's position thus: "God has given man the power of acting as a true first cause, and has thus placed him beyond the reach of true power, even the divine power, as a determining cause of his volitions."[4]

One can easily see that the principles upon which Taylor was building his theological system were fundamentally the same as those guiding the revivalist C. G. Finney. Although there were no links between the two men, the free-wheeling evangelist and the urbane scholar were both subjecting traditional views on depravity and grace to the bar of human rationalism, and in that court they could not survive. The logical connection between the two movements eventually became apparent. Within five years after the New Lebanon conference, the deeper implications of the new measures controversy were surfacing, and the developing schism was seen to be no longer geographical. The orthodox Calvinists, on the one hand, were lined up against the, more or less, Arminian position, whether found in the East or West. The "New Haven Theology" was only the New England manifestation of a much larger revolt against orthodoxy.

Asahel Nettleton was totally in disagreement with Taylor's views, and, although they had been friends, he took issue with him as soon as his theories began to spread among the Yale fraternity. While he was labouring with Beecher in a revival at Litchfield, he heard that the whole Yale faculty seemed to be denying that infants were sinners. He was so concerned that he wrote a letter to Taylor on the subject, warning him that he was planting a time-bomb by promoting such views. "You may speculate better than I can," he said, "but I know one thing better than you do. I know better what Christians will, and will not, receive; and I forewarn you, that, whenever you come out, our best Christians will revolt."[5] When Nettleton received no satisfaction from Taylor, he concluded that the whole matter was a "trick of the adversary to send Br T. on a wild goose chase after what he will never find, and, if found, would not be worth one straw".[6]

In the summer of 1828, Taylor decided to make a formal defence of his view and thus throw down the gauntlet to his brethren who disagreed with him. At the commencement of the Yale academic year in September, he preached the annual *Concio ad Clerum* in which he stated his position. He quoted Calvin, Bellamy, Edwards and "the Westminster divines", but he failed to convince his opponents that he really stood in this tradition. When his views became widely circulated, they were embraced with open arms by the Methodists. Wilbur Fisk, president of Wesleyan University, said to Eleazer Fitch, one of the New Haven men, "Your Calvinism is my Arminianism", a statement that embarrassed Fitch and Taylor not a little.[7]

Following Taylor's sermon, the opposing camp was in a state of agitation, fearing that his influence would carry New England as a whole to his position. But they were also confused as to what step to take next, now that the discussion was public. Where would the orthodox take their stand and who would lead the way? Some suggested Nettleton, but he felt frankly unequal to the task. He felt that the writing and answering of lengthy pamphlets was too arduous an undertaking for him now.

Nevertheless, he did not ignore Taylor's position or do nothing to oppose it. When Rice and the men in Virginia heard from the Yale students, they were shocked and Nettleton was embarrassed. He not only sought to refute Taylor's notions, but also assured Rice that Taylorism was not the prevalent view in New England. He came back to New England in the spring of 1829 and immediately went to New Haven to try to convince the men there of their errors. He also counselled with those of his own view, such as Caleb Tenny and Leonard Woods of Andover. Still he felt that someone else should head the anti-Taylor movement.

The first to attempt an answer to Taylor was a minister at Westchester, Connecticut named Joseph Harvey, who wrote a review of Taylor's sermon in the form of a pamphlet. Nettleton and Tenny had advised Harvey not to take on Taylor, and his effort did in fact prove him to be inadequate for the job. But at least it served to trigger open discussion on the issues in the *Christian Spectator*, a magazine which was owned by the Yale men, and the *Spirit of the Pilgrims*, which voiced the views of the older orthodoxy.

One who had been reading Taylor's views in the *Christian Spectator*, and thoroughly disapproved, was Bennet Tyler, who had succeeded Edward Payson as pastor of the Second Congregational Church of Portland, Maine. On 18th September, 1829, he wrote to Asahel saying, "Since I saw you, I have thought much of the New Haven divinity. I

The Congregational Church of Farmington, Connecticut.
Asahel Nettleton preached here in 1821 and a great revival occurred.

Bennet Tyler
Nettleton's close friend and biographer.   He was the first president of The
Theological Institute of Connecticut, and a defender of orthodox Calvinism
against the New Haven theology.

wish to see you in relation to that subject very much. . . . There is much in that with which I cannot agree. But I cannot go into particulars now. I hope I shall see you before long." Tyler soon sought to disprove Taylor's views in a pamphlet in which he states a belief that Taylor had "swerved from the faith of the pilgrim fathers".[8] Tyler's *Strictures* were reviewed in the *Christian Spectator*, and so the debate was under way.

The man most qualified to handle the New Haven theology controversy was the professor of theology at Andover Seminary, Leonard Woods. Intellectually he was on a par with Taylor, theologically he was solidly in the opposite camp, and he enjoyed great popularity throughout the East. After his attention was drawn to the New Haven problem, he set about to examine Taylor's position in the form of a series of eight letters to him, published at Andover in 1830. He accuses Taylor of teaching, by his views on sin and ability, that sinners are not "dependent on God" for their salvation.[9] According to the New Haven School, it is "impossible" for God to preserve men from sin, for this would destroy their moral freedom.[10] "And to speak of God's actually converting *any*, would be to speak of that which, in the nature of things, is impossible."[11]

Taylor's theory logically led to the deduction that regeneration is by moral suasion, a view which Finney held, rather than an inward renovation of man's nature by the Holy Spirit. Nettleton refuted the Taylor-Finney concept by using much the same line of argument as Woods. In a sermon on John 1 : 12, 13, he said, "*Persuasion* is not sufficient to make men new creatures. If the Holy Spirit operates on the minds of men, only by setting motives before them, be the kinds ever so diverse, or well adapted to this purpose, yet after all, it depends on the will of man, whether he shall be regenerated or not. On this scheme the glory of regeneration belongs to ourselves. No new taste, no new spiritual discernment, springs from persuasion. If regeneration comes thus, then a man begets himself – he is born of himself – he makes himself to differ from others."[12]

The discussion on grace, sin, and free will continued in various Christian periodicals for several years, but it ended in an impasse, for neither side was convinced that it was wrong. It eventually led to an open rift in New England, though many of the antagonists remained good personal friends. Through the New Haven defection, Nettleton's personal ties with Tyler and other pastors of like sentiment were strengthened, and he also formed close new alliances with men such as Leonard Woods, who had emerged as the chief theologian of the Edwardian school.

CHAPTER 32

BEECHER'S DEFECTION

In May of 1828 the Presbyterian General Assembly met in Philadelphia. It provided an occasion for some behind-the-scenes skirmishing between the new measures group and their opponents. Lyman Beecher found out that some of "Finney's friends were laying their plans to make an impression on the General Assembly".[13] Also, they were hoping to take advantage of a vacancy in the pulpit at the Second Church of Philadelphia, by getting one of their men to preach there. Beecher had been asked to supply that pulpit, so when he heard about the plan of the Finneyites, he offered to preach there during the General Assembly. His suggestion was taken, and, as a result, the plot failed and, as Beecher said, "That blocked somebody's wheels; it blocked a good many wheels".[14]

While the convention was going on, however, Beecher decided to make a move toward conciliation. He consulted a number of men who had been involved in the controversy and decided that the debate should be suspended. He believed "that if the war could only stop, they would grow cool".[15] A proposal was drafted which said, "The subscribers, having had opportunity for free conversation on certain subjects pertaining to revivals of religion, concerning which we have differed, are of the opinion that the general interests of religion would not be promoted by any further publications on those subjects, or personal discussions, and we do hereby engage to cease from all publications, correspondences, conversations, and conduct designed or calculated to keep those subjects before the public mind, and that, so far as our influence may avail, we will exert it to induce our friends on either side to do the same".[16] The statement was

signed by Lyman Beecher at the head of the list, followed by
Dirck Lansing, S. C. Aiken, A. D. Eddy, C. G. Finney,
Sylvester Holmes, Ebenezer Cheever, John Frost, Nathan
S. S. Beman, Noah Coe, E. W. Gilbert and Joel Parker.

This list reveals that of the nineteen members of the
New Lebanon convention, only six were involved in the
truce statement. And of these six, only Beecher, who initiated
the peace move, had been on the side of the Nettleton
position. This means, in short, that the Philadelphia conciliation was not a broad based settlement but a capitulation
by Beecher alone. With regard to the controversy itself, the
situation remained unchanged, because the bulk of the
anti-new measures group had not altered their opinions.

Beecher was, of course, sensitive to what Nettleton's
reaction would be, and he wrote him a long letter explaining
the statement and giving his reasons for issuing it. But
Asahel was not satisfied with the letter, and was not persuaded to cease in his opposition to the western revivals.
The problems in New York were as great as ever. Churches
were still being split over the new measures, and opposition
continued to mount wherever they were introduced.
Nettleton now became the undisputed leader of the older
revivalism and his relationship with Beecher began to cool.

But Beecher's defection did give a great boost to Finney
and his methods of revivalism. The whole implication of
Beecher's action was that there was nothing seriously wrong
about the new measures movement. Beecher did not justify
it, but neither would he now condemn it. This was all that
Finney and his friends were looking for. The gate to New
England was now wide open to him.

Having disengaged himself from the cause of Nettleton,
the most stalwart of the New England orthodox, Beecher,
was now ready, strategically, for the developments at New
Haven. Only four months after the Beecher's truce, Taylor
delivered the *Concio ad Clerum*, in which the New Haven
theology was affirmed and defended. On this issue Beecher
had no equivocality or ambivalence. He stood squarely with
Taylor, and had done so for many years.

Lyman Beecher's attachment to N. W. Taylor was both
personal and theological. Harriet Beecher Stowe said that
her father had "an unbounded and romantic attachment"
to Taylor, and Stuart C. Henry, a Beecher biographer, says
that Taylor was his "first friend and dearest idol".[17] They

had first met in Timothy Dwight's study, when Taylor was amanuensis to him and Beecher was pastor at East Hampton, Long Island, a post he held before coming to Litchfield. Together they spent many hours discussing the theology of Jonathan Edwards and the emerging theories of free will and depravity. They came out more or less together, denying the sinfulness of infants and teaching that "God governs mind by motive and not by force".[18] Force to them meant an inward influence of the Holy Spirit on the soul.

Beecher had not tried to conceal his belief that man had not inherited a corrupt nature. In January of 1822 he had written to Nettleton, who was at the time involved in a revival, that he was having trouble with infant depravity. "For some time past," he concedes, "I have noticed a leaning of my mind to *heresy* on this long-disputed and very difficult topic."[19] "I must confess I cannot accede to the common views of the doctrine of original sin. Voluntary agency seems to me indispensable to accountability. Without voluntary exercises or affection, there can be neither holiness nor sin."[20] In the same letter he revealed his peculiar relationship to Taylor. He seemed fearful that he would pronounce these views in such a definite and public way as to be drawn into open debate. "Brother Taylor," he said, "must be guarded."[21]

Beecher was a shrewd student of the theological and ecclesiastical problems of New England, and he foresaw the coming conflict over New Haven theology. It was a conflict he dreaded. In December of 1821, nearly seven years before Taylor's famous commencement speech, Chauncey A. Goodrich, one of the professors of Divinity at Yale, delivered a speech to a class of students, in which he propounded the new theology. News about this flew all over New England, and it was this which upset Nettleton when he was with Beecher in the revival at Litchfield. When Beecher saw Nettleton's concern, he knew that this was only the beginning. After Goodrich denied original sin and infant depravity, he "saw the end", and when he contemplated it, he "never felt so bad".[22] He feared that the Presbygational churches would be upset, the revival spirit dampened, and the Unitarians given grounds to rejoice. The debate came as he anticipated, and all these results followed.

In the eighteen-thirties, Beecher became a pronounced advocate of the Finney-Taylor theology, and his influence in that direction was great. Single-handedly he opened many of the pulpits of New England to Finney and helped push him to acceptance and fame. His old threat to meet him at the Massachusetts state line and fight him every inch of the way to Boston was forgotten; in fact he even helped Finney carry his "streak of fire" in 1831. Some of Beecher's deacons in the Hanover church in Boston wanted to hear Finney, and put pressure on him to invite the evangelist. About the same time Beecher's daughter, Catherine, saw Finney, who said to her, "Your father vowed solemnly at the New Lebanon Convention he would fight me if I came to Boston, and I shall never go there till he asks me".[23] Now the stage was set for Beecher to retract his vow. This he did when he invited Finney to preach for him in August of 1831.

From this point on, the paths of Beecher and Nettleton parted and each went his own way. A new alignment was shaping up, which had nothing to do with New England as opposed to other parts of the country. Those who were legitimate followers of Edwards joined with the Old School Calvinism at Princeton in an alliance which sought to perpetuate the basic truths of Reformed theology. Yale became the centre of gravity for the whole liberal movement, which was rooted fundamentally in a rationalistic approach to Scripture and theology.

Both Beecher and Finney left the East and became heads of schools. Beecher became president of Lane Seminary of Cincinnati in 1832, where he attempted to establish a citadel for the new school views in the West. Finney, after experience both as an evangelist and a pastor, became president of Oberlin College, Ohio, where he developed his famous Oberlin Theology based on the concept of sinless perfection. The views of Taylor and Finney on depravity produce a doctrine of Christian perfectionism when they are applied to the experience of believers. By the time Finney had become president of Oberlin College, he had long since recognised that the Presbyterian Church was no place for him, and he had left its ranks. It is certainly one of the ironies of history that he claimed for so long to be a member of a church whose doctrinal standards he had denounced so vehemently all the while.

CHAPTER 33

THE ANXIOUS SEAT

In 1831, Charles G. Finney was preaching in Rochester, New York, in what was his most successful revival campaign up until this time. But, in spite of the large numbers of people who were professing faith in Christ, he felt that something was lacking in his evangelistic techniques. For some time he had pondered about the need of sinners to make an open decision about their relationship to God. He was coming to the conclusion that something new and different was needed to "bring sinners to a stand", or in other words, to focus in their minds, in a bold and decisive way, the issues between them and God.[24] He felt that this should be public and physical, so that no one, especially the sinner, could doubt where he stood as far as salvation was concerned.

Then, suddenly, he had a sort of brainstorm. It occurred to him that a method, which was already widely in use, would be more than adequate. The *anxious seat*, which had long been popular in the South, would be a natural and convenient tool to crystallise his evangelistic strategy. Shortly thereafter, he began to call upon convicted sinners to come forward to certain prearranged seats as a sign that they had given themselves up to God, and were saved.[25] He found this technique quite successful, and many responded when he issued this invitation after preaching.

The history of the emergence of the anxious seat, or public invitation, as a device in American evangelism is an interesting study, and certainly this method has been crucial in the evolution of contemporary evangelistic techniques. It is generally recognised that nothing of this sort was used in the first great awakening of the seventeen-forties. The great

voices that called men to God during this period, such as
Jonathan Edwards, George Whitefield and Gilbert Tennent,
saw thousands converted, but they first made their professions of faith in private, as they counselled with pastors who
discussed with them their experiences. In all local churches,
where the converts made their stand, they did so after prior
interviews with ministers and in accordance with procedures
that were already arranged. By the use of this method,
spontaneous or "spur of the moment" professions were
avoided, for the pastors and evangelists could examine the
candidates and seek to determine which were apparently
genuine.

But among certain groups who were involved in great
spiritual awakenings about the beginning of the nineteenth
century, especially among the Methodists and Baptists of the
South, the practice emerged of asking sinners under conviction to come to the front of the congregation for prayer.
This procedure was used in the very conservative and
Calvinistic Kehukee Baptist Association of North Carolina.
The following reference is found in the history of this Association: "Giving the people an invitation to come up to be
prayed for, was also blessed. . . . The ministers usually, at
the close of preaching, would tell the congregation that if
there were any persons who felt themselves lost and condemned, under the guilt and burden of their sins, that if
they would come near the stage and kneel down, they would
pray for them . . . numbers apparently under strong conviction would come and fall down before the Lord at the
feet of the ministers, and crave an interest in their prayers."[26]

Such altar services were universally used among the
Methodists in their famous camp meetings and were, in fact,
at the very core of their evangelistic appeals. Although not
in use, at first, during the revivals of the North, the "anxious
seats caught on rapidly among the churchfolk of north-
western Pennsylvania and northeastern Ohio in 1831".[27]
This method was also used by some of the evangelists in New
York in what became known to New Englanders as the
"western revivals".

Charles Finney claims that he never used the anxious
seat specifically until 1831, although he had, prior to this,
on occasions, "asked persons in the congregation to stand
up", to indicate a determination to be saved.[28] One can
detect in Finney's reasoning on the utility of the anxious

seat a modification of the older concept. The Methodists and Baptists had, up until this time, only employed it as a way of identifying sinners for prayer. By their coming forth and kneeling at the front, the sympathies of all were drawn out and united prayer for their specific cases could be made to God. But Finney saw in the anxious seat a purpose more fundamental than identifying the lost for prayer. To him it was useful as a *means of grace*, a test of piety.

In Finney's *Lectures on Revivals of Religion*, he explains how he focused the attention of the sinner on the anxious seat. "Preach to him, and at the moment he thinks he is willing to do anything; he thinks he is determined to serve the Lord; but bring him to the test, call on him to do one thing, to take one step that shall identify him with the people of God. . . . If you say to him, 'There is the anxious seat, come out and avow your determination to be on the Lord's side', and if he is not willing to do so small a thing as that, then he is not willing to do *anything*, and there he is, brought out before his own conscience. It uncovers the delusion of the human heart, and prevents a great many spurious conversions, by showing those who otherwise imagine themselves willing to do anything for Christ, that in fact they are willing to do *nothing*."[29] Thus Finney began to make the anxious seat a kind of crux in the dilemma of those who were not converted, a "test" of their sincerity. The physical act of coming to the front of the church was projected as the outward sign of submission to God. To fail to move to the altar or anxious seat was rebellion against God.

The spiritual and theological implications of Finney's new and advanced interpretation of the anxious seat are obvious. This approach to the sinners' problem tended to switch his attention away from a relationship to God and direct it to a spot at the front of the church. "Coming to Christ," which is the condition of salvation, is a spiritual act and it was this which had been the object of traditional evangelistic appeal up to this time. Repentance and faith were regarded as the imperative obligations of unconverted men, and the preachers urged all to comply with these terms of salvation. Finney himself was a strong preacher of repentance and faith as the means of getting right with God. But these are inward exercises and thus lie in the secret and mysterious regions of the soul. To know whether one has truly repented and received Christ or not requires some understanding of the

Bible, acquaintance with one's own heart, and illumination
of the Holy Spirit. But movement to the front of a church is
a simple, physical act, easily perceptible by sensual experience, and one need never wonder whether he has
performed such a bodily function.

Furthermore, the human psyche is such that when outward and visible exercises are made to be tests or signs of
conversion, the distinction between those exercises and the
spiritual qualities they are supposed to symbolise becomes
blurred. If the anxious seat is the test or sign of one's sincerity in wanting to become a Christian, then the ordinary
man might conclude that if he has complied with the test he
is certainly saved. If refusal to come forward is rebellion
against God, then willingness to do so is submission to God.
Thus a conspicuous occasion of delusion is introduced into
evangelism. Finney's anxious seat, which he said took the
place of the ancient practice of baptism,[30] became in the
minds of simple people the way to God.

The orthodox Calvinists were quick to discern the
potential dangers in Finney's attitude toward the anxious
seat and his use of it in evangelism. In 1832 William Sprague,
a graduate of Princeton who pastored the Second Presbyterian Church of Albany, New York, published a book of
Lectures on Revivals. This volume was designed to be a positive
exposition of what genuine revival was, and a check to the
new methods in evangelism which were rapidly gaining in
popularity. A number of prominent educators and ministers
contributed letters for an appendix which was to add
personal experiences in revivals by these men. Among these
were quite a number who had been associated with Nettleton
and who had witnessed at first hand his gifts in evangelism.
The list included Francis Wayland, Alvan Hyde, Noah
Porter, Heman Humphrey, and Edward Griffin. Nettleton's
evangelism is commended several times.

In this volume, Sprague addresses himself to the danger of
confusing the spiritual act of coming to God and a physical
act in a public church service, which was an obvious
reference to the anxious seat problem in the new revivalism.
He said, "There is a danger that the individual will sub-
stitute what is considered an external expression of anxiety
for his soul, for the internal workings of genuine conviction;
or if there be something of true conviction, there is danger
that he will mistake the physical act of taking a particular

place or posture, which is spoken of as peculiarly favourable to conversion, for the spiritual act of yielding up the soul to the Saviour".[31]

Nettleton viewed the anxious seat with suspicion and believed that it tended to produce spurious conversions. In a letter to Samuel Miller of Princeton, he assures him that he never used it "in a single instance".[32] In one of his more pointed comments he says, "And I have no more doubt that the bustle and trepidation attending the call to anxious sinners to come out before a public assembly is calculated to efface conviction of sin and induce false conversions than I have of my own existence".[33]

But Finney recognised the value of his anxious seat method to his own philosophy of evangelism, and such intended checks as were found in Sprague's book did not change him. In fact, his strategy of calling men to a crisis of public decision has been interpreted by many as the crowning touch to his whole theory of salvation. William G. McLoughlin, Jr., in *Modern Revivalism*, says that Finney and his followers "believed it to be the legitimate function of a revivalist to utilise the laws of mind in order to engineer individuals and crowds into making a choice which was ostensibly based upon free will".[34] Considering the fact that the Finney-Taylor theology was posited on the supposition that man can convert himself, the anxious seat was indeed a handy and effective technique. If, as Finney believed, the direct agency of God is not needed in regeneration, then the preacher is compelled to produce quick and easy conversions. The shifting of the body from one place to another is a convenient way of translating man's decision into action.

Many have attributed Finney's views of free will and auto-conversion to the spirit of the age in which he lived. McLoughlin interprets the revivalism which Finney initiated as a kind of religious counterpart of the Jacksonian movement, with its emphasis on the dignity and moral worth of man and democratic principles in politics. "Finney was a child of his age," he says. "The basic philosophical and social principles underlying his thought were essentially the same as those associated with Jacksonian democracy."[35] Finney more or less democratised the kingdom of God, making man sovereign and putting God up for vote. McLoughlin says, "Because in American democracy all the complex problems of freedom and power were reduced to voting for, or against, one of two candidates, Finney applied the political metaphor to religion: 'The world is divided into two great political parties; the difference between them is that one party choose Satan as the god of this world. . . . The other party choose Jehovah for their governor.' Conversion was the decision to vote for Jehovah and to support his administration. . . . In this metaphor, God proposed and man disposed. Instead of his electing men to heaven, they elected him to rule the world."[36]

If Finney can be identified with the philosophy of American democracy, then Asahel Nettleton can be identified as a defender of Biblical theocracy. As an orthodox Edwardian he fully believed in the responsibility and moral agency of man, but he preached that God was sovereign in the universe and he upheld the Calvinistic doctrine of gracious, as opposed to remunerative, election. If C. G. Finney's evangelism rode the waves of confidence in man's abilities, Asahel Nettleton clung tenaciously to the rock of the older view that man is totally corrupt and cannot save himself. The symbol of one type of evangelism is the anxious seat, to which men were publicly pressured to repair. The symbol of the other is an inquiry meeting, where trembling sinners were pointed to Christ and admonished to go home, not "talk by the way", and seek peace directly with God.

CHAPTER 34

A TRIP ACROSS THE ATLANTIC

Following his return from Virginia, Nettleton continued to be involved in evangelistic preaching in various places in New England. His ministry was greatly appreciated at one community, Monson, Massachusetts, where a revival began about the middle of July 1829. The pastor, "Rev. Dr Ely", told Bennet Tyler in 1844 that Nettleton had "been raised up by the great Head of the Church, to accomplish His purposes of mercy in the revival of pure religion, and in the conversion of sinners".[37] He testified that the revival in Monson was "powerful and still, and rapid in its progress". "There was," he said, "less animal excitement – convictions of sin were more thorough, and conversions were more clear and decided, than in some other seasons of revival which we have enjoyed. We had but little to do, but to stand still and see the salvation of God."[38] "He always left behind him," said pastor Ely, "a sweet savour of Christ."[39]

In the autumn of 1829 the evangelist returned to the South for the benefit of his health. He spent time and preached in Charleston, South Carolina, and in the north-central section of North Carolina at Chapel Hill, New Hope, and Hillsborough. So far as the record shows, Charleston was the southernmost point of Nettleton's travels. Concrete information about the results of his preaching during this period is scarce, though Tyler "understood" that "his labours were crowned with success".[40]

In the winter of 1830-1831, he was in the New York City area, preaching for Gardiner Spring, Baxter Dickinson and others whose churches were experiencing revivals. Spring was a Hopkinsian, who agreed with Nettleton's view that the unconverted should not be told to "use the means" but to submit to God. He began his career as a lawyer, but abandoned the legal career and attended Andover Seminary in 1809 and 1810. He was ordained pastor of the Brick Presbyterian Church of New York City, where he remained until his death. He saw many revivals in his church between 1814 and 1834, and was decidedly of the Nettleton cast as far as theology and methods were concerned. He was one of the antagonists of N. W. Taylor.

In the spring of 1831 a number of Asahel's friends, such as Nathaniel Hewit, George A. Calhoun, and J. W. Douglas, began plans to make a trip to England. These men seemed to be interested in preaching there as opportunity afforded. They approached Nettleton about the idea, and after some hesitation he decided to go with them. Not only did the idea of visiting England appeal to him, but he felt that an ocean voyage might be beneficial to him physically and mentally. He made it clear, however, that if he went it was to rest and travel, not preach. He also thought this might be a good opportunity for him to promote *Village Hymns* in England and, with that in mind, he brought along a large shipment of the books. Before his departure he wrote widely to his friends, expressing fond farewells, thinking that perhaps he might not return alive.

On 30th May, 1831, he received a note from G. P. Shipman, stating that a steamboat would be at the foot of India wharf in New York City at six-thirty the next morning, waiting for the passengers, who would be conveyed to the ship *Great Britain*, on which they were scheduled to sail. On 31st May, the ship sailed from New York Harbour for Liverpool, England.

Among the evangelical leaders of England in 1831 were William Jay of Bath and John Angell James, pastor of Carr's Lane Church at Birmingham. Robert Murray McCheyne and Andrew Bonar were divinity students at Edinburgh. The Christians of England and Scotland had, since colonial days, kept in constant touch with the religious picture in the United States, and were well aware of the great revivals which had occurred there. When it was reported that one of America's leading revival preachers was in the United Kingdom, they wanted to meet him and hear him preach.

Nettleton soon discovered that American revivalism had obtained a rather negative image in Britain. Travellers in America had witnessed the camp meeting type of awakenings, and had reported some of the excesses to the British press. One "excellent man", about fifty years of age, who was well known and highly respected, travelled to America and gave a damaging analysis of what he observed in the "protracted meetings". This man, a preacher from Sheffield, wrote back: "Terrific sermons and other means are artfully contrived to stimulate the feelings of ignorant people. In compliance with the call given at the period of the highest excitement, they repair to *the anxious seat* by scores. As their fears are soon aroused, they are generally as soon calmed; and, in a few days, may profess to entertain hope. Many such converts soon lose all appearance of religion; but they become conceited, secure, and gospel proof; so that while living in the open and habitual neglect of their duty, they talk very freely of the time when they experienced religion."[41]

As soon as Asahel established contact with pastors and Christian lay people in the United Kingdom, he was confronted with such reports and put in a position of trying to explain American revivals. It seemed to be the universal impression in Great Britain that "the anxious seat" was the outstanding feature of evangelism in the United States and everyone there approved of it. As a result, most of the sound Christians had no confidence in American revivals.

Thus, Nettleton, who had come to England for rest and diversion, had to deal almost immediately with the vexatious problem of the new measures. In correspondence with the friends back in America, he revealed how troubled he was that 'the imprudence of a few zealous individuals, is doing more mischief to the cause of Christ in this kingdom than all the opposition of open enemies could ever effect".[42] But he did his best to explain the situation and defend American revivals. He assured them that he had never used any of the methods that had been complained of, and those who do "must alone answer for the consequences".[43] He describes himself as "almost exhausted" in his efforts to remove the stigma from American evangelism, a statement that is reminiscent of his efforts in the Albany area in 1827.

At Glasgow he had breakfast with some Christian friends and they discussed the anxious seat and other matters at great length. In England, they assured him, only the Methodists and "Ranters" practiced this method. (The Ranters, as they were disparagingly called, were a fanatical sect during the seventeenth century in England who were antinomian in theology and libertine in morals. They believed that they were incapable of sinning, thought they were in the same state as Adam before the Fall, stripped themselves naked during their public meetings and gave themselves up to violent bodily manifestations.) When Nettleton told them that "the best ministers in New England" did not practice the calling of people to the anxious seat, they seemed surprised and wanted him to hold a meeting to educate the public mind on the question.

Nettleton discovered that the chief source of the information which had been responsible for the attitudes he found in England was the *New York Evangelist*, a magazine which was sympathetic to Finneyism. He wrote to William Sprague explaining the difficult situation in England and placing the blame on this periodical, stating that it had done a great deal "to destroy the confidence of the good people in that kingdom, in the genuineness of the American revivals".[44]

While at Islington, he attended a meeting of more than forty evangelical Anglican clergymen at the house of Rev. Daniel Wilson. He was asked to give an account of the revivals he had experienced, beginning with the 1820 revival at Yale. In the course of his speech he mentioned that he had heard of a young American minister who had come to England for his health but had, so he had heard, died near London. He asked if any knew anything about this young man. Mr Wilson raised his hand and said, "I knew him. I received a note informing me that a young minister from America – a stranger, dangerously sick, desired to see me. I visited him twice, and prayed with him. He died on the third day after I first saw him. I brought his remains and buried them in my church yard."[45] Nettleton then told them that this young man, whose name was Sutherland Douglas, had been one of the converts of the Yale revival. Many of the Anglican ministers were touched, and wept.

During his stay in Great Britain, he not only toured parts of England and Scotland, but Ireland as well. As usual, when he tried to suspend pulpit labour because of his poor health, he found it impossible because of the insistence of others that he preach. Although his preaching was greatly appreciated and there were several cases of conversion, there were no great revivals which commenced through his labours in Great Britain, such as he had seen at home. During the eleven months he ministered here, his preaching was

Nettleton's home
built in 1837-1838 at East Windsor Hill, Connecticut.
The exterior is virtually unchanged.

Bennet Tyler's house
built in 1835, shortly after he became president of the
Theological Institute of Connecticut.

relatively ineffective compared to the results which accompanied his efforts in the United States. How does one account for this disparity?

A. A. Bonar, who produced the English edition of his biography, discusses this question. "His vigour of body was not what it had been," he notes, "nor could his mental energy be equal to what it was in the days of strong health; and this may account, in some measure, for the impression made by his preaching having been far less than was expected."[46] Undoubtedly his physical weakness was a handicap, but he witnessed great revivals in America after his typhus attack, and indeed even after his return to his homeland. Another reason Bonar suggests is as follows: "Besides, he was unable to hold any *series* of meetings, a measure to which he attached much importance."[47] There is an element of truth in this, for Asahel did, as a rule, spend some time in a community in preparing people for revival before it came. But, in fact, he never depended greatly on consecutive services; rather revivals usually broke out in the course of ordinary church meetings.

Was his style unacceptable to the British? There is no evidence that this was the case. The letters he received from those who heard him in England and Scotland indicated that he was greatly appreciated and that he made warm friends there. No available data indicates that his pulpit manner ran against the grain of British believers. Perhaps, in the end, one must leave the matter where Bonar did, after finally looking at it from a purely spiritual standpoint. "At the same time, the Lord may have intended to prevent His people attaching too much importance to any instrument; and to this cause, as much, at least, as to anything in his style not being so suitable to this country as to America, may be ascribed the comparative inefficiency of his preaching."[48] The accolades Asahel received among his own countrymen were more than enough to entitle him to immortality, even without the kind of success he would have desired in England.

Bonar does give one specific instance in which one of his sermons made a powerful impression. It seems that while he was preaching in Edinburgh, a "pious woman" who was sitting in a remote part of the house, became so "affected" that she left her seat, walked up in front of the pulpit and spoke to him. "Dear Sir," she exclaimed, "don't forget that

'God so loved the world that He gave His only begotten Son, that whosoever believeth on Him might not perish, but have everlasting life'."[49] In reply Nettleton repeated the explanation of the awful condition of men outside Christ and concluded, "But, stop! the uplifted arm of vengeance is yet stayed. The collected wrath yet waits a moment. A voice from the mercy-seat – a warning voice is heard. The Saviour calls. Haste, then, O sinner! Haste to Christ, the only refuge from the storm, and covert from the gathering tempest. Then safe from the fear of evil, at a distance, you shall only hear the thunders roll; while pardon, peace, and eternal life are yours."[50]

As effective as Asahel was as a preacher, there was nothing in either his style or content that would guarantee results. The first year of his ministry in eastern Connecticut was not accompanied with great results, and even during the revival period of 1812-1834 his success was unequal. But when a greater Power seized his personality and his preaching he became one of the most outstanding human instruments in the history of revivals.

In addition to his only moderate success in preaching, his hymnbook venture ran into some difficulty in England. Since he was not widely known there, publishers were reluctant to take responsibility for publishing a large number of the books. He did succeed in getting a limited edition of 500 copies printed in London, but the tremendous interest which had been demonstrated in America was not repeated.

Nettleton was the last of the American party to return from England. Hewit left in the autumn of 1831 after hearing that his daughter had died of "inflammation of the brain".[51] Nettleton stayed until August of 1832, when he returned to New York.

CHAPTER 35

THE THEOLOGICAL INSTITUTE OF CONNECTICUT

When Nettleton returned from England, he found that the controversy over Taylorism had come to a head and that an open division between the two camps was taking shape. The orthodox party was convinced that the New Haven theology was heretical, and had conceded that Yale was firmly in its grip. The first move was to establish a magazine which would expound their views. Although *The Spirit of the Pilgrims* had printed articles which espoused the Edwardian position, its primary intention was to combat Unitarianism, and with men like Beecher turning to the Taylor camp, it withdrew from the controversy. This left a vacuum which needed filling.

In 1832 such men as Caleb Tenney, Timothy Gillett, Chester Colton, Joseph Harvey and Isaac Parsons combined to sponsor *The Evangelical Magazine*. Its purpose was to "explain and defend the system of revealed truth commonly denominated Calvinistic".[52] This theology was believed by its sponsors to be "the one which . . . the Bible teaches, the one which is most consistent with the dictates of enlightened reason, and therefore the one which we propose to advocate".[53] They all signed their names to the first preface, in which their loyalty to orthodox theology was declared.

The next procedure was to organise an association of orthodox ministers. A preliminary meeting was held on 9th January, 1833, at which resolutions were passed and articles were drawn up pursuant to their purpose. Agents were appointed to secure the support of ministers throughout the state of Connecticut. A committee was chosen to arrange for a conference of ministers which would meet in September at East Windsor Hill for the purpose of forming a union of orthodox clergymen.

The historic conference took place on 10th September, 1833, at East Windsor, as had been planned. About fifty ministers from throughout the state were present. This group was by no means all of the conservatives in Connecticut, but it did represent the majority of those who had risen up and spoken out against Taylorism. Asahel Nettleton was among these fifty ministers. He had written to Bennet Tyler, who was then at Portland, Maine, inviting him to come, "knowing that he would be interested in the business of the meeting",[54] but the letter did not reach Tyler in time. More were not invited to this initial meeting because East Windsor Hill was a relatively small village and it would have been difficult to provide accommodation for a larger group.

At the first session, a committee of six was appointed to draw up the organisation plans for the Pastoral Union. The committee produced a tentative constitution and Articles of Agreement, which were adopted, and the Union was legally formed for the purpose of promoting "ministerial intercourse, fellowship and pastoral usefulness, the promotion of revivals of religion, the defense of evangelical truth against prevailing error". Most importantly, the Union was established for "the raising up of sound and faithful ministers for the supply of the churches".[55]

The last sentence reflected the seriousness of the situation in New England, as viewed by the participants in this conference. Most of these men were Yale graduates and their ties there were strong and tender. But Yale could no longer be counted on to produce the kind of ministers they believed the churches should have. Clearly, a new institution was needed.

On 11th September, the Pastoral Union met and took up the most important business which lay before it, the matter of the founding of a seminary. The name and purpose of the institution was quickly decided upon. It would be called the Theological Institute of Connecticut, and its purpose would be the training of ministers and "the teaching of sciences preparatory to, or connected with a collegiate course of study".[56] The management of the school was to be in the hands of a board of trustees consisting of twelve ministers and eight laymen. The trustees were to serve for one year, and they were subject to re-election.

Asahel Nettleton was honoured by being the first trustee to be elected.

Following the conference, plans moved quickly for the actual formation of the seminary. Finance was the first and obvious problem. From the outset it was decided that the school would not be heavily endowed, and that it would depend for its support upon contributions from friendly churches. The founders believed that in this way the school and the churches could feel a direct responsibility to each other. It was felt, however, that, in order to begin, it would be necessary to raise some money, and the sum of twenty thousand dollars was decided upon.

The leaders of the movement began immediately to dig into their own pockets. Asahel Nettleton gave an outright donation of five hundred dollars and pledged one hundred annually for the next five years. Two years later he gave five hundred dollars, and in 1839 an additional one thousand dollars. His total contributions of two thousand and five hundred dollars made him the greatest single donor to the seminary fund, with the exception of Erastus Ellsworth, a retired New York business man, who was also a member of the Board of Trustees. The original target of twenty thousand dollars for the school was very soon reached.

Mr Ellsworth, who had settled at East Windsor Hill, had recently purchased a tract of land in the town which was only a short distance from the "corners". The Board of Commissioners of the school, which had been elected to transact any business, decided to purchase this tract of land from Mr Ellsworth as a suitable site for the seminary. They bought it from him at the price of two hundred and fifty dollars. East Windsor Hill was the birthplace of Jonathan Edwards and site of the church of his father, Timothy Edwards. The plot for the future seminary was not far from where the old Edwards parsonage had stood.

Having secured the pledge of sufficient funds for the school and decided on the location for its buildings, the Commissioners began the important task of selecting a head for the seminary. To many of the ministers, Asahel Nettleton seemed a logical choice. However, his health was still poor, and he would not allow his name to be considered for the post. Nathan Perkins of West Hartford was also suggested, but due to his age his name was dropped.

As time went on the thoughts of the Connecticut men

turned more and more toward the Maine pastor, Bennet Tyler. He was himself a native of Connecticut and knew intimately most of those involved in the Pastoral Union. Furthermore, he had had valuable experience in his years as president of Dartmouth College, at Hanover, New Hampshire. He was completely in sympathy with the theological sentiments of the Pastoral Union and had been one of the most outspoken opponents of New Haven theology. Since Tyler's writings had had no small part in the developments in Connecticut, it seemed fitting that he should be offered the position of president of the seminary which was being founded to expound his views.

Tyler was Nettleton's choice; in fact he had never considered anyone else. Since the school house revival of 1812 they had been intimate friends and had stayed in close contact with each other. After the September conference at East Windsor Hill he had written to Tyler and asked him if he would accept the position of president of the seminary should the trustees offer the job to him. Tyler replied that he would have to receive more information about the school. He assured Asahel, however, that if he accepted the post he would want Nettleton to be associated with the school. Meanwhile, Nettleton asked him what provisions he would require for coming, particularly in the way of salary. Tyler replied that a thousand dollars per year, plus house rent and moving expenses, would be adequate.

On 16th October, 1833, at the first regular meeting of the Board of Trustees, Bennet Tyler was elected president of the Theological Institute of Connecticut. Nettleton was appointed to approach him about the matter. Tyler replied that he would like to come to East Windsor Hill to discuss the new school and his relationship to it. The week following his election, he came to Connecticut and acquainted himself with the situation. After talking with Nettleton and the others involved, he accepted the appointment. The Theological Institute of Connecticut had a president.

CHAPTER 36

OCCASIONAL INSTRUCTOR

One of Bennet Tyler's first official acts as president of the
Theological Institute of Connecticut was to suggest to the
trustees that Nettleton be elected to the faculty as the
instructor in Pastoral Duty. In compliance with Tyler's
wishes, the Board extended this invitation to him by a
unanimous vote in January of 1834. Nettleton was in the
South at the time, where he had become accustomed to
spend his winters since 1829. In a written reply, he expressed
his desire to be connected with the school, but was hesitant
about establishing such a fixed relationship. He questioned
"whether my habits and the state of my health will permit
me to sit down to close study, and to all the requisite preparation for that department". He also indicated that he had
been "wishing for some time past, to shun public observation
and to retire more into solitude".[57]

He decided to decline the position of teacher in the school,
for the reasons he had given. In response to this refusal, the
trustees suggested that he become a sort of unofficial instructor, with occasional lectures to the students, as his health
would permit. They asked him to spend as much time as
possible at the seminary, speaking on the subject of evangelism, revivals, and other topics with which he was con-
versant. This arrangement would only commit him to a
limited schedule of teaching and would leave him free to
follow his evangelistic work if he wished.

To this he consented, since it suited him better than the
original proposal. Since he served on the Board of Directors
of the school, and was also an ad hoc faculty member, East
Windsor Hill became a sort of home base for him. He spent

more time there than anywhere else, and devoted a great
amount of his time and energy to the seminary. Although he
never formally accepted a chair as an instructor in the
school, he was always considered to be a member of the
faculty by all who were connected with it.

Evangelism was Nettleton's field and this was the primary
theme of his lectures at the school. The faculty members and
students alike considered themselves very fortunate to have
in their midst one who had had such a long and varied
experience in revival activity. As a teacher on all aspects of
personal religion and practical divinity, his messages were
highly prized. He discussed what doctrines were eminently
useful in winning souls, how evangelistic services should be
conducted, and what problems might arise. He gave them
advice on how to handle people who were in various stages
of conviction and how new converts should be instructed.
Nettleton's entire approach concerning methods to be
employed in dealing with churches and pastors was, of
course, explained in detail to the students.

Nettleton proved to be an extremely valuable asset to the
seminary, and one would surmise, given his reputation
throughout the East, that his occasional presence there was
a great attraction to bring students to East Windsor Hill.
His many years of experience as a preacher made him a
nearly inexhaustible reservoir of information to all who
came and went from the school. It was soon discovered, after
he began his work of lecturing, that his love for young
preachers was as great as his love of ordinary lay people had
been. He took a personal interest in each of the students
and when he was in town he tried to seek out each one of
them and make personal acquaintance with him. He
devoted many hours to visiting in their homes and discussing
their problems with them. As a result of the personal attention he gave the students, he actually had a closer bond with
them than the official faculty members. Erastus Ellsworth,
who was known as the business genius of the seminary,
looked after the physical well-being of the students, and
"Nettleton cared for their souls".[58] As George Hugh Birney
said, Nettleton was "the father confessor to the campus,
even more than President Tyler".[59] How little Nettleton's
temperament and interests changed over the years can be
seen by comparing his relationship with the students at the
Theological Institute and his relationship with his class-

mates at Yale during the 1807-1808 revival. After 30 years
he was still a carer for souls.

Nettleton continued to do evangelistic work during the
eighteen-thirties, but revival activity was waning, and in
fact had been on a slow decline since the peak year of 1821.
This change is reflected in the statistics of the Presbyterian
church for this period. In the years between 1826 and 1832
there was a rapid increase in membership, averaging eleven
thousand per year, "But in the succeeding five years the
accessions by faith declined at an accelerating rate to an
average of only two thousand two hundred a year".[60]
Between 1834 and 1836 the church actually lost members,
partly due to the withdrawal of some to the Congregational
Church, but also because of the absence of such revivals as
had previously taken place.

Nettleton did not hesitate to put a good part of the blame
for the spiritual recession upon the watered down theology
emanating from Yale and the "new measures" type of
evangelism. Occasionally he visited areas where the new
type of revivals had been held, and there he found little
evidence of real conversions. In a letter from him, dated
6th February, 1838, to an unidentified correspondent, he
says, "I have but just returned from labouring a little in a
place made waste by a series of protracted meetings and
revivals of modern stamp! Many of the subjects of those
revivals are now all *unconverted*, and some of them have come
out joyful, and now do solemnly declare that they have
never before been under conviction of sin or known anything about regeneration". He adds, "I cannot give you
particulars, only that they now declare that the doctrines
which they have been taught they do know to be false from
their own personal experience".[61]

Nettleton was not alone in his negative analysis of the
situation in evangelism. In 1836 Lyman Beecher, with whom
Asahel was still at swords drawn over theology, spoke out
against "itinerant preachers" at a meeting of the General
Associations of the Congregational Churches of Connecticut
and Massachusetts. At this very meeting the Association
passed a resolution barring abolition agents, speakers for
benevolent enterprises, and itinerant evangelists from the
pulpits of New England.[62] Such was the reputation of
evangelists ten years after Edward Griffin prophesied that
the world would be converted by revivals.

The prevailing discouragement over the spiritual condition of the country generally was echoed even by the master spirit behind the new revivalism, Charles G. Finney. In the same year that itinerant preachers were barred from New England, he declared in a lecture, which was published in the *New York Evangelist*, that, of all the converts of the revivals of the preceding ten years, "the great body of them are a disgrace to religion. Of what use would it be to have a thousand members added to the Church to be just such as are now in it".[63] According to William McLoughlin, this indictment against the quality of church members did not mean that he believed the revivals were spurious, but simply that there was a "low standard of piety" among the Christians.[64] Nettleton claimed that, in many instances, they were simply not converted at all. It was exactly "ten years" since the beginning of the controversy over western revivals and nine since he stood up in New Lebanon, New York, and warned against the consequences which now were admittedly present.

During his days as an instructor at East Windsor Hill, Nettleton engaged in extensive correspondence with old and new friends about the state of religion in America and New England in particular. Among these communicants were William Sprague, who eventually became known as, "The biographer of the Church", because of his series, "Annals of the American Pulpit", Leonard Woods of Andover, the chief spokesman for New England Calvinism, and Samuel Miller and Charles Hodge of Princeton. He also spoke throughout the country, though his activity was seriously curtailed because of bodily weakness.

Much of the written exchange was about the Finney-Taylor theology. As time went on he became, if anything, even more opposed to New Haven theology and more unmoveable in his adherence to the old orthodoxy. Although he and Taylor never ceased to be personal friends, he wrote extensively against his views in personal letters and in reviews which were published in current periodicals. Taylor seemed, all the while, to be avoiding controversy with him. According to a letter to Leonard Woods, dated 14th July, 1835, Taylor tried to make out that there were no real differences between them. Nettleton's reply was: "And yet I have disputed you face to face, day after day and night after night whenever I met you ever since 1821, with feelings of deep concern, as God knows, and as your own conscience will sooner or later testify."[65]

Nettleton's intransigence in the theological controversies of the eighteen-thirties has earned for him, with some historians, the reputation of a crabby old man who stubbornly defended an obsolete system of Calvinism.* But by men, such as Bennet Tyler, Heman Humphrey, and Leonard Woods, he was regarded as a champion for the true gospel, a defender of the faith once for all delivered unto the saints. Unquestionably, a departure from the doctrines and methods he used in evangelism was accompanied with a great decline from the strong and vibrant evangelicalism of a former generation. He and his friends went to their graves contending that the departure and the decline were inter-related.

*Charles C. Cole, Jr., in *The Social Ideas of the Northern Evangelists*, 1826-1860 (New York, 1954), says that Nettleton was "out of step with the times, doctrinally speaking". Also, "His verbose letters give the picture of a crabby, old man fighting vainly for the status quo". (*Op. cit.*, p. 23.) His contemporaries, even his antagonists, did not look upon him in this light.

CHAPTER 37

END OF A LONG JOURNEY

During all the years of his evangelistic ministry, Nettleton never had a real home. Following his mother's death in the spring after his graduation, his brother Ambrose had assumed the responsibility for the home in Killingworth. This released him from any domestic duties and he was free to go from place to place and preach as opportunity afforded. He was always given lodging and meals by the host Christians in the churches where he was preaching. During his recovery from typhus, he had made the home of Philander Parmele his abode, but after his friend's death he could not even do this.

After the organisation of the Theological Institute at East Windsor Hill, this town became more or less headquarters for him. He decided to make this his permanent residence and build a house of his own. In this he was assisted by his brother Ambrose, who came from Killingworth to supervise the construction. James F. Skinner, a carpenter, was hired to erect the structure. Asahel already owned some land, a wooded lot on the east side of town, but this was not suitable. Birney says, "It was the custom in the town to portion-off sections of the worthless land, to which this tract belonged, to those who did not already hold property, in order to insure the owner's the right to vote."[66]

Asahel began to look around East Windsor for a more suitable farm to purchase. He found a piece of land on the west side of the highway, running north and south, just below the old cemetery of the Timothy Edwards' church. There he built a two-storied house with a barn behind it. The construction of the house took nearly a year and cost about three thousand dollars. The final bill was issued and paid on 25th April, 1838. About the same time that he took care of this expense, he paid a bill to Benjamin Cook of East Windsor for forty dollars, to pay for the boarding of his brother Ambrose.

Nettleton's house was a typical, frame, New England house with shutters and simple decorations over the doors and windows. Here he lived for the rest of his life. Since he never married, he lived alone. Early in his life he and Samuel Mills had taken a resolve not to enter into any "entangling alliances", since they thought that by remaining unmarried they could be better missionaries. Although he never went to foreign fields, he did, for several years, serve as a missionary of a sort, since he did evangelistic work in "waste places". He was stricken with illness at the age of thirty-nine and did not expect to live. These are some of the reasons for his voluntary celibacy.

Although Asahel was only fifty-six when he moved into his new house, he settled into what was a virtual retirement. He was never able to lead a vigorous life after 1822, and although there were times when he felt good enough to resume some preaching activity, he was, for the final twenty-two years of his life, a broken vessel. In spite of considerable travel abroad and in the South, which helped somewhat, there was, as the years went by, a general recession in his stamina. Mrs. Parmele invited him to Bolton in 1839, but he declined. His response to her revealed that much of the spark of life was gone. "I have journeyed so long and so far in this wilderness world, and have passed through so many scenes of alternate storm and sunshine, that I am worn out with languor and fatigue, and have long since concluded to retire, and journey as little as possible, except so far as duty and the state of my health seem to demand."[67] He was able to retire in comfortable circumstances, because of substantial royalties on *Village Hymns*.

Although his work schedule was greatly diminished during these final years, honours continued to come his way. In 1839, two colleges sought to confer upon him the Doctor of Divinity degree. These were Hampden-Sidney College of Virginia, where he had spent so much time, and Jefferson College in Pennsylvania. He had never sought such a distinction and was evidently embarrassed by these moves. He did not appreciate titles for the clergy, nor did he want to be called "Doctor". Yet he appreciated the gestures of these schools, and recognised that it would not be polite to refuse. He recalled a statement that Ebenezer Porter had made when he had received a similar honour. "Too much noise to get rid of this contemptible honour," he said, "was not worth the trouble that it would cause."[68] Asahel gratefully, though reluctantly, accepted the honorary doctorate and was henceforth known to contemporaries as Dr Nettleton.

In the late eighteen-thirties Nettleton's interests turned more and more to the seminary and its students. He had become the "grand old man" of revivalism of New England and students naturally frequented his house, where they sat at his feet and listened in awe as he told of the glorious revival days of the past. He seemed to be greatly beloved by them and they often spoke of him in later years with the highest esteem.

In July of 1843 the students of the seminary established a new organisation known as the "Nettleton Rhetorical Society". Nettleton evidently did not have a direct hand in the formation of this organisation; it simply showed the great respect in which he was held. The purpose of this society was stated in the preamble to the constitution. "Fully aware that the religious teachers of the age should be well versed in biblical learning – that they should be able and skillful defenders of the truth; we are equally convinced that they should be lovers and efficient supporters of General Literature – that in manner of address – in force and aptness of illustration – in Elegance of Style and vivacity of thought, they should be able to arrest, to interest, and instruct."[69]

This honour probably pleased Nettleton more than the Doctor of Divinity degree, considering his strong attachment to young ministers and his desire to influence them for good. He acknowledged the compliment by presenting the society with a handsome leather ledger in which the records of their meetings were kept. All the faculty of the Theological Institute were honorary members, but "there was one of them who was almost always present – he for whom the society was named".[70]

In spite of his poor health, Nettleton's spirit seemed to prosper during his retirement years. Although he had had many trials and had been subjected to numerous unpleasant circumstances, he had lived, all in all, a happy and prosperous life. No one could match him as far as revival recollections were concerned. He turned a great deal to his books and enjoyed reading immensely, something he had not had enough time for previously. Among the books he studied were D'Aubigne's *History of the Reformation*, Gaussen on *Inspiration*, Tracy's *History of the Great Awakening*, the works of the younger Edwards, the works of Nathaniel Emmons, and the works of Andrew Fuller. Perhaps his favourite author of all was John Bunyan. Tyler said, "He was a great admirer of the writings of Bunyan, and often referred to them in illustration of his own opinions."[71] He once said, "More of my life is written in Bunyan's *Grace Abounding to the Chief of Sinners*, than anywhere else."[72]

But in his later years, he remained what he had been all his life, a student of the Bible. He often said, "There are many good books, but after all, there is nothing like the Bible."[73] It was especially precious to him in his twilight years. He not only read portions of the Scriptures every day for his own private devotion, but he made a "close and critical study" of them in the original as well. He kept his Greek Testament and concordance by him constantly. He told Bennet Tyler, on one occasion, that reading the Bible in a translation is like taking water from a vessel, whereas studying it from the original languages is like "drinking water at the spring".[74] Whenever his friends visited him, he always sent them away with interesting and instructive comments and remarks on portions of Scripture.

Although he remained, till the end of his life, reticent about his own inward experiences, he obviously enjoyed great peace of mind as he hastened toward death. "He expressed entire submission to the will of God – a willingness to be in His hands, and to be disposed of according to His pleasure. He spoke of the great deceitfulness of the human heart, and the danger of self-deception; but intimated that he had no distressing doubts and fears."[75] He continued to affirm strong adherence to the doctrines of grace and to all the evangelical truths which had been his mainstay during his days of active ministry. They seemed to be a great comfort to him as his natural powers failed.

In 1841 Asahel became seriously ill with what was diagnosed as gall-stones. For more than a year he tried practically every remedy available, but he became no better and suffered acute misery with this affliction. At length it was decided, as a last resort, to try surgery. In those days of primitive medicine, an operation was considered an extreme measure and was reverted to only with great caution and reluctance. But finally, following the recommendations of friends, he decided to go ahead with the operation. He went to New York and underwent surgery on 14th February, 1843.

For a time the operation seemed successful, though he continued to suffer greatly. After some time it became apparent, however, that he was growing worse again. The doctors advised a second operation, which took place on 8th December. Again his prospects of recovery seemed bright at first, but he soon relapsed and it became evident that the struggle for life was being lost.

For the last few months of his life, he was an invalid. Henry Blake, one of the students, often sat with him at night and was like a nurse to him. He could not sleep much and talked often about the scenes of revival that seemed to come continually before his mind. The days and nights by Nettleton's bedside made a deep impression on Blake, especially the accounts he heard from him about the days when God was visiting the towns of New England in such a remarkable way. Blake later said, "I have always cherished the impressions received from Dr Nettleton during the months and years he lay dying in that hallowed chamber as among the most valued results of my theological course."[76]

Another frequent visitor to the bedside of Nettleton was the President of the seminary, Bennet Tyler. They reminisced about their long association together and past experiences. They discussed the general state of the church and religion and the prospects of the new school. Asahel spoke often of his love for the school and the seminary church, sometimes with tears filling his eyes. He also talked about what it is like to face death and the importance of building a firm hope for eternity in days of health rather than waiting until a time of illness or approaching end to life. He stated that he had little confidence in people who were religious only when they became ill.

As the time for his departure seemed to be obviously drawing near, Bennet Tyler was with him. "You are in good hands," he said. "Certainly," Nettleton replied. "Are you willing to be there?" Bennet asked. "I am," said the dying evangelist. He seemed to have no parting counsel to give to those he was leaving behind, except the truths he had always preached to them. He spoke of a farewell sermon he had delivered in Virginia from the text, "While ye have the light, walk in the light". As he quoted this verse once again, his face shone with "peculiar lustre". He told his old friend Bennet that he had no worry at the prospect of death and testified a few hours before the end, "It is sweet to trust in the Lord".[77]

The last twenty-four hours of his life he said little. He made his last earthly communication with Tyler on the evening before his death. Bennet asked him if he enjoyed peace of mind. He nodded in the affirmative. Throughout the night he became weaker and at eight o'clock on the morning of 16th May, 1844, after much severe suffering, he died. He was buried in the little cemetery behind the chapel building at East Windsor Hill. Fourteen years later, Bennet Tyler died and was laid to rest just a few feet away from Nettleton's grave.

Nettleton's will revealed that he had accumulated a considerable estate, largely the income from his hymnal. His house and property were worth nearly six thousand five hundred dollars. His total estate, which included investment in bank stock, real estate in the new country of Illinois, and other interests was valued at twenty-one thousand six hundred and twenty-five dollars. Had he not refused so much money early in his life he probably would have died quite wealthy.

His will included bequests for his brother and sister in Killingworth, and small amounts to some of his friends, including Mrs Parmele and his college roommate, Jonathan Lee. The balance he willed to the seminary and to the American Board for Foreign missions, which, as Birney says, were the institutions "which represented the causes closest to his heart".[78] By the terms of the will, the income from *Village Hymns* formed a part of the annual income of the Theological Institute of Connecticut.

CHAPTER 38

THE NETTLETON LEGACY

Some idea of Nettleton's reputation at the time of his death can be seen by the reaction of the religious public upon the publication of his *Memoir* by Tyler in 1844. It was hailed throughout America by evangelical leaders as a welcome addition to the store of Christian biographies.* In October, 1844, the *Biblical Repository*, said, "We have seized this book just issued from the press, with great interest, and perused it with uncommon satisfaction. We are sure it will be read by thousands who have been savingly profited by Dr Nettleton's labours, and by thousands who have heard the report of his labours, and his success as a minister of the gospel".[79] The *New York Observer* said of him, that he was "one of the most extraordinary preachers of the gospel with whom God has ever blessed this country".[80] Christians of all denominations commended the publishers and extolled the life which was enshrined in this volume. Even the *New York Evangelist* spoke of him as "an extraordinary man", who had "served a glorious purpose in his day and generation. Few men, since the apostolic days, have been honoured with such signal success in preaching the word, and in the conversion of sinners as he . . .".[81]

In 1846 the school he helped to establish made another move to honour his memory. The trustees decided to set up a professorship as a memorial to him. Eleven thousand dollars were set aside by some people associated with the school, to which four thousand dollars were to be added by the institution itself, to secure the income for the salary of a Professor of Biblical Literature. This professorship was first

* This biography, in the Andrew Bonar edition, was reprinted in Scotland in 1975 by The Banner of Truth Trust.

filled by Professor William Thompson, and was intended "to testify to our respect and affection for the memory of one of the early friends and benefactors who loved this institution unto the end".[82] It was known as the "Nettleton Professorship of Old Testament" and was perpetuated for the generations following. Thompson's connection with the seminary continued until his death in 1889, and "to his wisdom, patience, self-denial, and teaching skill, whatever success the institution has had is chiefly due".[83]

But the passing years have not been kind to Nettleton, in so far as perpetuating his memory is concerned, and the respect of historians has not been equal to that of his contemporaries. There were later editions of Tyler's biography both in America and Great Britain, but a century passed before there was another study of his life and ministry, Birney's doctoral thesis, and it was never published. Although Nettleton was a household word at the time of his death, by the turn of the twentieth century his name and life had fallen into oblivion.

To modern students of revivalism in America, he is generally known as an antagonist to Finney, who is credited with being the "Father of Modern Evangelism". All serious studies of American Church History devote some place to his ministry, but few credit him with contributing much to the evolution of religion. He is considered a part of a bygone age and culture, a kind of roadblock in the path of progress. Unfortunately, the evangelical church has also seemed content to leave Nettleton in the graveyard of forgotten warriors. In contrast, Finney, who outlived Nettleton by thirty years, has been published, studied, quoted, and copied endlessly. While Finney's right to fame is unquestionable, Nettleton's fate seems totally unwarranted.

Adequate reasons, though not necessarily justifiable, for Nettleton's plunge into anonymity are not hard to find. One is the fact that he left no personal literary legacy. He was admittedly no writer, and unfortunately there are no really accurate copies of his sermons. His sermon notes were published in 1845 by Tyler, but they were taken from his manuscripts and from personal notes of his hearers and they give no adequate representation of his preaching, as the introduction to the volume plainly says. Tyler was among the first to lament "that he did not commit more of his thoughts (to writing)".[84]

Part of the reason, no doubt, is theological. The tides of change that began in Nettleton's day continued to rise, and eventually washed away many of the landmarks of the great revival eras. Nettleton saw the beginnings of the great decline in the influence of Calvinism as a significant force in American religion; in fact, by the end of the nineteenth century evangelicalism as such had been expelled from most of the great educational institutions of the United States. New England led the way in the great theological and spiritual apostasy of the late nineteenth and early twentieth centuries, and became totally dominated by the liberalism which had been exported from Germany. The playground for the "new measures" experiment in the eighteen-thirties became the wasteland of Unitarianism in later years.

The renascent evangelicalism of the twentieth century has not returned to the roots of the Puritan era in America, but has largely been attached to the Keswick and prophetic conferences of the later nineteenth century and the Scofield type of dispensationalism. Neither of these has shown much respect for the heritage of the past. The twentieth century heirs of the Reformed tradition have been generally of the Princetonian school, which became increasingly intellectual and philosophical, and not much interested in revivalism. With the religious institutions of New England in the grip of rationalism, there has been no one around to perpetuate the philosophy, or even the memory, of one of her noblest native sons, Asahel Nettleton.

The neglect of him by the evangelical church is a misfortune that has overtaken the entire movement of which he was a part. Today, secular writers give more attention to the great awakenings than do evangelical historians, though they are understandably critical. They always seek to explain the heroes of these movements, such as Whitefield, Tennent, Nettleton, McGready and Cartwright, from a social and psychological perspective. The testimonies and experiences of the subjects of these great revivals are drawn out and examined as coldly and critically as a scientist looking at a dead spider under a microscope. In a large measure, American Christians do not know there were such experiences, and what they do read about they cannot understand.

The whole New England school has virtually been forgotten. Books such as Frank Foster's *Genetic History of the*

New England Theology, which was written just after the turn of the last century, is purely academic and is referred to only by a few scholars. Who has heard of Samuel Hopkins, Joseph Bellamy, Edward Griffin, Leonard Woods, Edward Payson, or Nathaniel Emmons, or read their writings? Only Jonathan Edwards has survived, but the image is one of a stern theologian at the top end of a string, dangling poor sinners over a burning hell. Recent studies and publications have revived an interest in him and shown the great contribution he has made to the American nation and church. Hopefully the value of some of his spiritual sons will once again be recognised. Asahel Nettleton led more people to God than any of them, and he was a much more effective preacher than the great master himself.

Many of the physical monuments to Nettleton's life and ministry are still standing. The school he helped to establish was, of course, moved to Hartford in 1865 and renamed the Hartford Theological Seminary. All his personal letters and effects are still housed in the tower of one of the buildings of that institution, which now takes up a city block in one of the exclusive residential districts of Hartford. As a training school for ministers, it was shut down in 1972, although there is still a foundation there named "Hartford Seminary Foundation". The buildings are now used as offices for community organisations and occasional conferences are held on the seminary premises. The huge library was put up for auction and sold to Emory University of Atlanta, Georgia. The vine-covered stone-grey buildings still reach toward the sky; a kind of gaunt reminder of a glory that is past.

At one time an elegant painting of the evangelist who made the school famous hung in one of the halls of the seminary. To look at this portrait today, one has to go to the attic of one of the buildings on the campus. There, leaning against one of the roof supports, is the portrait of Asahel Nettleton, seeming to stare sadly into the darkness. The fate of his picture seems almost symbolic of what has happened to his testimony in America.

The old seminary building was torn down in 1936, but its facade still may be seen as the portico of the Ellsworth school in East Windsor Hill. Behind the school, which was once the site of the seminary, a brown-spotted tomb marks the final resting place of Nettleton. His house still greets travellers along the historic old boulevard which runs through town, and is seemingly no worse for the years. The exterior, now painted green, is original, as are the shutters.

Many of the church buildings where he conducted his great revivals are still being used. The quaint little Congregational Church structure in Milton, where he saw one of the first of the great spiritual transformations, houses occasional religious services. Noah Porter's church at Farmington, which in its day was considered one of the finest outside Boston, is in use and one of the historic landmarks of Connecticut. At Lenox, Massachusetts, the building in which Samuel Shepherd and Asahel Nettleton pleaded for God, rises above the highway. It is now known as "The Church on the Hill". Nearby is a graveyard where Shepherd and his wife were interred.

Visitors to such churches today, as the one at Lenox, who know what went on within their walls, can, with the use of a little imagination, create a different scene and setting than these buildings now have. As the vision begins, the electric power lines, automobiles, and modern houses disappear and another picture unfolds. Carriages, horses, and people on foot fill the church yard. Men in top hats, frock coats, and knee breeches, and women in bonnets, shawls, and full skirts press toward the meeting house. Enter the building and you find a huge throng of people filling the sanctuary and the galleries above. After a few hymns sung by the congregation, the scriptures are read and prayers offered; a stillness falls across the audience. The hush is in anticipation of the appearance of the speaker.

Then, slowly and deliberately, the preacher steps behind the pulpit. A glow is upon his face, as if he, like Moses of old, had been in higher regions talking with his God. He begins to speak in a slow conversational tone, but there is such earnestness and sincerity in his manner that you dare not miss a word. He keeps your eyes glued upon him.

As his message unfolds, he seems to be touched as by a fire from the heavenly altar. The theme is noble and vital. It centres about the great realities of God. He talks of the holiness of "the Supreme Being", the awful guilt of sinners and the way of salvation through Christ. He pleads with sinners to submit to God, with a pathos you have never heard before. He speaks to you as though he knew your very thoughts, and tells the whole crowd exactly how you feel.

The words that pour from the pulpit pierce your heart like
a shot from an arrow, and stay there, burning inside. You
look around and others are also touched. Some are weeping,
others are quietly praying that God will take them up into
His arms of love.

Suddenly you awake from your vision. The great crowd
melts away. The carriages vanish and the electric lines,
automobiles and houses emerge again. Once more the old
church is empty and stands in lonely vigil over the graves of
her sons. The walls no longer ring with the songs of happy
people, but are quiet and deserted. You drive away, but
cannot help thinking, "What a tale these walls could tell!"

Much could be said about Asahel Nettleton as a man.
He was the quiet, contemplative type, and seemed, to many,
austere and abstract. He usually had little to say to people
he did not trust, but he had warm and tender feelings
toward his intimate friends. He cherished his close associa-
tion with people like Philander Parmele, Jonathan Lee, and
Bennet Tyler. Some of those with whom he was personally
acquainted were the leading religious figures of his day,
which shows what a strategic place he had in American
Church History. This list, which includes Timothy Dwight,
Samuel J. Mills, N. W. Taylor, Lyman Beecher, Charles
Finney, Francis Wayland, William Sprague, and Edward
Griffin is a "Who's Who" in early nineteenth century
American Christianity.

His life was a strange mixture of monumental successes
and extreme tragedies. The revivals he helped to initiate
were the wonders of his age and put him in a unique and
highly privileged class as a preacher. Many evangelical
ministers would count it a great blessing to be instrumental
in *one* awakening, such as those that were commonplace in
the first ten years of Nettleton's evangelistic labours. But
such a position as he held did not come without a price. He
was buffeted by many storms, which, like God's blessings
on his ministry, came in a giant size. One can trace six
major crises in his life, each being totally different from the
others. The first was the *spiritual* struggle which issued in his
conversion. The second was *domestic*, for he lost both his
father and mother in his youth. The third, the period of
depression which briefly interrupted his college career, was
partly spiritual but mostly *psychological*. The period in 1818,
when his *moral* integrity was in question, was the fourth great

trial, and may well have been the worst of his whole life. The fifth was the typhus attack of 1822 which robbed him of his *physical* health, and made him a semi-invalid for the rest of his life. And the *theological* debates in which he was involved, beginning in 1826, were prolonged, vexatious, and unsettling. This was the final adversity, and it followed him to his grave. In spite of the fact that he is mostly remembered in history because of his part in the Finney-Taylor dispute, he was no lover of controversy and never sought for an opportunity to disagree or debate.

He seemed to love young people, a feeling that was quite mutual. Many of the people who were converted in his great revivals were teenagers. They seemed attracted to him, and liked to be around him. He was a favourite of the theological students in the Institute at East Windsor, who cherished his counsel.

Much could be said about him as a theologian. Although he was not an original thinker, he was a profound Biblical scholar and few evangelists in church history had as thorough a knowledge of "experimental divinity" as he. He drank deeply from the springs of evangelical truth, especially those that related to the experience of salvation.

But in none of these areas can a legitimate claim for fame and uniqueness be staked out for him. As a private personality or abstract thinker he had only average abilities. It is as a preacher, evangelist, and soul winner that he made his niche in history. As a soul surgeon, as a communicator of gospel truth, and as a promoter of true revivals, he had and has few peers. He has been, and will continue to be remembered as one who did a great deal to establish true religion in the hearts of men and advance the Kingdom of God on earth.

His evangelism has been disparaged because it did not touch the great urban centres of America. It is true that many of his revivals were in small communities and villages. Although he preached in Newark and New York, most of his ministry was around Hartford, which was one of the few Connecticut towns which had more than five thousand inhabitants in 1820, and New Haven which numbered just over eight thousand.[85] Admittedly, Nettleton never reached the great cities of the East in his preaching, but discerning students of American revivalism have been of the opinion that the evangelistic efforts of even the best-known American revivalists have never made much impact, from a spiritual and moral standpoint, upon the great metropolitan areas.*

The fact is, that given the extent of his exposure, and the permanence of his converts, he very well may have been, next to George Whitefield, the most effective evangelist in the history of the United States. The ratio of his converts to the population of America in his day is very revealing. Although there is no way of knowing how many were brought to salvation through his preaching, a conservative estimate would be twenty-five thousand. Based on the reports of first hand witnesses, and pastors who laboured in the communities where his revivals took place, sometimes examining the situation thirty years later, only a small fraction of these converts were spurious. The population of the United States in 1820 would have been around nine million, including about half that many in the old coastal North.[86] The population of the country today is approximately two hundred and twenty million, or over twenty-four times as many as in 1820. An ingathering of new believers in modern times, proportionate to the success of Asahel Nettleton, would be over six hundred thousand. That many genuine conversions in contemporary society, through one human instrument, would indeed be phenomenal.

Although the name of Asahel Nettleton has suffered eclipse since his death, this will unquestionably change. It will certainly change if the United States is once again blessed with an evangelical awakening, comparable to the first two, or the last great awakening, the prayer revival of 1857-1859. Such spiritual upheavals, which were characterised by power, purity, and permanence, have always turned the minds of Christians to the quality type of evangelism which is illustrated in the ministry of Asahel Nettleton.

---

*McLoughlin's estimate of American evangelists from Finney on can be summed up in his statement on Moody's revivals. "He boosted the morale of the regular churchgoers, but he did not reach the masses and he did not add appreciably to the numerical growth of the churches." (*Op. cit.*, p. 265.) See also pp. 266-281.

[1] From a letter to Bennet Tyler, cited by Birney, p. 200.
[2] *Ibid.*, p. 155.
[3] Stuart C. Henry, in *Unvanquished Puritan*, p. 135.
[4] *A Genetic History of the New England Theology* (New York, 1907), p. 172.
[5] Ms. Letter to Leonard Woods, cited by Birney, p. 158.
[6] *Ibid.*, pp. 158, 159.
[7] Mss. Notes on *Spirit of the Pilgrims*, cited by Birney, p. 160.

8 Cited by Birney, p. 170.
9 *The Works of Leonard Woods, D.D.*, in five volumes (Boston, 1851), Vol. IV, p. 383.
10 *Ibid.*, p. 384.
11 *Ibid.*, p. 386.
12 *Memoir*, p. 278.
13 *Autobiography*, Vol. II, p. 103.
14 *Ibid.*, p. 103.
15 *Ibid.*, p. 103.
16 *Ibid.*, p. 104.
17 *Unvanquished Puritan*, p. 133.
18 *Autobiography of Beecher*, Vol. II, p. 157.
19 *Ibid.*, Vol. I, p. 472.
20 *Ibid.*, p. 473.
21 *Ibid.*, p. 472.
22 *Ibid.*, Vol. II, p. 157.
23 *Ibid.*, Vol. II, p. 108.
24 Finney, *Memoirs*, p. 288.
25 *Ibid.*, p. 288.
26 *History of the Kehukee Baptist Association* (1802), by Lemuel Burkett and Jesse Reed, p. 145, cited by David Scott, in "The Invitation System: a Survey of its Beginnings, its Causes and its Acceptance", in *Baptist Reformation Review*, Spring, 1976, p. 34.
27 *The Frontier Camp Meeting, Religion's Harvest Time* (Dallas, 1955), by Charles A. Johnson, cited by David Scott in above, p. 36.
28 Finney, *Memoirs*, p. 288.
29 *Lectures on Revivals of Religion*, by Charles G. Finney (New York, 1898), p. 254.
30 *Ibid.*, p. 254.
31 *Lectures on Revivals of Religion*, by William B. Sprague (London, 1959), pp. 225, 226.
32 Birney, p. 411.
33 Birney, pp. 413, 414.
34 McLoughlin, p. 86.
35 McLoughlin, introduction to Finney, *Lectures on Revivals of Religion* (Cambridge, 1960), cited by David Scott in *Baptist Reformation Review*, Spring, 1976, p. 39.
36 McLoughlin, *Modern Revivalism*, pp. 69, 70.
37 Tyler, *Memoir*, p. 192.
38 *Ibid.*, p. 192.
39 *Ibid.*, p. 192.
40 *Ibid.*, p. 194.
41 *Ibid.*, pp. 195, 196.
42 *Ibid.*, p. 196.
43 *Ibid.*, p. 196.
44 Birney, p. 208.
45 Tyler, *Memoir*, p. 197.
46 Bonar, p. 286.
47 *Ibid.*, p. 286.
48 *Ibid.*, p. 286.
49 *Ibid.*, pp. 286, 287.
50 *Ibid.*, p. 288.
51 Birney, p. 209.
52 Birney, p. 185.
53 *Ibid.*, p. 185.
54 *Ibid.*, p. 186.
55 *Ibid.*, pp. 186, 187.
56 *Ibid.*, p. 187.
57 Tyler, *Memoir*, pp. 200, 201.
58 Birney, p. 193.
59 *Ibid.*, p. 193.
60 McLoughlin, p. 145.
61 Birney, p. 399.
62 McLoughlin, p. 146.
63 *Ibid.*, p. 147.
64 *Ibid.*, p. 147.
65 Birney, p. 381.
66 Birney, p. 211.
67 *Ibid.*, p. 212.
68 *Ibid.*, p. 213.
69 *Ibid.*, p. 214.
70 *Ibid.*, p. 214.
71 *Memoir*, p. 306.
72 *Ibid.*, p. 306.
73 *Ibid.*, p. 304.
74 *Ibid.*, p. 305.
75 *Ibid.*, pp. 305, 306.
76 Birney, pp. 216, 217.
77 Tyler, *Memoir*, pp. 312, 313.
78 Birney, p. 217.
79 Supplemental advertisement, in *Remains of the Late Rev. Asahel Nettleton, D.D.*, p. 10.
80 *Ibid.*, p. 10.
81 *Ibid.*, p. 10.
82 Birney, p. 218.
83 Williston Walker, in *A History of the Congregational Churches in the United States* (New York, 1899), p. 360.
84 Preface to the *Remains*, p. iii.
85 These statistics are found in *The Second Great Awakening in Connecticut*, by Charles R. Keller, cited by Bernard A. Weisberger in *They Gathered at the River* (Boston, 1958), p. 67.
86 *The Growing Years*, p. 146.

INDEX